Thanks to Renée and all t lation of information on t Knowing when and how t can neither ignore these c the matter of gender and how it was designed by our Creator—a desires men and women to value and complement each other as we work together to make King Jesus famous.

Dave Hamlin, lead pastor, Shelby Christian Church

Renée has compiled the thoughts and discoveries of learned theologians and practical disciple makers to explain why this topic of gender is so vital and to give a framework for understanding it from a biblical perspective. Although God does speak on this topic, much of the world (even within the Christian community) is largely ignoring his perfect ways. Thank you for publishing this resource for church leaders and everyday Christians. This gives me a one-stop guide and the language I need to disciple women in our current culture.

Michelle Eagle, women's discipleship minister,
Harpeth Christian Church; women's coach, Renew.org

Renée elegantly takes one of the most volatile and debatable subjects in our time and handles it with grace and clarity. A must-read for those pursuing faithfulness and truth in these confusing times.

Joel Singleton, lead minister, San Jose Church of Christ

Now more than ever, the North American church is being flooded with ideas about what it means to be made in the image of God and how we as Christians are to show the world the glory of God's design. *Male and Female* offers much-needed clarity to today's complex conversations around biblical manhood and womanhood. It is deeply biblical, relevant, and refreshingly countercultural, offering hope and conviction to disciples living out their faith in a post-Christian society.

Daren Overstreet, senior minister, Anchor Point Church

At a time when traditional views about all things gender seem to be in upheaval, here is a deep dive that is worth the read. This book will challenge many cultural and biblical assumptions and give you plenty of food for thought. Read it. Wrestle with it. Just don't ignore it.

Jimmy Adcox, discipleship minister, Southwest Church of Christ

A fantastic book that provides evidence from several sources for acknowledging the significant roles that both men and women are blessed with. The evidence and real-life stories point to what it means to be created as a man or a woman and how important both are in God's plan for us.

Tim Cook, church planter, 419 Ministries Canada;
church relations, Maritime Christian College

In *Male and Female*, Renée Webb Sproles cautions the reader to avoid merely "feeding on a handful of passages," in order to stay away from stereotyping men and women. Well done on expanding our knowledge of Scripture and challenging our stereotypes! The challenge to examine the "theological triage" in our marriages (see Chapter 11) was a reminder that these issues are where the tire meets the road. In the words of the author, "This information is not just good news for a world full of hurting marriages. It's the best news around!"

Rowlie Hutton, vice president and relationship manager,
The Solomon Foundation

RENÉE WEBB SPROLES, General Editor

MALE & FEMALE

A BIBLICAL LOOK AT GENDER

Forewords by Chad Ragsdale *and* Richard Oster

RENƎW.org
Male and Female: A Biblical Look at Gender

Requests for information should be sent via email to Renew. Visit Renew.org for contact information.

In SWS, unless otherwise noticed, all Scripture quotations are taken from the NRSV.

Italics have been added to Scripture quotations by the author.

ISBN: 978-1-959467-02-1 (Paperback)
ISBN: 978-1-959467-12-0 (Hardback)
ISBN: 978-1-959467-03-8 (Kindle)
ISBN: 978-1-959467-04-5 (ePub)

Cover and interior design: YouPublish (youpublish.com)

CONTENTS

FOREWORD

BY CHAD RAGSDALE

A good referee is essential to having a good basketball game. Sure, you need skilled players, clever coaches, and functional equipment, but without a good referee, a game can quickly devolve into frustration and chaos. The referee's job is to know and enforce the rules of the game. If there is a foul or a violation, the referee blows his whistle to temporarily stop the game so that order can be restored. In this way, the referee exercises a necessary authority over the game.

A referee is needed as well when seeking clarity on difficult biblical and theological issues. Who gets to blow the whistle as we are arriving at conclusions on contentious questions? Whom do we count on to tell us when our understandings are in-bounds or out-of-bounds? What is our authority when we're trying to decide what we believe about issues like the death penalty, the legalization of marijuana, or abortion? What about the topic of this particular book? There are few issues more contentious in our world today than gender. The mere mention of "gender identity" or "gender roles" elicits a fight-or-flight response in many of us. This immediate, visceral reaction makes clarity even more elusive. We get busy readying ourselves for a fight rather than discerning the truth. We need a referee.

Our problem may not be as simple as only needing a referee, however, because the truth is everyone already has one. Every person already makes decisions about difficult issues in light of an authority. There are no exceptions. The difficulty is not the lack of an authority but the presence of *too many* authorities. For some, their authority is tradition. Our present interpretations are indeed shaped by the traditions handed down to us through the Christian generations. For others, their authority is their contemporary community of faith. Their first concern is for what *we* believe about this issue. Some put the whistle in the hand of human reason. As such, all interpretations should conform to "what makes sense." In reality, this most often means "what makes sense to our contemporary culture." Still others place their trust in what we could call intuition or experience. This very popular referee blows the whistle when an interpretation doesn't *feel* right.

Each one of the referees in the previous paragraph can be valuable and helpful in their own ways. Tradition, or what G.K. Chesterton admiringly called "the democracy of the dead," gives modern Christians historical roots. Tradition reminds us we are a part of a grand legacy that didn't begin with our generation. There is wisdom to be found in listening to those who have gone before us in faith. Our faith communities are also essential in helping us discern truth. The Bible is a community book. We need the help that comes from reading the Bible together especially when we are dealing with complex or controversial issues. Reason and intuition are also helpful. Untangling complicated issues often requires careful reasoning and reflection on lived experiences. We may rightly see the dangers of these last two authorities—reason and experience—but we should also admit that our own interpretations are regularly shaped by them.

For all of their benefits, however, all these authorities are inadequate and potentially misleading on their own. These competing authorities, or referees, also cause conflict. When each person is listening for a different whistle, there are bound to be irreconcilable conflicts and frustrations. What we need is to attune ourselves to a common authority. For those of us who are committed to following Jesus in all of the complex issues of our day, the God-breathed Word useful for "teaching, rebuking, correcting, and training in righteousness" (1 Timothy 3:16) is that authority. We seek out truth not in our own wisdom or understanding. No, we listen to God's Word.

One of my preaching professors in college drilled this point into his students with regularity: whatever you say in a sermon, make sure *the text always wins.* The text must have the final say. The text is the one holding the whistle. That is the goal of this volume: to listen carefully to the text and to let it win. We recognize that biblical interpretation, or exegesis, is not simplistic.

This is especially the case when it comes to the type of complex issues and controversial texts this book covers. We know that people of good faith have studied these issues and have come to different conclusions. That's why we must keep coming back to the text using every interpretive tool at our disposal to understand it well, something this book does admirably. More than anything, however, we must come to the text time and time again with what Eugene Peterson calls "sustained humility." We come to the text not to speak, but to listen; not to dictate, but to respond. The text always wins.

Chad Ragsdale (DMin, Talbot School of Theology)
Executive Vice President of Academics, Ozark Christian College

FOREWORD

BY RICHARD OSTER

Henny-Penny, we are told in various versions of the story, was a chick hit upon the head by a single falling acorn. She concludes the "sky is falling" and precipitates mass hysteria among her fowl colleagues. It is clear to us and to the crafters of this tale that Henny-Penny reached an unfounded conclusion based upon a one-off experience.

But, you know, sometimes the "sky *is* falling." The city of Memphis, where I live and work, did experience a celestial collapse upon its citizens, its commerce, and its very future as a city. It was the late 1870s, and a Yellow Fever crisis spread through the lower Mississippi Valley. In 1878 alone, there were over 5,000 deaths in Memphis. The city was de-charted by the State of Tennessee and all citizens urged to leave. Clergy and physicians came from other states to assist the city; many of these also fell to the Yellow Fever, whose cause and cures were still unknown. Bodies had to be simply tossed out into major streets so wagons could pick them up and bury them, unmarked, in pit graves in Elmwood Cemetery. Those caring men and women who placed the bodies in the street one day were sometimes placed in the same street a few days later. So, was "the sky falling" on Memphis during those years? Absolutely!

Only those plagued with abysmal ignorance of Scripture and church history could ignore the places where the early church's devotion "to the apostles' teaching" (Acts 2:42) was later ignored. Not unlike the rapid and unmitigated speed of the Yellow Fever by mosquitoes in late nineteenth-century Memphis, false teachings that spring up to interfere with God's mission in the world have often "spread like gangrene" (2 Timothy 2:17).

In our times, an important element of God's truth to provide his blessing to humanity has come under attack, and that is the eternal, two-fold truth imbedded in God's creation. These two truths are God's goodness in creation and God's order in creation. While some pagan religions in apostolic times promoted self-harm (e.g., cutting), it was the apostle Paul who argued that "asceticism and severity to the body" had no place within believers' efforts to become more spiritual and closer to Christ (Colossians 2:23). Our bodies are good and aren't available to abuse and misuse as ways to recapture Eden. It was Paul, again, who argued that those who deny the goodness of sexual expression within marriage have abandoned the faith (1 Timothy 4:1–5) and rejected the divine creation of the two becoming one in sexual expression. Due to adverse cultural influences on the churches of Paul's time, he also addressed more than once the importance of congregations following God's order in creation in addressing the roles of men and women in Christian ministry and leadership (1 Corinthians 11:2–16; 14:33-35; 1 Timothy 2:8–15).

These matters of faith and lifestyle that required apostolic attention and Paul's use of the creation theology are not strangers to us modern believers, especially in the West. In some places in the West the "sky has fallen" on creation theology and the related topic of gender. Additionally, further disregard for the inspiration of all Scripture and its use as "profitable for teaching, for reproof, for correction, and for training in righteousness" (2 Timothy 3:16) has hastened the arrival of a plethora of harmful teachings.

This helpful book, *Male and Female: A Biblical Look at Gender*, attempts to address these many recurring false teachings that stem from churches' neglect or denial of clear apostolic teaching on God's creation. Renée Webb Sproles's style is intentionally popular and no one should be distracted from appreciating her work due to expecting a lot of academic jargon and hard-to-follow arguments. This work contains sixteen sections with a summary and conclusion by Bobby Harrington and Sproles with autobiographical accounts of their spiritual journeys and very challenging guidelines about what it means to be a Christlike husband in headship and Christlike wife in submissiveness. In addition to the sections written by Harrington and

Sproles, there are several guests writers who bring important information to the conversation.

The real value of this work is its attempt to have a serious and informed advocacy of a biblical theology of God's design and order of creation and gender relationships. In addition to teachings about a twenty-first century practice of Ephesians 5, it engages topics such as "women elders," the "LGBTQ+" movements, the "Transgender Debate," the recurring topic of women preachers, and a critique of the impoverished alternatives offered by "Modern Western Culture." To my knowledge not a single contributor to this important work would defend the practices of earlier generations of believers who, in the name of God, mistreated sexual minorities, supported ungodly interpretations of the roles of men and women, and shut out women from ministry gifts given to them by God. The various contributors do, however, think that on these issues the "sky has fallen" in some places, and that it is not hysteria to point out the obvious and attempt to avert it happening repeatedly.

Richard Oster (PhD, Princeton Theological Seminary)
Professor of New Testament, Harding School of Theology

INTRODUCTION

BRAVE NEW WORLD

As I write this, it is the middle of June, which is now widely celebrated as Pride Month.

Target is currently selling a line of pro-trans clothing for adults and children, which includes chest binders (to flatten the breasts of girls and women) and packing underwear (which adds padding to the crotch to create the appearance of a bulge between the legs).[1]

New York Governor Kathy Hochul announced that all sixty-four SUNY (State University of New York) campuses are being directed to update policies to ensure that a person's chosen gender identity and pronouns are used. The student's chosen name and pronouns will appear in campus portals, class rosters, and student email addresses. And students will be able to select "X" when asked to provide gender by the college.[2]

Rainbow flags, including the "trans flag" colors, are everywhere from the Tampa Bay Rays' uniforms to Oreos. [3]

---

1. Laken Brooks, "For Pride Month, Target Is Selling Compression Tops and Packing Underwear," *Forbes*, May 16, 2022, www.forbes.com/sites/lakenbrooks/2022/05/16/for-pride-month-target-is-selling-compression-tops-and-packing-underwear/? (accessed September 25, 2022).
2. "'Equality and Respect': SUNY to Implement Chosen Name and Pronouns Policy," *NBC New York*, June 8, 2022, www.nbcnewyork.com/news/local/equality-and-respect-suny-to-implement-chosen-name-pronouns-policy/3725453/ (accessed September 25, 2022).
3. Amanda Prestigiacomo, "Rays Pitcher Who Did Wear 'Pride Night' Logo Defends Teammates for Opting Out: 'Different Beliefs Exist,'" *Daily Wire*, June 8, 2022, www.dailywire.com/news/rays-pitcher-who-did-wear-pride-night-logo-defends-teammates-for-opting-out-different-beliefs-exist (accessed September 25, 2022).

Yes, Oreos.

The pride sandwich cookies packaging is covered in multi-colored sayings that capture the spirit of our age well:

> *You can be anything, do anything, love anyone.*
> *You're perfect. Change for no one.*
> *It takes courage to be your authentic self.*
> *Love knows no boundaries.*

There's even a blank space for you to add your own truth to these "real words from proud allies."

TIMID AND CONFUSED CHURCHES

Since the publication of our book, *On Gender,* just a handful of years ago, the topic of sex and gender in America—and even in the church!—has become more misunderstood and confused, not less.

This was made all too clear to me when I was invited to speak at a forum on women in leadership at a prominent, historic local church this winter. I presented a complementarian position while two college professors presented the egalitarian position. This was followed by a Q&A from the audience. The general sentiment of the pastors and church leaders in attendance (and articulated by the moderator) is shared by an increasing number of Christians. It goes something like this.

> *The issue of what we believe about men and women isn't gospel-level important. The most important thing is Jesus. And besides, it's hard to know what the Bible says about men and women. It's complicated. And we've been wrong before. Men have made some big mistakes in their marriages and in our churches. We need to make up for that. Shouldn't we err on the side of caution and just let everyone choose for themselves what to believe? If we're just sincerely following what we think is true, isn't that enough?*

As a woman raised in a church tradition that failed to recognize women in big and small ways, I empathize with this reasoning. I really do.

And yet.

The only way I can follow Christ right now, and for all eternity, is as a *woman*. I won't be married at the resurrection, but I will always and forever be female. What Scripture says about creation, sin, and salvation point to very important *secondary* truths that were once taken for granted.

For example, no one claiming to follow Jesus would have questioned, until recently, that believing in "the Maker of heaven and earth" (Psalm 115:15) would also include believing that we have been made male and female in his image (Genesis 1:26–28) or that marriage is ordained by God as between one man and one woman (Genesis 2:23–24; Matthew 19:4–6).

When something as significant as sex and gender is placed into the category of opinion and then dismissed as something so minor that Christians can all have wildly differing opinions on it, serious consequences will follow.

They already have.

A recent nationwide survey of America's Christian pastors—the American Worldview Inventory 2022—shows that just slightly more than a third (37 percent) possess a biblical worldview, while the majority—62 percent—hold a worldview they describe as "syncretism." (Syncretism is when you combine different religions, cultures, or schools of thought.)[4]

As go the churches, so go the parents in them.

A portion of this inventory released some weeks later points out shocking statistics about parents. Overall, it found that only 5 percent of parents have core beliefs and behaviors in harmony with a biblical worldview. For example, only one-fourth of parents with preteens (26 percent) contend that human life is sacred. A little over half of them (54 percent) believe that human beings can be understood as God's creation, made in his image, but fallen and in need of redemption. When it comes to "beliefs and behavior

4. Tracy Munsil, "New Study Shows Shocking Lack of Biblical Worldview Among American Pastors," Arizona Christian University, May 12, 2022, www.arizonachristian.edu/2022/05/12/shocking-lack-of-biblical-worldview-among-american-pastors/?mc_cid=d27768fdf2&mc_eid=217eb0e707 (accessed September 25, 2022).

concerning sin, salvation, and one's personal relationship with God," only 5 percent hold a consistently biblical view.[5]

According to Barna, "Parents these days often feel guilty 'imposing' their views on their children, having bought into the notions that imparting inviolable guidelines to their children is overbearing and intolerant, and that it takes a village—which we know as our culture—to effectively raise a child these days."[6]

As go the parents, so go the children.

Christian adolescents are leaving their homes without the spiritual muscle to survive in a culture that has embraced lies about sex and gender. About 75 percent of "churched Christian" Gen Z teens (born from 1999 to 2015) don't believe that sex before marriage and homosexual behavior are morally wrong.[7]

I could go on, but I think you get the idea. We're weak, confused, and largely being swept away by the culture.

And yet.

If you're a disciple of Jesus, you have no reason to be timid or confused about your convictions if they're grounded in his teachings. Are you his disciple? Do you believe he is, in addition to Messiah and Son of God, the wisest

5. See George Barna, "American Worldview Inventory 2022: Release #2: The Strengths and Weaknesses of What Pre-Teen Parents Believe and Do," Arizona Christian University, March 29, 2022, www.arizonachristian.edu/wp-content/uploads/2022/03/AWVI2022_Release_02_Digital.pdf (accessed September 25, 2022). For more information on biblical worldview, see Bobby Harrington and Daniel McCoy, "What is a Biblical Worldview? Definitions, Dilemmas, and Dangers," Renew.org, www.renew.org/what-is-a-biblical-worldview/ (accessed September 25, 2022).

6. Barna, "American Worldview Inventory 2022."

7. "Churched Christians have attended church in the past six months but do not hold to the following criteria to qualify as 'engaged Christians' based on these beliefs: The Bible is the inspired word of God and contains truth about the world. I have made a personal commitment to Jesus Christ that is still important in my life today. I engage with my church in more ways than just attending services. I believe that Jesus Christ was crucified and raised from the dead to conquer sin and death." "Gen Z and Morality: What Teens Believe (So Far)," *Barna*, October 9, 2018, www.barna.com/research/gen-z-morality/ (accessed September 25, 2022).

man who ever lived? If so, then take your convictions and courage from him and learn to live from him. Jesus gives us a clear solution for this cultural moment: believe in him and obey his teachings.

GROUNDING CONVICTIONS IN THE TEACHINGS OF JESUS

When Jesus told his disciples to make disciples of all nations, he didn't just tell them to stick with the basics of the faith. He told them to teach people to obey *everything* he commanded (Matthew 28:18–20).

Theologians have called this the "hermeneutics of obedience": we come to understand the Scriptures best by obeying what they say. Similarly, child psychology calls this "actions preceding beliefs." Young children gain understanding *after* they obey again and again.

> Moral training is progressive. That is, all virtues placed in the heart of a child develop from the general to the specific. For example, when learning the virtue of honesty, a three-year-old child will first learn, "Thou shall not steal." At five, the understanding of the virtue broadens. "Thou shall not steal" includes "Thou shall not manipulate a situation to gain an advantage over another child's toy." By age seven, different specific meanings include, "Thou shall not extort from another." At twelve, the meaning expands further, continuing the progress until the child comes to the fullness of that virtue.[8]

Perhaps this was part of what Jesus meant when he said, "Unless you change and become like little children, you will never enter the kingdom of heaven" (Matthew 18:3b). Part of following Christ is obeying him even when we don't want to or when his commands don't make sense to us, just like young children with their parents.

Abiding in Jesus leads to ever-increasing fellowship with him and fruitfulness in our lives (John 15:1–17). Loving him means obeying him (John 15:9–10). Doing these things is my heart's desire. I believe that if you're reading this book, they are your heart's desire, too. Amid the current confusion, let's do

8. Gary and Anne Marie Ezzo, *Growing Kids God's Way: Reaching the Heart of Your Child with a God-Centered Purpose* (Louisiana, MO: Growing Families International, 2008), 21.

our best to obey and understand everything Jesus commanded us, especially in something as significant as sex and gender.

STEREOTYPES AND ARCHETYPES

There is likely no more loaded question these days than this: *What does it mean to be a man or a woman?*

When Tennessee Senator Marsha Blackburn asked Supreme Court Justice Ketanji Brown Jackson if she could define what a woman is during her nomination process, she was met with the reply, "I'm not a biologist."[9] Jackson knew better than to try and answer a "gotcha" question like that in our current cultural moment.

It's easy to be suspicious of these gender questions as "gotchas" within churches, too. This is because, unfortunately, many Christians have taken concepts of masculinity and femininity from the archetypes described in Scripture and collapsed them into stereotypes.[10] It's been all too easy to reduce maleness or femaleness to particular social roles. An archetype is the original pattern or model of which all things of the same type are representations or copies. Meanwhile, a stereotype is a fixed image, an oversimplification, of an original.

Catholic philosopher Peter Kreeft encourages us to set aside the stereotypes and return to the archetypes. In so doing, we can avoid a common misstep: equating gender with stereotypes that paint one group as superior and the other as inferior. Kreeft notes that both chauvinists and egalitarians assume that "all differences are differences in value." Both see *sameness* or *superiority* as the only options. The chauvinist argues that the sexes are different in *nature*, therefore they are different in *value*, so that a "male chauvinist," for example, sees men as superior to women. The egalitarian argues that the

9. Jonathan Weisman, "A Demand to Define 'Woman' Injects Gender Politics into Jackson's Confirmation Hearings," *NY Times*, March 23, 2022, www.nytimes.com/2022/03/23/us/politics/ketanji-brown-jackson-woman-definition.html (accessed October 19, 2022).
10. Peter Kreeft, "Is There Sex in Heaven?" www.peterkreeft.com/topics/sex-in-heaven.htm (accessed September 26, 2022).

sexes are not different in *value*, therefore they are not different in *nature*, with men and women being basically interchangeable.[11]

Kreeft explains,

> It is easy to see how foolish both arguments are. Of course not all differences are differences in value. Are dogs better than cats, or cats than dogs? Or are they different only by convention, not by nature? Chauvinist and egalitarian should both read the poets, songwriters, and mythmakers to find a third philosophy of sexuality that is both more sane and infinitely more interesting. It denies neither the obvious rational truth that the sexes are equal in value (as the chauvinist does) nor the equally obvious instinctive truth that they are innately different (as the egalitarian does). It revels in both, and in their difference: *vive la difference*![12]

Archetypes exhort men and women to assume sex-based behaviors and roles, while simultaneously recognizing a spectrum of giftings, talents, and inclinations. Stereotypes, on the other hand, cause confusion and frustration by requiring rigid role-playing between men and women and oversimplifying the wide spectrum of giftings among both sexes.

It is easy for us to see the transgender movement using stereotypes of men and women, as if the essence of femininity were breasts, makeup, and fancy clothing or the essence of masculinity were a flat chest, muscles, and body hair. The underlying assumption is that women and men are interchangeable. That to have equal value, maleness and femaleness must be, at root, social constructs.[13]

But the church, too, has been guilty of stereotyping men and women. When we focus women exclusively on how to be feminine or what they are in relation to men, we paint an incomplete picture of womanhood. When we focus men exclusively on leadership, bravery, and strength, we paint an incomplete

11. Peter Kreeft, "Is There Sex in Heaven?" 2022.
12. Peter Kreeft, "Is There Sex in Heaven?" 2022.
13. Maria Baer, "What Are Women For?" *Breakpoint*, March 28, 2022, www.breakpoint.org/what-are-women-for/ (accessed October 19, 2022).

picture of manhood. When we reduce marriage to men leading and women submitting, we oversimplify the dynamic and beautiful complementarity of a husband and wife.

Throughout this book, we will find ourselves being called back, over and over, to God's design for maleness and femaleness. It's crucial to note that this will stretch *all of us*. If you tend to see maleness and femaleness as basically interchangeable, studying God's design will stretch you. If you tend to see maleness and femaleness as tied to social stereotypes, studying God's design will stretch you. As general editor of this book, I have learned a ton and at times have had to allow Scripture to inform and even correct what is natural for me. In a culture confused about sex and gender, if we are disciples of Jesus, we must embrace the truth of God's good design. The primary calling of both men *and* women is to glorify him. And, yes, how we work out this calling will be marked by our maleness and femaleness, but our calling shouldn't be reduced to male and female stereotypes.

Before we dive into the contents of the book, let's define some key terms we will use.

IMPORTANT TERMS: COMPLEMENTARIAN, EGALITARIAN, SEX, AND GENDER

Throughout the book a few key terms will be used again and again. Because the culture often means something very different when they use these words, I'm going to define them as they are used throughout the book.

Term #1: Complementarianism

Complementarianism is the view that men and women are created equal in their being, value, and personhood, yet they *complement* each other with different roles and responsibilities as manifested in marriage, family life, and the church.

Note that there are two variations in the complementarian viewpoint.

We at the Renew Network believe that many complementarians have proven to be tradition-bound and overly restrictive, failing to make room for many of the important roles women play in the Bible. Many traditional churches are frozen in a rigid church leadership culture that prioritizes one set of Scriptures about gender, especially 1 Corinthians 14 and 1 Timothy 2, while de-emphasizing other Scriptures that describe important areas of church ministry in which women were involved. Women in these churches might never be asked to pray or read Scripture in the presence of other men. Consequently, they may hesitate to speak up in class or small groups, leaving the conversation for men alone. And if women are asked to teach at all, it is likely to be in the nursery or elementary classes. I know a woman who was asked to stop teaching the sixth-grade class when her son was baptized at age twelve. Why? Because this boy was considered to have more spiritual authority than his own mother after his baptism! Sadly, this rigid stereotyping of men and women can cause men to take a low view of women in their marriages and at church. One way to describe this approach is "hard complementarianism."

In contrast to this view, there are those who hold to a more moderate or softer form of complementarianism ("soft complementarianism"). Moderate or soft complementarians see a principle-based posture in Scripture, more than that captured by clear-cut rules or laws. This approach envisions the ambiguity of missional settings and circumstances where strict rules are not as important as pursuing God's heart and his normative principles. It also advocates the active participation of women throughout the ministries of the church, while holding that the main preacher-teacher role and elder role are only for qualified men.

We hold to soft complementarianism at the Renew Network. We are a multiethnic network with leaders and churches throughout North America and in other countries beyond.

This soft complementarianism seeks to stand against the impulses of a chauvinistic, dominating, and sometimes abusive traditionalism on the one side, and the impulses of a sex-blind, gender-leveling egalitarianism on the other side.

So what is egalitarianism?

Term #2: Egalitarianism

Like complementarianism, egalitarianism holds that men and women are created equal in their being, value, and personhood. But egalitarianism diverges from complementarianism by teaching that there are no unique roles for men and women in the home and church. In this view, men and women have interchangeable roles and adhere to mutual submission toward each other.

Egalitarian concepts emerged in philosophical and political circles in the 1700s and are just now coming to dominate most aspects of Western civilization. The initial impulses have great merit with a focus on equal treatment of each individual. In fact, equality of persons as made in the image of God finds direct support in biblical teachings, and we can celebrate anywhere we see this principle lived out.

Yet unchecked egalitarianism, grounded in a developing secular philosophy, is now becoming a trump-card consideration used to override additional biblical principles. And sadly, Christian egalitarians are now arguing that what the Bible teaches is in step with this advanced secular egalitarian thought.

When it comes to church leadership, egalitarianism means that women do everything in the church that men do. They should be championed as pastors, preachers, and elders. Similarly, egalitarianism in the home translates into no unique roles for men or women; mutual and interchangeable submission is the standard. Egalitarianism in the church is a relatively new belief system, growing quickly in our Western culture, which first valued these ideals in philosophy and psychology.[14]

Up until recently, mostly theologically progressive (liberal) churches adopted egalitarianism. But that is changing rapidly, especially in the last ten years, as more and more evangelical, Bible-believing churches and ministries follow suit.

---

14. See Carl Trueman, *Strange New World: How Thinkers and Activists Redefined Identity and Sparked the Sexual Revolution* (Wheaton: Crossway, 2022) and *The Rise and Triumph of the Modern Self: Cultural Amnesia, Expressive Individualism, and the Road to Sexual Revolution* (Wheaton: Crossway, 2020).

We at the Renew Network believe that, by and large, these evangelical churches and ministries will end up on the same path that the mainline, progressive denominations have followed. However, they will travel there not by first denying the authority and infallibility of the Bible, as the mainline churches have done. Rather, they will get there by introducing new methods of interpretation that are easier to adopt in a post-truth, post-critical thinking culture.

We at Renew.org admit that, at first glance, a purely egalitarian position sounds like good sense. Even good news. Our culture has conditioned us for it. An egalitarian favors equality: people should get the same, or be treated the same, or have the same authority.[15] It can just feel right to embrace these exact ideas in our churches and marriages.

But a straightforward reading of *Scripture* with good exegesis (more on this in future chapters, particularly Chapter 4 and forward) offers a more nuanced way. It recognizes equality of personhood, noting that men and women equally reflect the image of God, while also maintaining differences for the sexes in marriage and ministry. It affirms a proper view of authority and influence based upon Christ's example as a suffering, loving, servant-like head. It upholds God's created order and the obvious biological differences between the sexes.

Making egalitarianism the lens for reading Scripture will lead us down a different path.

Unchecked egalitarianism will promote the interchangeability of men and women and even challenge the concept of authority with a call to mutuality. As we will show in this book, equality is a good impulse, but it goes bad when it is used to override other scriptural principles. And bad ideas create victims in various ways.

15. Richard Arneson, "Egalitarianism," *The Stanford Encyclopedia of Philosophy*, summer 2013, www.plato.stanford.edu/entries/egalitarianism/#:~:text=Egalitarianism%20is%20a%20trend%20of,as%20equals%2C%20in%20some%20respect.

Term #3: Sex

Kreeft cuts through the confusion: "Sex is something you are, not something you do . . . we have trivialized sex into a thing to do rather than a quality of our inner being. It has become a thing of surfaces and external feeling rather than of personality and internal feeling."[16] In this book, when not referring to sex as an activity, the words "sex" or "sexuality" will mean a person being biologically sexed as male or female.

Term #4: Gender

Gender is how we live out our biological sex. It's how we act in light of being male or female.[17] As Christopher West notes in his excellent book, *Theology of the Body for Beginners*, the root of the word "gender" (gen) means to produce or give birth to. We see this in words like genesis, generous, genetics, genealogy, and genitals. "A person's *gen*-der, therefore, is based on the manner in which that person is designed to *gen*-erate new life."[18]

In this cultural climate, it has become common to separate sex from gender and then customize gender in ways that match a person's inner feelings, regardless of their sex. As we'll explain throughout this book, this separation is not good for those who believe God created us male and female. As Williamson and Radcliff explain in Chapter 15 ("Thoughts of a Theologian and a Therapist on the Transgender Debate"), a person's gender identity ought to be "anchored to biological sex. We embrace the body as a good gift of God."

One final note before we begin.

Because the Renew Network desires to equip churches to choose a better way when it comes to gender than an ineffective traditionalism or a culturally dominated progressivism, we have published the following formal statement on gender.

---

16. Kreeft, www.peterkreeft.com/topics/sex-in-heaven.htm.
17. Todd Wilson, *Mere Sexuality: Rediscovering the Christian Vision of Sexuality* (Grand Rapids: Zondervan, 2017), 61.
18. Christopher West, *Theology of the Body for Beginners: Rediscovering the Meaning of Life, Love, Sex, and Gender* (Sandy, UT: Wellspring, 2018), 40.

> *We believe both men and women were created by God to equally reflect, in gendered ways, the nature and character of God in the world. In marriage, husbands and wives are to submit to one another, yet there are gender-specific expressions: husbands model themselves in relationship with their wives after Jesus's sacrificial love for the church; and wives model themselves in relationship with their husbands after the church's willingness to follow Jesus. In the church, men and women serve as partners in the use of their gifts in ministry, while seeking to uphold New Testament norms, which teach that the lead teacher/preacher role in the gathered church and the elder/overseer role are for qualified men. The vision of the Bible is an equal partnership of men and women in creation, in marriage, in salvation, in the gifts of the Spirit and in the ministries of the church but exercised in ways that honor gender as described in the Bible.*

The authors of this book uphold this statement.

Much of this edition is formatted in a Q&A format so that you can quickly find answers to your most pressing questions. Feel free to read straight through or jump around. More resources can also be found at Renew.org.

1

WHAT DOES NATURE TELL US SEX AND GENDER ARE FOR?

RENÉE WEBB SPROLES

I'm going to set up this section of the book with a series of questions and answers:

Can you use a cell phone to drive a nail into the wall?
Yes.

Is that what the cell phone was made for?
No.

Is using a cell phone the most efficient way to hammer a nail?
Of course not.

Will the cell phone be damaged in the process of hitting the nail?
Very probably, yes.

Before we can discern if men and women are "working" the way God intended, we need to know what sex and gender were made for. Without a clear understanding, we may find ourselves using cell phones to hammer nails, so to speak. We'll be wondering why we are confused about our identity, frustrated in our relationships, and getting hurt in our churches. I suggest we can find the answer to what sex and gender were made for in three distinct places: nature, culture, and Scripture.

We'll look at nature and culture in this chapter and the next, before devoting several chapters to Scripture.

WHAT NATURE SAYS SEX AND GENDER ARE FOR: BODIES AND BEHAVIOR

In America, we have come to believe that our physical bodies are subordinate to how we imagine ourselves. We often want to do any "what" with our bodies without giving heed to the "why" of our design. We, especially women, can come to believe that our bodies hinder our flourishing. We can even believe that our bodies lie to us.

A Christian view of nature, however, sees our sexuality (male or female) not as a *hindrance* to our flourishing but as a *clue* to God's design and purpose for us in the world he made.[19]

In his excellent article, "Natural Complementarians: Men, Women, and the Way Things Are," Alastair Roberts notes that there are "family resemblances" for each sex. These resemblances are traits that are generally recognized amongst men and others that are generally recognized amongst women. "Recognizing differences in the physical, sexual, and hormonal ordering of male and female bodies helps us to understand broader behavioral and social differences that correlate with these."[20] Put simply, our behavior is affected by our bodies.

One clue our bodies give us is that humans were made as a duality.

Duality

Complementarity is woven throughout creation. God made the *heavens* and the *earth* (Genesis 1:1). He separated *light* from *darkness*, making *day* and *night* (Genesis 1:3–5). He made waters in the *heavens* and on

19. Joe Rigney, "What Makes a Man—or a Woman? Lost Voices on a Vital Question," September 9, 2020, www.desiringgod.org/articles/what-makes-a-man-or-a-woman (accessed October 19, 2022).

20. Alastair Roberts, "Natural Complementarians: Men, Women and the Way Things Are," *The Calvinist International*, September 13, 2016, www.calvinistinternational.com/2016/09/13/natural-complementarians-men-women/ (accessed October 19, 2022).

the *earth* (Genesis 1:6–7). He gathered the water into *seas*, setting apart the dry *land* (Genesis 1:9–10). God made the *sun* and *moon* to govern the *day* and the *night* (Genesis 1:16). He made *sea creatures* and *land creatures* (Genesis 1:20–25). And as the pinnacle of creation, he made *man* and *woman* in his image (Genesis 1:26–27).

Complementarity is found within our individual bodies as well. There is a sense in which our body needs duality to function in its most basic ways. Our eyes see two images, layering each one on the other to gain perspective and clarity. Our hands do slightly different things, so using them in unison is more powerful than using them individually. Our ears work best in stereo, making sounds clearer, providing direction and depth perception.

In the same way, our bodies give us clues that we were made with complementary masculine and feminine tendencies. Let's look at these more closely.

Infants

Male and female fetuses differ in testosterone concentrations beginning as early as week eight of gestation. This early hormone difference exerts permanent influences on brain development and behavior. Contemporary research shows that hormones are particularly important for the development of sex-typical childhood behavior, including toy choices, which until recently were thought to result solely from sociocultural influences.[21]

Children

Masculine and feminine natures can be observed in their raw forms very early in life. Christine Hoff Sommers has an excellent article in *The Atlantic* titled, "You Can Give a Boy a Doll, but You Can't Make Him Play With It." In it, she notes:

> Children, with few exceptions, are powerfully drawn to sex-stereotyped play. (*Boys are powerfully attracted to large-group, rough-and-tumble play; and girls are attracted to intimate theatrical play.*)

21. Melissa Hines, "Sex-related variation in human behavior and the brain," *Trends in Cognitive Sciences,* August 18, 2010, www.cell.com/trends/cognitive-sciences/fulltext/S1364-6613(10)00172-5 (accessed October 19, 2022).

> The female preference for nurturing play and the male propensity for rough-and-tumble hold cross-culturally and even cross-species (with a few exceptions—female spotted hyenas seem to be at least as aggressive as males). Among our close relatives such as vervet and rhesus monkeys, researchers have found that females play with dolls far more than their brothers, who prefer balls and toy cars. It seems unlikely that the monkeys were indoctrinated by stereotypes in a Top-Toy catalog. Something else is going on.[22]

Long before their bodies change at puberty, little girls and little boys tend to display behavioral differences. What is written in every cell of their bodies is displayed in their personalities and interactions with the world. Charles Murray notes, "Both sexes have all the major sex hormones to some degree, but *androgens* are the ones most identified with males (testosterone being the most famous) and *estrogens* are the ones most identified with females."[23] Professor Melissa Hines, who studies gender development at Cambridge University, writes about the influence that pre-natal hormones have on post-natal behavior. She writes:

> The effects of the early hormone environment also extend to personality characteristics that show sex differences. Probably the best-established links in this area involve empathy, which is typically higher in females, and physical aggression, which is typically higher in males.[24]

Hormone concentrations contribute to substantial differences between boys and girls.[25] Testosterone permanently changes brain tissue and is correlated with higher levels of confidence, status assertion, risk-taking (physically and intellectually), and sex drive.[26] Estrogen also affects brain development

22. Christian Hoff Sommers, "You Can Give a Boy a Doll, but You Can't Make Him Play With It," *The Atlantic*, December 6, 2012, www.theatlantic.com/sexes/archive/2012/12/you-can-give-a-boy-a-doll-but-you-cant-make-him-play-with-it/265977/ (accessed October 19, 2022).
23. Charles Murray, *Human Diversity: The Biology of Gender, Race, and Class* (New York: Twelve, 2020), 98–100.
24. Hines, "Sex-related variation in human behavior and the brain."
25. Hines, "Sex-related variation in human behavior and the brain."
26. Murray, *Human Diversity*, 100; Roberts, "Natural Complementarians."

and is associated with the ability to recognize different emotions and facial expressions, as well as increased language capacity.[27] When this hormone dump is interrupted for boys or girls, sex-specific behaviors are less pronounced, again demonstrating the biology-behavior link.

Scientists are discovering (or more accurately, rediscovering) that our behavior is not solely socially constructed. Peter Kreeft puts it this way: "Biological sexuality is innate, natural, and in fact pervasive to every cell in the body. It is not socially conditioned, or conventional, or environmental; it is hereditary."[28]

Adolescence

And let's not forget the rollercoaster of adolescence. No matter what we wish or think about our biological sex, our bodies change and develop according to a chromosomal reality (XY or XX) powered by hormones. Changes in body shape and voice, pubic and facial hair growth, and sex organ development all occur during puberty.[29]

I was listening to a recent episode of the *Strong Women* podcast titled "Sexual Discipleship" (How's that for an interesting title?!) where Dr. Juli Slattery, author of *Rethinking Sexuality: God's Design Matters,* noted the crucial role that the biological process of puberty plays in our sexuality. It's a lengthy quote but worth the read:

> Sexuality is about so much more than what we are doing with our bodies. It's the aspect of humanity that God has given us that draws us to share ourselves, into intimacy. If you think about a child who reaches puberty at 11, 12, or 13 years old, male or female, something happens where they begin pursuing relationship and thinking about relationship. Boys become obsessed with sexual desires and urges, which has challenges, but we need to see that it's actually a good

27. "The Influence of Estrogen on Female Mood Changes," *Eurekalert,* January 22, 2012, www.eurekalert.org/pub_releases/2012-01/sicp-tio010912.php (accessed October 19, 2022).
28. Smith, "Is There Sex in Heaven."
29. "The Growing Child: Teenager (13 to 18 Years)," Stanford Children's Health, www.stanfordchildrens.org/en/topic/default?id=the-growing-child-adolescent-13-to-18-years-90-P02175 (accessed October 19, 2022).

> thing. As girls become sexually awakened, it's channeled more into the romance stories and daydreaming about the boy they like.
>
> Imagine if there was no sexual awakening for adolescents and young adults. We would be content with jobs and hobbies and really self-gratification and chasing down what we want without moving toward people. So, our sexual desire and sexuality are about moving us toward intimacy here on earth, and they point us toward the intimacy and covenant we are supposed to have with God.
>
> Our sexuality is telling the story that you were not made to do life alone. This is true not only in marriage but also in singleness and friendships, which drive us to be vulnerable, wanting to be loved, wanting to be embraced, and all of the expressions of being male and female.[30]

The human drive for intimacy and connection, amplified by adolescent changes, coincides with the naturally observable truth that maleness and femaleness complement and are attracted to each other.

Drawing Us Toward One Another

And for those who would argue that masculine and feminine traits are not always allotted evenly to each man and woman, I agree. But these exceptions prove the general rule. In later chapters, we'll see how Scripture gives restraining and exhorting guidelines for each sex *in spite of* as well as *because of* their natural tendencies.

By adulthood, these biological differences can be especially pronounced in both men and women: there is no escaping the biological reality that men and women have unique roles in intercourse and procreation. Alastair Roberts explains it this way:

> Male identity, in contrast to women's, and across human societies, is far more consistently invested in demonstrating robust external agency in the world . . . . Men do not have the same profound physical

30. Dr. Juli Slattery, "Sexual Discipleship," *Strong Women Podcast*, September 9, 2020.

> and emotional bond to their offspring that women have. Women's own bodies are the site where the chief end of their sexuality can be realized, as a man is united to them, a child can be conceived and gestated within them, and where that child can later [be] nurtured by them. Men's bodies, by contrast, are directed outside of themselves sexually, towards ends realized elsewhere. As a result, their powerfully outward-oriented sexual impulse and natural energies are much more easily waylaid where they are not assisted by healthy social norms.[31]

Sex as an action is a pleasurable, baby-making activity meant to be practiced within a marriage. The first chapter of Genesis shows us how God intended sex to be used: "God blessed them and said to them, 'Be fruitful and increase in number; fill the earth and subdue it'" (Genesis 1:28a).

Dr. Jennifer Roback Morse, founder and president of the Ruth Institute, a global non-profit organization that defends the family at home and in the public square and equips others to do the same, points out that the "sexual revolution's" ideologies have changed our view of sex in three fundamental ways:

- The "contraceptive ideology," which separates sex from childbearing
- The "divorce ideology," which separates sex and childbearing from marriage
- The "gender ideology," which eliminates all distinctions between men and women except those that individuals explicitly embrace[32]

Alastair Roberts notes that linking the action of sex with babies is a crucial biological reality that elevates its status from mere pleasure to purpose.

> Procreation means that sex is never just about us: it draws us out into the world in responsible and committed action. Procreation presents us with a world with stakes, where actions have consequences. Procreation means that we must approach sex—like life, like truth,

31. Roberts, "Natural Complementarians."
32. "The Sexual State: How Elite Ideologies are Destroying Lives," Family Research Council, January 22, 2019, www.frc.org/university/the-sexual-state-how-elite-ideologies-are-destroying-lives.

> like God—from a position of commitment and responsibility to something greater than our own will and pleasure.[33]

As we will see in later sections where we examine Scripture, this act is about *more* than continuing the human race, but it's certainly not *less* than that.

It's worth noting that those of us who aren't having intercourse *are* fully human and fully sexual. Otherwise, Paul and Jesus would not have been fully men. Whenever we imitate Christ by sacrificially giving up our bodies for others, we are expressing in other ways the body's spousal meaning.[34]

So to return to our question at the beginning of this chapter, what does nature show us our complementary, biological sex, as male or female, is for?

Nature hints that our createdness as male or female is for attraction to intimacy and relationships. It's also for making babies. Just like electrons and protons, there are opposite forces that draw us together, helping us understand and impact the world in ways superior to just going it alone. In fact, many times it's in the context of male/female relationships that we *better* understand what it means to be either a man or a woman.

Through nature, God has revealed clues of who he is and what he wants. Creating humanity in his image is a major way that God has revealed himself in creation (what theologians have called "general revelation," because all people have access to these truths). Likewise, these observable behavioral and body differences are also part of what God has revealed in creation, and we do well to take the hint instead of rebelling against his created order.

Unfortunately, humans are the most stubborn of his creation, as Isaiah 1:3 explains, "The ox knows his master, the donkey his owner's manger, but . . . my people do not understand." Commenting on this, Old Testament scholar John N. Oswalt describes how God has given us his standards, and we tend to vilify those who point them out to us. Yet, "to require a railroad engine to stay on its tracks is not some infringement of its basic rights; it

33. Alastair Roberts, "Rescuing Christian Masculinity," *Alastair's Adversaria,* November 12, 2014, www.alastairadversaria.com/2014/11/12/rescuing-christian-masculinity/.
34. West, *Theology of the Body*, 56.

is merely to define the circumstance under which that machine must operate if its potential is to be realized."[35] We need to take the hints God makes through creation.

In the next chapter, we'll take a look at the hints various cultures give us about what sex and gender are for.

35. John N. Oswalt, *Isaiah,* NIV Application Commentary, edited by Terry Muck (Downers Grove: Zondervan, 2003), 75.

2

WHAT DOES CULTURE TELL US SEX AND GENDER ARE FOR?

RENÉE WEBB SPROLES, EMMA JANE GOODWYN

This might seem like an impossible chapter. How can "culture" teach us what sex and gender are for—when cultures can range from rigid to fluid, from traditional to experimental when it comes to sex and gender? In fact, in the next chapter, Daniel McCoy will draw a "you are here" map of sorts when it comes to contemporary Western culture's view of sex and gender. As you'll see, we're not advocating for letting this particular culture be our reliable guide for the purpose of sex and gender.

Culture is a shared way of living, and cultures can range from healthy to self-destructive. Joe Rigney describes the power and purpose of culture this way: "Culture is the expression of nature (and, for Christians, also of Scripture) in a particular time and place. It includes customs and traditions that testify to the natural tendencies of our nature."[36] What we describe in this chapter isn't limited to one particular culture; rather, we offer insights we learn about sex and gender from culture to culture (i.e., cross-culturally). In particular, this chapter will highlight two cross-cultural norms we learn about sex and gender.

Before we arrive at those two central norms, here are some facts we see across cultures (even if some cultures work to downplay them):

36. Joe Rigney, "What Makes a Man—or a Woman? Lost Voices on a Vital Question," Desiring God, September 9, 2020, www.desiringgod.org/articles/what-makes-a-man-or-a-woman (accessed October 19, 2022).

First, being born male or female is a biological fact. Only a fraction of one percent of infants are born with chromosomal abnormalities that would make their sex difficult to determine by their genitalia.[37] Yet our culture is increasingly embracing the idea that sex has no relation to gender. Indeed, in 2021 the American Medical Association's LGBTQ+ advisory committee recommended that hospitals remove the sex of a baby from the public-facing portion of birth certificates because "assigning sex using a binary variable and placing it on the public portion of the birth certificate perpetuates a view that it is immutable."[38] Why just the public-facing portion? Why not leave it off altogether? Because doctors cannot give appropriate care unless they know what kind of body, male or female, they are treating.

Next, we have categories of masculine and feminine. These are the tendencies and aptitudes of the sexes that are observable among men and women. Each of us has masculine and feminine tendencies in varying degrees. We all know women who have more masculine tendencies and men who have more feminine tendencies. This simply confirms that there is a spectrum of what it looks like to be a man or a woman.

Then there is the state of being a man or a woman. Boys are not yet men; and girls are not yet women. Being a man or a woman involves growth and maturity. This can be purely biological: a growth from infancy to childhood to adolescence to adulthood. But becoming a man or woman can also involve spiritual, intellectual, social, and emotional growth.

Then, there is the question of what it means to be a *good* man or a *good* woman. Many thanks to Alastair Roberts for the concise observation that "those who are good at being 'manly' are often bad men."[39] Some of the current confusion around what it means to be a man or a woman arises from the right impulse to correct abuses perpetrated by men and women behaving

---

37. Leonard Sax, "How Common Is Intersex? A Response to Anne Fausto-Sterling," National Library of Medicine 39, no. 3 (August 2002): www.pubmed.ncbi.nlm.nih.gov/12476264/ (accessed October 19, 2022).
38. Frankie de la Cretaz, "American Medical Association Recommends Removing Sex From Birth Certificates," *Them*, August 5, 2021, www.them.us/story/american-medical-association-recommends-removing-sex-from-birth-certificates (accessed October 19, 2022).
39. Alastair Roberts, "2 Stories of Manhood," *The Gospel Coalition*, June 13, 2022, www.thegospelcoalition.org/reviews/men-we-need-good-be-man/ (accessed October 19, 2022).

badly. The natural strength and power of men is good for others when it arises from love and is exercised with care, but unchecked masculinity can be harsh, scary, and even dangerous. The gentleness and relationality of women are good for others when they emerge from love and are exercised with strength. But unchecked femininity can be weak, petty, and undermining. Instead of creating a never-ending list of gender categories, we should be asking what it means to be *good* in conjunction with the reality of being a man or a woman. Often, it means taking on some of the other gender's natural strengths to balance our own.

TWO CROSS-CULTURAL NORMS

Again, gender is the expression of our bodily reality as biological males and females (our sex) in our culture (although some try to disconnect their gender from their sex and ground their gender in their inner feelings). The distinct roles of men and women, known as gender norms, are culturally agreed-upon standards by which people live. Much of feminism in the last few decades has declared that these norms are totally made up and should be abandoned. Are they right?

I want to show you that there are agreed-upon standards across cultures and that they do have something to do with our bodies. While the particularities of gender norms like clothing or speech may differ from culture to culture, as we look across cultures, we see two norms emerge that differ between men and women: *protecting and preserving families.*

Men are particularly suited to the protection of families, while women are particularly suited to the preservation of families. Families are the building blocks of culture. When the family collapses, civilization eventually follows. Nicknamed "The Enforcer" by her five children, Barbara Bush said as much at her commencement address to Wellesley students on June 1, 1990: "Your success as a family, our success as a society, depends not on what happens in the White House, but on what happens in your house."[40]

---

40. Casey Quackenbush, "On Family, Giving, and Life in Politics: Here are Some of Barbara Bush's Most Memorable Quotes," *Time*, April 18, 2018, www.time.com/5244413/barbara-bush-most-memorable-quotes/ (accessed October 19, 2022).

So what has happened in our "houses" across history? A Yale study summarizing gender differences in division of labor, political, and warrior roles across the centuries found that there were some near-universal patterns for men and women:

- Men almost always hunt and trap animals, fish, clear land, prepare soil for planting, butcher animals, make nets and rope, and collect honey.
- Women almost always care for infants. They also usually gather wild plants, cook, prepare dairy products, fetch firewood or other fuel, launder clothes, spin yarn, and care for children.

Just a cursory glance at the biological differences between males and females can help explain this phenomenon. Heavy work like hunting, trapping, and clearing land is incompatible with caring for infants, not to mention the loss of reproductive potential for a society if females were killed in battle. Even with the archeological confirmation of the legendary Amazonian and Greek female warriors, women are estimated to amount to less than 1 percent of all warriors in human history. This gender difference is more of a cross-cultural universal than almost any other gender difference in societies.[41]

Modern Western culture is striving to free men and women from the constraints of gender norms. But is that truly liberating? Christina Hoff Sommers, author of *Freedom Feminism*, notes:

> In a 2008 study in the *Journal of Personality and Social Psychology*, a group of international researchers compared data on gender and personality across 55 nations. Throughout the world, women tend to be more nurturing, risk averse, and emotionally expressive, while men are usually more competitive, risk taking, and emotionally flat. But the most fascinating finding is this: Personality differences between men and women are the largest and most robust in the more prosperous, egalitarian, and educated societies. According to the authors, "Higher levels of human development—including long and

41. Carol R. Ember, Milagro Escobar, Noah Rossen, and Abbe McCarter, "Gender" in C. R. Ember, ed. *Explaining Human Culture*, November 18, 2019, www.hraf.yale.edu/ehc/summaries/gender (accessed October 19, 2022).

> healthy life, equal access to knowledge and education, and economic wealth—were the main nation-level predictors of larger sex differences in personality."[42]

Yes, countries that have made the *greatest strides* in gender equity report *larger sex differences* in men and women. Not smaller.

If you think gender norms are just socially constructed, these cross-cultural results seem counterintuitive. Even confusing. But the confusion evaporates when we allow ourselves to acknowledge that these cross-cultural norms are grounded in biological facts—and all the more so when we see a purposeful Creator who set up the biological facts in the first place. As it turns out, when granted greater freedoms, "both sexes become freer to do what comes naturally."[43]

In the remainder of this chapter, we will explore how observing culture helps us see how preserving and protecting families are for our good.

HEALTHY CIVILIZATIONS

Dr. Richard Oster has noted that ancient civilizations, whether pagan or Christian, recognized the significance of protecting and preserving families. "They valued organization and rule in the home because they understood that without properly functioning homes and marriages, civilization would not continue. There would be chaos." (For more on this, see Chapter 10 of this book.)

It's in the context of protecting and preserving families that men and women build healthy civilizations. The biological realities of men, such as increased testosterone and greater muscle mass, make them especially dangerous when not attached to women in families.

> Tying men to women and children harnesses men's energies to the construction and protection of society, where otherwise they might

42. Christina Hoff Sommers, "Defending Freedom Feminism," *Reason,* January 18, 2014, www.reason.com/2014/01/18/saving-feminism/ (accessed October 19, 2022).
43. Murray, *Human Diversity*, 36, 42.

> run amok. Where men are not tied to women in such a manner, men often try to prove their masculinity in destructive and socially damaging ways. The violence of dysfunctional masculinity is much more of an immediate threat to culture than dysfunctional forms of femininity: women's violence is more likely to be directed against their own bodies. Women and the children that they bear exert a centripetal social force upon men, drawing them toward the service and protection of society.[44]

Gail Collins, the first female editorial page editor at the *New York Times*, noted in an NPR interview on her book *America's Women* that the most important role women have played in the history of our nation is "to make men behave one way or another."[45]

Skeptical?

Collins gives an example from our nation's history. When the first colony was established in Jamestown, two hundred men were sent over to do the work. Instead, what ensued was what Collins called "a rowdy fraternity party in the wilderness." One visitor even found the men bowling in the streets! Investors in the colony, less concerned about gender norms and more concerned about salvaging their investment, decided to offer women of marriageable age free passage and appealing hope chests to entice these "fraternity boys" into becoming diligent, hardworking, productive men.

It worked. Behold the socializing power of wives and mothers.

First Things journalist Glenn Stanton notes:

> Women create, shape, and maintain human culture. Manners exist because women exist. Worthy men adjust their behavior when a woman enters the room. They become better creatures. Civilization arises and endures because women have expectations of themselves and of those around them.

44. Roberts, "Natural Complementarians."
45. Gail Collins, "America's Women," interview by Juan Williams, *NPR*, October 9, 2003, www.npr.org/templates/story/story.php?storyId=1459945 (accessed October 19, 2022).

> This is not just a conservative or traditionalist idea. . . . Anthropologists have long recognized that the most fundamental social problem every community must solve is the unattached male. . . . Men settle down when they get married; if they fail to marry, they fail to settle down.[46]

We need each other!

BRINGING OUT THE BEST IN EACH OTHER

As we look at family across cultures, we will see many families that are more a source of hurt than stability. But when done well, families create societies where we can live in harmony and thrive. Feminist cries like "A woman needs a man like a fish needs a bicycle" give voice to injustices that women have suffered under dysfunctional masculinity, but it's not fundamentally true. When we recognize biological realities, embrace God's image in us, and follow his path for men and women, we bring out the best in each other.

In America, it might be easy to think that this emphasis on family unfairly marginalizes single adults. That might be true if you think of family as simply the nuclear family of father, mother, and children, but this model is a relatively recent cultural invention. David Brooks, in his article, "The Nuclear Family Was a Mistake," argues that *extended* family groups have been the (very healthy) norm for countless civilizations, including ours. Summarizing the changes in family structure over the past century, Brooks notes:

> We've made life freer for individuals and more unstable for families. We've made life better for adults but worse for children. We've moved from big, interconnected, and extended families, which helped protect the most vulnerable people in society from the shocks of life, to smaller, detached nuclear families (a married couple and their children), which give the most privileged people in society room to maximize their talents and expand their options. The shift from bigger and interconnected extended families to smaller and detached nuclear

46. Glenn T. Stanton, "Why Men and Women Are not Equal," *First Things*, August 26, 2016, www.firstthings.com/blogs/firstthoughts/2016/08/why-man-and-woman-are-not-equal (accessed October 19, 2022).

> families ultimately led to a familial system that liberates the rich and ravages the working-class and the poor.[47]

American culture tends to believe that we can pay someone to do the relational work of childrearing for us.[48] This stream of thought leads to the belief that parenting is an interchangeable activity. Even one that we can hire out to any competent adult—rather than a mother's love and a father's love, any person can lovingly raise a child.

Wealthy nuclear families can outsource and pay for many services that protect and preserve their family, whereas this is difficult for others. Brooks argues that extended families traditionally provided a socializing force and a resilience to weather unexpected burdens. If the nuclear family faced the death of a parent or a ruptured relationship between a parent and child, then aunts, uncles, cousins, and grandparents were there to fill the breach. This extended network also socialized its members, teaching them what is right and wrong and how to behave toward others.

American culture also largely teaches us that children are a lot of trouble. That they're an inconvenience. And we typically wait to have kids until we are ready to be inconvenienced on *our* terms. They are expensive and, many people quip, if society really cared about babies, it would make having one entirely free.

But the best things are never free, or easy, or even fair. For children, there is no adequate substitute for the family. (And by family, we mean married, biological parents, when at all possible.) Katy Faust and Stacy Manning note the critical roles of mother (female) and father (male) in their excellent book, *Them Before Us: Why We Need a Global Children's Rights Movement*:

> Decades' worth of research affirms how dramatically male and female differences manifest in the family, the relationship in which the two

47. David Brooks, "The Nuclear Family Was a Mistake," *The Atlantic*, March 2020, www.theatlantic.com/magazine/archive/2020/03/the-nuclear-family-was-a-mistake/605536/ (accessed October 19, 2022).
48. Jennifer Roback Morse, *Love & Economics: It Takes a Family to Raise a Village* (Lake Charles, LA: Ruth Institute Books, 2008), 161.

> sexes are required to cooperate most intensely. . . . Mothers and fathers differ in smell, voice, physique, and their interactions with their kids.[49]

A father's love is critical in preparing his child to launch into adulthood; and a mother's love is critical to ensuring her child's physical and emotional well-being. In families, children learn how to attach to others, how to love, and how to cooperate. Even adoption—a beautiful concept fleshed out in the gospel—addresses the fact that every child needs a family.

Think about it. If you could dream up your perfect childhood, what would it look like? We'd guess it would be in a happy, loving family with a mom and a dad.

STARTING NOW

Here's the good news: If you didn't have a healthy, happy childhood, you can provide one for your kids. By saying *no* to your own sleep, you're saying *yes* to easing your infant's hunger. By saying *no* to workaholism, you're saying *yes* to your role as a mother or father: the only mother or father that child has. By saying *no* to scrolling on your cell phone at every free moment, you're saying *yes* to the hard and important conversations with your teen.

When we are reconciled to God through Jesus, we become part of one big, extended, beautiful family. We gain ancestors we can look to for inspiration and courage: men and women who through faith conquered kingdoms and administered justice and whose weakness was turned to strength as they faced jeers, flogging, prison, and stoning (Hebrews 11:33–37). We gain brothers and sisters, mothers and fathers, grandparents, aunts and uncles who can provide a place for the single adult and nuclear family alike to be preserved and protected. The early church shared everything they had with one another so that there were no needy people among them. They were characterized by grace and unity—the hallmarks of a healthy family (Acts 2:42–45). We can live that way too. As a matter of fact, I (Renée) have.

49. Katy Faust and Stacy Manning, *Them Before Us: Why We Need a Global Children's Rights Movement* (New York: Post Hill Press, 2021), 60.

My husband and I experienced the power of God's extended family in our church's small groups throughout many stages of life.

A female friend who never married invested in my daughter's life during the critical teen years. She was able to speak to her in ways that I couldn't, from a perspective I didn't have, and with spiritual giftings different from mine. She did the same for my daughter-in-law.

In our thirties, our small group helped one another through the death of a beloved mother and friend—taking care of her children, feeding the family, driving her to doctor's appointments, and some of us sitting with her as she died. We've weathered post-partum depression, porn addiction, learning disabilities, job loss, teen rebellion, marital conflict, and more. We ate in each other's homes, watched each other's kids (and corrected them when needed!), fixed each other's broken appliances, and prayed for each other. Those with special training in medicine, or physical therapy, or finance, or home improvement, or education, or gardening, or counseling provided their professional help graciously and freely again and again. Those with broken nuclear families have learned to be the men and women God calls them to be as we live life together.

Behold the power of God's extended family.

Christian author Rosaria Butterfield calls this way of life in God's big, extended family "radically ordinary hospitality."

> Radically ordinary hospitality is done for the good of everyone—the host included. . . . [It] lives out your transparent, authentic faith before the watching world, knowing that too many people are dying of crushing loneliness, both within the church and without, and taking comfort in being both earthly and spiritual good to others. . . . [It] focuses on bearing the image of God. It seeks to simultaneously build up the family of God as it adds and includes those who do not yet know Christ.[50]

50. Tilly Dillehay, "Rosaria Butterfield Calls You to (Radically Ordinary) Hospitality," *The Gospel Coalition*, June 11, 2018, www.thegospelcoalition.org/article/rosaria-butterfield-radically-ordinary-hospitality/ (accessed October 19, 2022).

So to return to our original question, what does culture show us that biological sex is for? Protecting and preserving families. And it shows us that family is good for us.

In a culture that downplays the biological realities of men and women; ignores the sacred gospel story written on our bodies (see Ephesians 5:25–33); considers children an inconvenience; and faces the catastrophic fallout from the disintegration of the family, we have *good news:* there is meaning and purpose when you embrace your God-given calling as a man or a woman.

What does it mean to be a man or a woman? It means we recognize that our biology affects our behavior. It means that our bodies are signs, pointing to God's love story of the gospel. It means that men and women can build a culture in the church that protects and preserves families, recognizing the extended family of God we are part of, whether single or married.

May God give us the grace to live as the men and women he made us to be.

We've looked at what nature and culture teach us about the purpose of sex and gender. In the following several chapters, we will look to Scripture to help us understand what sex and gender are for. But first, we're going to take a quick "you are here" look at modern Western culture's predominant worldview, which undergirds its view of sex and gender.

3

DOES MODERN WESTERN CULTURE HAVE THE ANSWERS?

DANIEL MCCOY

One summer, I unintentionally made myself go prematurely bald. How? I was giving myself a haircut with some electric clippers when I discovered that they needed to be oiled. I removed the guard, oiled them, and went back to buzzing my hair—forgetting to put the guard back on.

That's the kind of result you can get when you insist on the do-it-yourself method.

When presented with God's way of doing things, our culture prefers the do-it-yourself method. When we remove any and all guards and structures put in place by God, we end up losing a lot more than we thought we would.

In the following chapters, we're going to explore what the Bible says about sex and gender. In a post-Christian culture, the gut response may be, "Why look at what the Bible says about these things?" Even if you're interested in what the Bible says about Jesus and salvation, why be interested in what the Bible says about sex and gender? Isn't the Bible the product of men who were hopelessly immersed in patriarchal and even misogynistic thinking? Why go back to the Bible for something like gender?

My purpose in this chapter is to warm you up to the idea that maybe this is an incorrect gut reaction. Maybe our modern Western culture is the wrong place to look to learn our views of sex and gender.

When it comes to sex and gender, there are important questions that will be answered. They will be answered by *someone*. The answers will be grounded either in our authority and our culture's authority or in God's authority. From somewhere, you will be told things like this:

- This is what you are.
- This is how to live.
- This is how to think.

In this chapter, I'm not trying to argue for a particular way to understand various Bible verses when it comes to gender. That comes in a later chapter. All I'm trying to do in this chapter is to zoom out to the two big-picture views of sex and gender in general—modern Western culture's view and a biblical view—and to warm you up to the idea that this culture is exactly the wrong place to get our views of sex and gender.

Now let me make clear what I'm not saying when I say that culture is the wrong place to ground our views of gender. I'm not saying that everything about gender in our culture is bad. On the contrary, I am grateful when I see women treated well and freed from oppression. I am grateful when I see women do well and succeed in their chosen profession. There's a lot in our culture regarding gender equality that we can be grateful for.

However, I do believe that culture is the wrong place to *ground* our views of gender. And I'll explain that in a minute.

First, I want to tell you a story about empowerment.

THREE METAMORPHOSES

Empowerment is taking somebody who hasn't had a voice and giving them a voice. It's taking somebody who hasn't had power and giving them power. Empowerment is often a wonderful thing. But if empowerment is the one thing we value as a culture above anything else, it turns into something destructive.

Here's a story told about empowerment. It's called "The Three Metamorphoses"—in other words, three transformations. The story goes like this.

There's a human spirit that will undergo three metamorphoses, or three transformations. First, the human spirit takes on heavy burdens like trying to be a good person when times are bad. That's a burden. Burdens like trying to love people who hate you. That's a burden. And thus, the first metamorphosis is for the human spirit to become a camel—a camel having to carry around a bunch of burdens.

The second metamorphosis is when the camel becomes a lion. Why a lion? Well, in the backdrop of this story there is a dragon. The dragon has a name: "Thou shalt." The dragon symbolizes commandments from above: thou shalt, thou shalt not. When the camel transforms into a lion, the lion pounces on the dragon and kills it and wins its freedom from the dragon who had told him how he could and couldn't live. Now the lion is free. That's the second metamorphosis.

The third metamorphosis is when the human spirit that was a camel and then a lion now turns into a child. You know how children like to play and make up games and have fun? Well, without the dragon telling the human spirit what to do, the human spirit now has childlike freedom to create and play and enjoy. It's innocence, it's forgetfulness, it's a new beginning.

Interesting story, but even more interesting is *who told the story.* The story was written by a German existentialist named Friedrich Nietzsche.[51] What is an existentialist? An existentialist is basically someone who says we can't really know what objective reality is, so we have to create our own reality. Put more technically, existentialism teaches that "existence precedes essence": *that* I am (my existence) comes before *what* I am (my essence). That I exist means that I can decide for myself what my essence will be.

"GOD IS DEAD"

Friedrich Nietzsche was an existentialist and an atheist. He believed that there's no God, and because there's no God, there are no set definitions of right and wrong. There are not even set definitions of true and false. So we get to create our own morality and our own truth. Nietzsche was the

51. Friedrich Nietzsche, *Thus Spake Zarathustra*, translated by Thomas Common (Ware, Hertfordshire: Wordsworth Editions, 1997), 21–23.

philosopher who made famous the idea that, culturally, "God is dead." And since God is dead, we are in charge. We are the child who can create reality however we like. Fast forward to today, and in the twenty-first century, that means we're creating our own reality of what it means to be male and female. We can create our own genders and identify as whatever we feel that we are. We're the creators.

Nietzsche saw himself as someone who had helped slay the dragon and was now a creator of reality to mirror his own desires. Nietzsche was not just a famous atheist, but he was perhaps the most logically consistent atheist you could ever read. He reasoned that if God doesn't exist, then we need to stop living as if he does.

Nietzsche lived in times in which basic Christian beliefs still framed the default worldview for most everyone. According to Nietzsche, the whole Christian idea about loving your enemies—it's garbage. We need to throw that out. And that whole Christian belief about treating people equally—it's ridiculous. We need to throw that out too. There were people whom Nietzsche called the "bungled and botched."[52] And he said it was ridiculous of Christianity to elevate these people, to give them eternal importance. As for women, Nietzsche could be brutal in his writings. He writes of women, "One-half of mankind is weak, typically sick, changeable, inconstant."[53] To Nietzsche, women were the "source of all folly and unreason."[54] He wrote, "Man shall be trained for war and woman for the recreation of the warrior. All else is folly."[55]

There are a couple things you'll want to remember about Nietzsche: First, he was an existentialist. He taught that we can't really know what reality is, so we get to create our own reality. Second, he was no friend of equality or of women. In fact, it's because of people like Nietzsche that feminism exists. There have been people—even Christians—who have oppressed women,

52. Friedrich Nietzsche, "Section 43," *The Antichrist* (Mineola, NY: Dover Publications, 2018).
53. Friedrich Nietzsche, *The Will to Power* (New York: Vintage, 1968), 460.
54. Leonard Lawlor and Zeynep Direk, *Jacques Derrida: Critical Assessments of Leading Philosophers* (Routledge, 2002), 139.
55. Bertrand Russell, *History of Western Philosophy* (London: Routledge, 2004), 690.

undervalued women, kept them down. And that's why there is feminism: the attempt to raise women up, to empower them, against these forces.

WAVES OF FEMINISM

There have been three major "waves" of feminism in Western culture. The first wave of feminism had to do with winning the right to vote for women, culminating in the Nineteenth Amendment in 1920. The second wave of feminism of the '60s and '70s had to do more with women's rights in the workplace and legalizing abortion. And the third wave of feminism, which started in the '90s and continues today, has to do with a feminism that lifts up people who experience intersecting oppressions.

Here's what I mean by intersecting oppressions. If you're a gender minority and a racial minority, then that's an intersection of oppression. Or if you're a religious minority and a sexual minority, then that's an intersection of oppression. Third wave feminism brings all of those factors together and tries to empower anyone living at these intersections. More and more, our post-Christian culture grounds its views of right and wrong in intersectionality. Instead of grounding their views of right and wrong in what the biblical God has revealed, they stake what's right and wrong in the lived experience of oppressed people. So this is an important concept to understand if you want to understand the dominant ethics of modern Western culture.

Intersectional, third-wave feminists tend to be very cynical about any group that has traditionally held power: for example, white people and men. There is also an intense cynicism toward traditional Christian morality in areas of sexual morality and gender identities and norms. If you're a Christian, heterosexual, and cisgender (i.e., your gender identity matches your biological sex), then you're likely seen as an oppressor by intersectional feminists.

DIGGING THROUGH LAYERS OF OPPRESSION

I've read a fair amount of the intersectional feminist literature. I'm friends with some intersectional feminists. And they are all about digging up injustice and tossing it away like dirt. In my own words, here's one of the first layers that intersectional feminism digs up and tosses away. It's called, "This is what you are." This is referring to anytime we are told, "You are a woman, and this is what that means," or, "You are a man, and this is what that means." According to intersectional feminism, dig that up and throw it out. Such claims are said to be ways that privileged people keep everybody else at the margins.

A second layer that intersectional feminism digs up and tosses away is called, "This is how to live." You say that sex is for marriage? That gender comes in twos? That marriage is for a man and a woman? No, we will live however we want to live. When it comes to anything that traditionally says, "This is how to live," they dig it up and throw it out.

A third layer dug away by intersectional feminism is called, "This is what to think." This is the rejection of capital-T Truth. *Don't tell me what to think. Instead, I'll believe* my *truth.* And with that last shovel dig, the intersectional feminist arrives at the core of empowerment. You can no longer tell me what I am or how to live or what to think. I am fully empowered because I no longer submit to any of the following pronouncements:

- This is what you are.
- This is how to live.
- This is what to think.

But here's the twist. Modern Western culture has dug its way to complete and full empowerment—rejecting all the "Thou shalts" and "Thou shalt nots." And we've wielded our shovel in the name of justice for the oppressed, equality for the underdog. Our culture has been trying to dig through these layers of, "This is what you are," "This is how to live," and, "This is what to think," *because* we're trying to lift up the oppressed.

And yet. Our culture digs to its destination and, there, it hears laughter. It's the laughter of surprise. We look around and see the source of the laughter. It's a man with a bushy mustache named Friedrich Nietzsche. Our culture has arrived where Nietzsche has been for over a century. The great irony is that we're here because we're trying to find equality and justice. Yet it was *Nietzsche*—hater of equality, disparager of women—who pioneered this descent. It was Nietzsche who said there's no set right and wrong. There's no capital-T Truth. We create our own reality.

Here's the point: The very steps that modern Western culture has taken to throw off the shackles of oppression are the very steps down the dark path to *enabling* oppression. The more godless our culture becomes, the less it will be about truth and the more it will be about power. If we reject God's definitions and God's ways, and we just do it ourselves, we're going to lose a lot.

What will we lose in the descent? For starters, we will lose the idea of humanity being made in the image of God. We will lose right and wrong being a part of reality, as they just become hurdles to get over. We will trade love and forgiveness for envy and resentment. A godless, post-Christian world has no way to ground these things in reality, and we will lose them. We will lose even manhood and womanhood themselves.

WHAT POST-CHRISTIAN MEANS

Do you know what a post-Christian culture becomes? A *pre-Christian* culture. And that's frightening for anyone who has read about the cheapness of life in the pre-Christian Roman Empire. Unwanted babies were left outside until the elements killed them, and this was done to girls more often than boys such that the boy-to-girl ratios of major cities were lopsided. Wives often went uncherished and even treated like property. Divorce and extramarital affairs were commonplace. Fornication was customary, public exposure was normalized, and many prostitutes gained celebrity status.

The further forward we move as a post-Christian culture, the faster we travel backward in time. And post-Christian becomes pre-Christian.

Feminists need to take a good hard look at how modern Western culture tends to assign worth to women: it vacillates between valuing women for how well they can please men; or how well they can become indistinguishable from men. Either way, this is a culture that reduces women to something far less than what they are. In a world that teaches them to weigh their worth by how closely they resemble the cover of a magazine or how successful they can be on the corporate org chart, Christianity tells women the truth: You are worth so much more than your exterior. You are worth so much more than how high a position you've accumulated. You are worth so much more than your ability to make men happy. And not only are you worth more than what your culture is telling you but your purpose is higher than what your culture offers you. God calls you to no less than joining him in redeeming all that's broken in this world.

So if you're assuming that modern Western culture is where we find solid answers on sex and gender, I would highly encourage you to revisit what God has to say.

4

WHAT DOES SCRIPTURE TELL US SEX AND GENDER ARE FOR?

RENÉE WEBB SPROLES

The bulk of the following chapters will explore what Scripture teaches us about sex and gender.

In this introductory chapter to the chapters that follow, we're going to look at a couple types of evidence the Bible gives us for what it means to be a man or woman. Alastair Roberts has made the helpful observation that there are two types of evidence in Scripture regarding men and women: circumstantial and specific.

The *circumstantial* evidence runs from the opening chapters of Genesis to the closing of Revelation and the wedding supper of the Lamb. The circumstantial evidence will be the focus of this chapter. And then there is the *specific* evidence, the teaching about men and women found in places like 1 Corinthians 11 and 14 and 1 Timothy 2. The specific evidence is like medicine, as it addresses gender-related issues that come up in marriage and the church.

What would happen to your body if you ate only medicine like Advil, Tylenol, or Aleve for breakfast, lunch, and dinner? Enough of that, and you would get very sick and probably die. Similarly, when the church tries to live day-by-day on the "medicine" of a handful of Scriptures, we also tend to get sick. Feeding on just a handful of passages, it's easy to stereotype men and women, creating narrow categories for the expression of masculinity and femininity.

In this chapter, we'll examine the circumstantial evidence about what it means to be a man or a woman, and then in several of the following chapters, we'll study the specific evidence: passages that address issues within marriage and the church. Especially if you're reading from a Western cultural context, as the writers of this book are, you'll find places in this chapter that might not feel right culturally. We live in a very different world from the world of the Bible: We elect our leaders. We no longer offer animal sacrifices. We underscore that men and women can do any job they put their mind to. We try to treat all our children equally when it comes to dividing up the inheritance. I could go on.

As we read snapshots of maleness and femaleness in the biblical narrative, we will run into legitimate debates about what our Creator values transculturally versus what merely represents ancient Near Eastern culture. The Bible narrates far more than it commends, and there is no reason to consider pre-Christian ancient Near Eastern culture as more moral or worthy of imitation than other cultures. With this caveat, what follows is my best attempt to gather principles of what God seems to commend in maleness and femaleness from stories and themes throughout the Bible, whether it's seen through his initiative in setting up institutions or his commendation of behaviors and attitudes.

CIRCUMSTANTIAL EVIDENCE

The Bible takes us on a journey from a wedding in an earthly paradise to a wedding in a heavenly paradise in the new heaven and new earth. Between these events, the prophets use boldly erotic images to describe God's love for his people. The love poetry of Song of Solomon redeems human love and gives us a glimpse into the things of heaven. The one-flesh mystery is explained in Ephesians 5 as pointing to Christ and the church. Spousal imagery is woven throughout Scripture.

Let's begin in Genesis 1–3. The apostle Paul returns to these chapters again and again when he's writing about what it means to be male or female and how we relate to one another, so it makes sense that we would familiarize ourselves with these chapters first.

GENESIS 1–2

In Genesis, we see the archetypal man and woman, Adam and Eve, enjoying God and being called to fill the earth and subdue it. They'll do this both face-to-face in intimacy and shoulder-to-shoulder in cooperative work. They will also both fail, and even this will give us insight into what it means to be a man or a woman.

Primogeniture. So man is created first. Who cares? Well, the original readers of Genesis would have cared. They would have noticed this order of creation. In the ancient world, there was a concept known as "primogeniture": this gave special rights and responsibilities to the firstborn son. In Deuteronomy, God recognizes this responsibility by requiring fathers to give their firstborn sons a double portion of the inheritance, even if the son is by a wife they don't love. Being a firstborn man meant using masculine strength to fulfill these responsibilities.

Priest. Adam performs a *priestly* role within the garden. As with the future priests in the Old Testament Levitical system, Adam teaches God's commands. In Genesis 2, Adam teaches his wife, Eve, the command about not eating from the tree of the knowledge of good and evil. This gives us a clue that being a husband, and perhaps a man in general, includes knowing God-ordained boundaries, teaching them to others, and upholding them yourself (see Ephesians 5:25–27).

Naming. Adam continues to bring order to the creation by naming the animals. As with primogeniture, naming in Scripture is a very important concept: it denotes relationship and responsibility from the namer to the one who is named. The animals are brought under Adam's protection and care as he names them. This suggests that being a man means being responsible for those in your care.

Strong help. God then creates a "strong helper" corresponding to, or opposite, of the man, created from his side. God brings the woman to the firstborn son as a bride. Face-to-face and as one flesh, they can now fulfill God's command to fill the earth. Shoulder-to-shoulder, they can fulfill God's command to subdue it. Being a woman means bringing strong help to fill the earth and subdue it alongside men.

Geography and sex. We also see that the man is created in the wider world and placed in a garden, while Eve is created from Adam inside the garden as his corresponding, strong help. In this sanctuary, Adam is being trained by God to work it and keep it. God is teaching the man, the firstborn son, to fulfill his calling to exercise dominion over the earth. Being a man means working to bring order to the world around you.

We see this reality played out in the marriage relationship. As we explored in Chapter 2, men tend to be more outward-facing; and women tend to be more inward-facing. When we talk in these general categories, it's easy to slip into stereotyping men and women instead of archetyping. But bear with me, and we'll unpack what this means.

Christopher West explains how these roles are reflected in the sexual union of men and women. A man's role is outside his body as he enters the woman. Woman's role is inside her body as she receives him and conceives new life, carrying it for nine months inside her body. We are meant to help complete each other, creating a third person who comes into existence.[56] This becomes a sign of an ultimate reality, of the story of God's divine love within the Trinity, of his love for each one of us, and of the eternal life he wants to conceive and birth within us. Being a woman means carrying new life into the world.

GENESIS 3

When the serpent comes to Eve, we see the order of creation start to be overturned. How did the serpent get into the garden anyway? And why did Adam stay silent when the serpent was deceiving Eve? Adam allowed the serpent into the garden unhindered and unaccompanied. He allowed the serpent to speak to his wife and mislead her. When he simply listened to Eve

56. West, *Theology of the Body*, 55.

and didn't speak up, didn't teach her, and didn't guard the garden or the truth of God's command, he failed. The whole order of the universe began to break down.

From this point on, the rest of Scripture will be spent showing the struggle to make things right again.

Dominion becomes domination. In the beginning, the power of the woman was in her voice and influence. But now there seems to be a firewall of sorts there where the man will no longer be so receptive to her. "Your desire shall be for your husband, but he will rule over you" (Genesis 3:16). Here, God explains that women will face resistance from men in a way that will be tragic.

Now there's nothing wrong with a husband listening to his wife, but if there is no sense of exercising his own judgment before following along, there's something wrong there. Echoes of this story are heard when Sarai takes her maid, Hagar, and gives her to Abram: "And Abram listened to the voice of Sarai" (Genesis 16:2, NASB).[57]

Adam's particular responsibility. Even though Eve instigates the sinful exchange and sins first, God comes to Adam, challenging him and holding him responsible for what both he and Eve did. Why?

Romans 5 gives the explanation: It's because Adam represents humanity. Not Eve. Paul calls Adam "the pattern of the one to come." We don't talk about Adamic-Evean humanity. The symbol for humanity is Adam and then Christ: "For if the many died by the trespass of the one man, how much more did God's grace and the gift that came by the grace of the one man, Jesus Christ, overflow to the many!" (Romans 5:15b).[58]

This distinct complementarity in the opening chapters of Genesis continues through the book with lots of men getting circumcised and lots of women having their wombs opened.

---

57. Alastair Roberts, "The Dance of the Sexes," *Home Fires Podcast*, February 14, 2022.
58. Roberts, "The Dance of the Sexes."

Moving into the rest of Scripture, we'll see a lot of importance given to being male and female. No matter the skills, gifts, or abilities, we will find that although masculine and feminine qualities overlap, the sexes are not interchangeable. We'll see examples of those who beautifully embrace and fulfill their masculinity and femininity, and we'll also see how some fail in their maleness and femaleness, as Adam and Eve did.

From here on, at the end of each section in this chapter, we will pause to ask what clues we find about what it means to be a man or woman. Please read these summary statements as snapshots of faithful (and sometimes unfaithful!) maleness and femaleness, rather than comprehensive definitions. And very importantly, try to read these stories and summaries through the lens of the chapter's title ("What Does Scripture Tell Us Sex and Gender Are For?") rather than through the often-different lens of what you think sex and gender should be for.

ABRAHAM AND SARAH

God called Abram out of his home country and promised to make him into a great nation: "I will bless you; I will make your name great, and you will be a blessing . . . and all peoples on earth will be blessed through you" (Genesis 12:2b–3). Indeed, Abraham is our father in the faith: "Understand, then, that those who have faith are children of Abraham . . . the man of faith" (Galatians 3:7, 9b).

Abraham's wife, Sarah, is held up as an archetypal female in the letter of 1 Peter. Why? Sarah respected Abraham in her actions (obeying him) and in her speech (calling him lord). What kind of submitting did Sarah do? Besides going with her husband in faith to a land God would show them, another big example comes to mind—one that actually underscores Abraham's weakness. Fearing for his life, Abraham selfishly put Sarah in jeopardy. He basically said, "You're so beautiful that the Egyptians will kill me and take you for themselves; so say you are my sister." Here, we see Abraham repeating the sin of Adam, failing to provide boundaries and protection. And because Abraham failed in this calling, God judged justly, sending plagues on Pharoah's household and ensuring Sarah's safe return home. This happens not once, but *twice.*

What does it mean to be a man? It means rising up to fulfill and enjoy the honorable status of husband and father. Like Abraham, you are a man of faith and follow where God leads. It means you protect your wife and your family.

What does it mean to be a woman? It means rising up to fulfill and enjoy the honorable status of wife and mother. Like Sarah, you trust God even when his promises seem impossible to fulfill or when your husband doesn't. You display quiet courage and fortitude, facing terrifying situations with grace.

NABAL AND ABIGAIL

Before he was king, David was on the run from King Saul, and one of the episodes in this season of his life involved an altercation with a rich man named Nabal. David's men came to Nabal, asking for hospitality. Nabal selfishly and rudely refused, putting his whole household in mortal danger, since David planned to kill the whole lot of them when he heard the news (1 Samuel 25).

The reaction of Abigail, Nabal's wife, to her wealthy, contemptuous, drunkard of a husband is worth noting. She sprang into action and went to David to intercede and ask forgiveness for her husband. Just as Abraham had failed to protect Sarah, Nabal was failing to protect his family, and his wife stepped up. Abigail shrewdly made amends for her husband's behavior by graciously offering gifts, an apology, and a blessing to David and his men. Nabal's sin was grievous and God struck him dead, and Abigail became the wife of the future king of Israel.

The story of Nabal and Abigail suggests that when men fail to use their power for good, women must assume traditionally male tasks.

What does it mean to be a man? It means protecting those for whom you're responsible and offering resources so that people can be fed, rested, and refreshed.

What does it mean to be a woman? It means protecting your family through hospitality, shrewdness in relationships, and generosity toward those in need.

PRIESTS

God set apart the Levites as the priestly tribe. All of Israel's priests were male. Does this tell us anything about men and women? I think that it does. It is noteworthy that priests used sacred violence without pity on behalf of God's holiness. They also taught the law to the people of Israel. Their leadership was authoritative and involved the elemental, boundary-making things of life. From the beginning, God expected the Levites to exercise discipline—even unto death. After the incident of the golden calf in Exodus 32, the Lord's instructions were for "Each man [to] strap a sword to his side. Go back and forth through the camp from one end to the other, each killing his brother and friend and neighbor" (Exodus 32:27b). Alastair Roberts notes,

> The priest's business was death. He was the man of knife, fire, cut flesh, and spilt blood. The priests were the crack troops who manned the moral and cultic boundaries of the nation, and were praised for being able to rise above all pity when judgment was necessary. The priest as the elite sword-wielder, who will not show mercy in the defense of truth when all others fail, and will not spare, pity, or compromise when others do, seems to be a pretty consistent theme in relation to priestly leadership in Scripture, yet rather noticeable by its absence in current understandings of pastoral ministry. The capacity to exercise agonistic, uncompromising, and strong leadership from the front, when such leadership is called for, seems to have been peculiarly characteristic of that which was expected of the priests, as the moral guardians of the nation.[59]

59. Alastair Roberts, "Some Lengthy Thoughts on Women Leadership," *Alastair's Adversaria,* www.alastairadversaria.com/2011/12/08/some-lengthy-thoughts-on-women-leadership/ December 8, 2011, (accessed October 19, 2022).

What does it mean to be a man? It means drawing and maintaining the boundaries of truth through uncompromising, masculine strength.

PROPHETS

Being a mouthpiece for the word of the Lord was often a dangerous calling. People frequently mocked, rejected, persecuted, and even killed God's prophets (Acts 7:52). Prophets who spoke falsely on behalf of God received the death penalty. Even so, not all prophets in Scripture shared a similar status or performed the same work. [60]

There were covenant-founding prophets who served as God's mouthpiece and ambassadors, such as Moses, Samuel, Elijah, and John the Baptist. All were male.

There were also prophets who received revelation preserved for us in the canon, such as Isaiah, Jeremiah, Hosea, and others. All were male.

Then there were helper/assistant/apprentice prophets, leaders of schools of prophets and their followers. These were male and female. Roberts again:

> There are some things that certain kings and prophets do that no queen or prophetess could do. A prophetess could not symbolize God's relationship to his people as Hosea did, or a queen as Solomon did in his Song. This is all related to the fact that God identifies himself as Father and Husband, and refers to himself using masculine pronouns.[61]

We again see signs of the complementarity of men and women in the lives and work of the prophets. After crossing the Red Sea, Moses and the Israelites sang a song of gratitude to God. After this, Miriam, called a prophet/

60. Sam Storms, "What Does Scripture Teach About the Office of Prophet and the Gift of Prophecy?" *The Gospel Coalition*, October 8, 2015, www.thegospelcoalition.org/article/sam-storms-what-does-scripture-teach-about-office-prophet-gift-prophecy/ (accessed October 19, 2022).
61. Roberts, "Some Lengthy Thoughts on Women Leadership."

prophetess in this context (Exodus 15:20), took a tambourine and led a procession of women in singing and dancing. There is also a "prophetess" in Isaiah 8:3 who remains unnamed but is Isaiah's wife. It's unknown whether Isaiah's wife was a prophetess in her own right or whether she was called this because she participated in her husband's ministry.[62]

In the New Testament era, on the day of Pentecost (Acts 2), the Holy Spirit was poured out on men and women, old and young, so that "they will prophesy" (Acts 2:18). Men and women were, indeed, praying and prophesying in the early church, and Paul did not forbid them to do so. Even still, there is a complementarity envisioned. As Dr. Richard Oster explains in Chapter 6 of this book,

> Paul says that every man who prays or prophesies with his head *covered* dishonors his head, but that every woman who prays or prophesies with her head *uncovered* dishonors her head. Paul is addressing a situation where men's heads are covered and women's heads are uncovered.
>
> And what does Paul say? He says it's a dishonor. It's communicating, visually and culturally, a misunderstanding of this headship relationship in verse 3, where Paul lays a theological foundation for his instructions on head coverings: "But I want you to realize that the head of every man is Christ, and the head of the woman is man, and the head of Christ is God" (1 Corinthians 11:3).

What does it mean to be a man? It means speaking God's truth so that the community has a clear vision of what it means to obey God.

What does it mean to be a woman? It means leading God's people in prayer, in celebration, and in praise to promote unity and strengthen the bonds of community.

62. Roberts, "Some Lengthy Thoughts on Women Leadership."

JUDGES

There are over a dozen judges in Scripture. All are male except one: Deborah. She is remarkable, to be sure, but the writer seems to want to make sure we grasp how unusual it was for a woman to act as judge by introducing her as "a woman, a prophetess, the wife of Lapidoth."[63]

Deborah's role arose as civil life in Israel had collapsed (Judges 5:7), and she seemed to be striving mightily to re-establish it, seeking to hand over guardianship to Barak.[64] Alastair Roberts notes that her distinctly feminine rule as prophetess and judge can be contrasted with the other male judges in several ways.

While the other judges *went out* to judge and lead Israel in battle, Israel *came* to Deborah to be judged and wanted a man to go into battle. She urged Barak, the hesitant and weak military leader, to go. But Barak abandoned his calling, and thus Deborah had to go into battle while another woman, Jael, killed Sisera. Ideally, Barak would have stepped up and done that.

In her victory song, Deborah saw herself as a *mother* whose purpose was to raise up *sons* who would be able to fight and represent the nation (Judges 5:7–9). This doesn't mean that Deborah didn't believe she could fight alongside Barak or shouldn't fight alongside him. But the forces that want to control society tend to go after the men, such as Pharoah and King Herod killing the baby boys so that a strong man couldn't rise to power; or Jacob's sons tricking the men in a city to get circumcised so they could easily attack and kill them to get revenge on behalf of their sister (Genesis 34).

Alastair Roberts rightly notes that Deborah knew Israel was better off when it had the strength of men protecting it, upholding it, and securing its safety, both civilly and nationally. She recognized that as Israel's men were conquered, the forces surrounding Israel gained power over them. Her rule was like that of a vice president in the absence of a president.[65]

---

63. Roberts, "Some Lengthy Thoughts on Women Leadership."
64. Roberts, "Some Lengthy Thoughts on Women Leadership."
65. Roberts, "Some Lengthy Thoughts on Women Leadership."

What does it mean to be a man? It means holding a guardian-type power that you exercise for the good of others.

What does it mean to be a woman? It means listening to God, using wisdom, and speaking the truth to those who should be using their power for others' good.

KINGS AND QUEENS

God made a covenant with Abraham and promised that kings would come from him (Genesis 17:2, 6). This would include the ultimate and final king, Jesus (e.g., Isaiah 9:6–7). Israel's monarchs were distinguished by gendered titles. Kings were male. Queens were female.

In egalitarian circles, much can be made of the fact that there were queens in Israel as well as kings. But upon further reflection, we see the complementary rule of kings and queens. Kings exercised authority, while queens exercised delegated authority. Or to put it another way, women exercised authority and leadership in relation to the men around them.

The queens of Israel were queen consorts (the wife of a reigning king) or queen mothers (like Esther and Jezebel). They had power, yes, but it was a delegated power. The exception to this is Athaliah, the wicked queen consort who reigned as queen after the death of her husband, King Jehoram. As a daughter of Ahab and Jezebel in the northern kingdom of Israel, Athaliah was not part of the Davidic line of kings and is treated as more of a usurper.

What does it mean to be a man? It means using your authority and power to bring blessing to those under your authority.

What does it mean to be a woman? It means using your position of delegated authority to bring blessing to those around you.

WISDOM AS A WOMAN

"Does not wisdom call out? Does not understanding raise her voice?" (Proverbs 8:1).

In a reversal of the serpent's deception of Eve, Proverbs personifies wisdom as a woman. In Chapter 31, we see her in her fullness of wisdom. She sums up the meaning of the book as not only the embodiment of wisdom but also the embodiment of a good wife.

What does it mean to be a woman? It means being wise. It means being "strong help" for those around you. It means being trustworthy, diligent, compassionate, hospitable, and business-minded.

SONG OF SOLOMON

The Song of Solomon holds out a beautiful complementarity between a man and a woman. Alastair Roberts notes that Song of Solomon lays out a kind of refresh of what life was supposed to be like between the sexes. It shows man and woman in a restored situation.

Here, the desire of the woman is for the man, and his desire is also for her. When he exercises his strength, he's not using it in a way that resists her. There's a sense in which his strength is always *for* her. It's like the relationship between Christ and his church, where Christ delights to build up and empower his church while the church responds in kind to Christ.

What does it mean to be a man? It means using your strength as a husband to love and empower your wife.

What does it mean to be a woman? It means submitting to the initiating love of your husband with love of your own.

GOD, THE FATHER

God's identity is revealed consistently throughout the entirety of Scripture as Father. Yet the Song of Moses says God is like "an eagle that stirs up its nest and hovers over its young" and when Israel thinks God has forgotten her, God asks, "Can a mother forget the baby at her breast and have no compassion on the child she has borne?" (see Deuteronomy 32:11a, 18; Isaiah 49:15a). Male *and* female metaphors are used for God and by God in Scripture. Kenneth E. Bailey further explains this in his book *Jesus Through Middle Eastern Eyes: Cultural Studies in the Gospels*:

> We know that God is Spirit and is neither male nor female. Yet in the Scriptures we are told that the believer is "born of God" (1 John 3:9). Here John uses female language to describe the relationship between God and believers. Similarly, when Jesus addressed God as "Father," he used a male metaphor/title to help us understand the nature of God. Scripture uses male and female images to enrich our understanding of God, who is Spirit and thereby beyond male and female.[66]

What does it mean to be a man or a woman? It means that we need each other to get a more complete image of God's protection and love for the world.

JESUS, THE SON OF GOD

Jesus, the image of the invisible God, is God's one-of-a-kind Son (John 3:16). Paul writes, "All things have been created through him and for him. He is before all" (Colossians 1:16b–17a). If we have seen Christ, we have seen the Father.

There are times that Jesus speaks with a motherly love: "Jerusalem, Jerusalem, you who kill the prophets and stone those sent to you, how often I have

66. Kenneth E. Bailey, *Jesus Through Middle Eastern Eyes: Cultural Studies in the Gospels.* (Downers Grove, IL: InterVarsity Press, 2008), 280.

longed to gather your children together, as a hen gathers her chicks under her wings, and you were not willing" (Matthew 23:37). And Jesus elevated women above the status given them by the Jewish rabbis, as well as by many Greek and Roman leaders. He often directly taught women who became his disciples. Jesus commended the faith of the Syro-Phoenician woman who requested that he heal her daughter. Jesus discussed worship with the woman at the Samaritan well. Jesus ate with Mary and Martha. Women traveled with Jesus as part of his larger group of disciples; and this team of women ministered to him.

Women remained at Jesus' side during the crucifixion even when the men fled for their lives. These women were the first to go to the tomb after Jesus' resurrection, the first to receive the announcement that Jesus was risen, and the first to report Jesus' resurrection to the other disciples.

And yet.

Jesus chose twelve apostles. All were men.

Jesus established the leadership of the early church with men.

(And as we will see in the coming section, there is a continuing pattern of male leadership within the church.)

What does it mean to be a man or a woman? Jesus shows us that men and women are welcome to learn and serve alongside him, with some particular, authoritative leadership roles being reserved for qualified men.

EARLY CHURCH

The early church was formed with the synagogue as its background. A careful reading of the book of Acts shows that the early church started in the temple courts and drew its earliest members out of synagogues. In this way, the synagogue is an extension of the Old Testament model where male priests were given the responsibility to be authoritative teachers. Prophets, male and female, appeared here and there. But the burden of teaching day-to-day in the Old Testament was on the male priesthood of Israel.

This helps explain why the early church was established by twelve apostles, all of whom were men. It also helps explain why, when Paul wrote to Timothy to describe the role of elders in the church, he explicitly wrote to men. (Do you know many women who must be told not to be violent, but gentle? See 1 Timothy 3:3.)

We also have a reference to a woman apostle named Junia. Romans 16:7 says, "Greet Andronicus and Junia, my fellow Jews who have been in prison with me. They are outstanding among the apostles, and they were in Christ before I was." Just as there were distinctions in the category of prophet, we see distinctions in the category of apostle, a word meaning "one who is sent." Alastair Roberts explains:

> There are apostles who are members of the Twelve, apostles who witnessed the resurrected Christ, apostles who were sent by a particular church, apostles who performed miracles and others who didn't, apostles who were personally commissioned by Christ and others who weren't . . . there were also [women] apostles who (probably like Isaiah's wife) enjoyed the title because they were made coworkers by their apostolically commissioned husbands. Even within the Twelve we find distinctions, with Peter as a sort of lead or chief apostle, and James and John as next to him. In my experience, arguments for women's ordination often treat these categories as if they were homogeneous, and do not take sufficient cognizance of the huge differentiations that can exist within them.[67]

Women prayed in the gathered church in the presence of men. They taught younger women, and Aquila and Priscilla taught Apollos. Women hosted churches in their homes. Women who were sixty years old or older could be appointed to the ministry of the widow and placed on the payroll of the church. This is in the same overall context of the work of elders and deacons.

67. Roberts, "Some Lengthy Thoughts on Women Leadership."

The early church had male and female deacons. Phoebe is called a "deacon of the church in Cenchreae" (Romans 16:1).

Men and women participated in many of the decisions made by the early churches. Acts 15 indicates that the entire church was assembled and involved in making important decisions regarding the mission to the Gentiles.

First Corinthians 11 affirms women praying and prophesying in the gathered church in the presence of men. Paul does not forbid women to do this; he only instructs them to "have authority on their heads" when they do.

What does it mean to be a man and woman? The early church shows us that men and women were praying, prophesying, and serving alongside one another, while a particular, authoritative leadership role is reserved for men.

MARRIAGE

Jesus affirms God's design for marriage by referring to the creation account.

> "Haven't you read," he replied, "that at the beginning the Creator 'made them male and female,' and said, 'For this reason a man will leave his father and mother and be united to his wife, and the two will become one flesh'? So they are no longer two, but one flesh. Therefore, what God has joined together, let no one separate." (Matthew 19:4–6)

Jesus defines marriage as between one man and one woman. But there's more.

In Ephesians 5, Paul calls spouses back to the original order of love through the redemption won for them in Christ. Headship is the divine calling of a husband to take primary responsibility for Christlike servant leadership, protection, and provision in the home. Submission is the divine calling of a wife to honor and affirm her husband's leadership and help carry it through according to her gifts.

The phrase "mutual submission" is used often when referring to the husband-wife relationship, since Paul begins his instructions to Christian families with the sentence, "Submit to one another out of reverence for Christ" (Ephesians 5:21). But our submission to one another is more nuanced than that. In terms of husbands and wives, our submission to one another is *gendered.* Paul shows that the way a wife submits to her husband is different from the way a husband submits to his wife. The wife submits to and respects her husband (Ephesians 5:22, 33). The husband loves his wife and gives himself up for her (Ephesians 5:25).

Paul calls this a "profound mystery," which can be literally translated *mega mystery.* It means large or great in the widest sense. And it is! In marriage, the husband represents Jesus, and the wife represents the church (Ephesians 5:31–33). What a testimony this could be to the watching world when done well!

Think about it. The way Christ submits to God's plan of redemption is different from the way the church, his bride, submits to him. Christ "loved the church and gave himself up for her to make her holy, cleansing her by the washing with water through the word, and to present her to himself as a radiant church, without stain or wrinkle or any other blemish, but holy and blameless" (Ephesians 5:25–27). The church responds to this initiating love by submitting to Christ's authority.

Looking further, we continue to see the model of "submission to one another out of reverence for Christ" played out in families as well as with slaves and masters. The way children submit to their parents is different from the way parents submit to their children. Children obey and honor their parents (Ephesians 6:1–3). Fathers are forbidden from exasperating their children and are commanded to bring them up in the instruction of the Lord (Ephesians 6:4). The way they submit is not interchangeable. Fathers don't obey their children, and children don't instruct their parents. Slaves were to obey their masters wholeheartedly with respect, fear, and sincerity while masters were to reciprocate without showing favoritism. Each of them was to recognize that they were serving the Lord (Ephesians 6:5–9).

Submission is established to accomplish something. Christ submitted to God's calling so that he could reconcile us with God. The church submits to each other (Ephesians 5:21), putting each other's needs first (Philippians 2:4), and the result is unity in Christ. In submitting to Christ, men provide headship for their wives; and women submit to their husbands' initiating love. Children submit to parents. On and on it goes.

What does it mean to be a man or a woman? It means we submit to one another in gendered, complementary ways as we reenact the gospel story in our marriages and families.

REVELATION

At the wedding supper of the Lamb, we see the church, male and female, representing the bride. Jesus is our groom. Andrew Wilson writes,

> Our future hope is one in which heaven and earth come together, with the glory of the one transforming the other (which is why most of the pairs of Genesis 1 are transcended in Revelation 21: there is no moon, no need for sun, no sea, no darkness, no sexual intercourse, and heaven and earth are beautifully married). The final destiny of the cosmos, and the marriage of Christ and the church, reflect neither conflict nor collapse but complementarity, as the glory of the one permeates and suffuses the other. Blessed are those who are invited to the wedding supper of the Lamb![68]

What does it mean to be a man or a woman? It means we recognize complementarity in all of creation that will eventually culminate in the church's wedding supper with King Jesus. There's no indicator that our resurrected bodies will be genderless in the new heaven and earth; in fact, when Jesus was raised from the dead, he remained a man. We will no longer be individually married (Matthew 22:30); the church will be collectively married to Christ.

68. Andrew Wilson, "Beautiful Difference: The (Whole-Bible) Complementarity of Male and Female," *The Gospel Coalition*, May 20, 2021, www.thegospelcoalition.org/article/beautiful-complementarity-male-female/ (accessed October 19, 2022).

This chapter's purpose was to look at the "circumstantial evidence" of what it means to be male and female throughout the pages of Scripture. We gathered principles of what God seemed to commend in maleness and femaleness from stories and themes throughout the Bible. Now, with the scope of Scripture in mind, we can move to the specific, teaching texts that address the problems between men and women in marriage and the church.

However, before we get to specific texts, it will be helpful to make one more stop to pause and consider a common but curious theme in Scripture when it comes to maleness and femaleness: the concept of "headship."

5

WHAT'S ALL THIS TALK ABOUT HEADS?

RENÉE WEBB SPROLES

I'd like to address one more concept before moving into a discussion of specific, teaching texts like Ephesians 5, 1 Corinthians 11, or 1 Timothy 2. There is an order in creation that Scripture calls "headship." For example,

> But I want you to realize that the head of every man is Christ, and the head of the woman is man, and the head of Christ is God. (1 Corinthians 11:3)

It's important to note that: Paul doesn't say Christ *should be* the head of man. He says Christ *is* the head of man.

- Paul doesn't say the man *should be* the head of woman. He says man *is* the head of woman.
- Paul doesn't say God *should be* the head of Christ. He says God *is* the head of Christ (see John 5:19; 12:49).

In 1 Corinthians 11, Paul reminds the Corinthian church about the nature of reality. He connects the principle of male headship all the way back to creation. That creation connection means headship is not just a cultural issue of Paul's time that can be ignored today. Male headship is not subject to change as culture changes. We can deny it. We can say it doesn't exist. We can say it was socially constructed. But no matter what you believe about gravity, if you step off the edge of a cliff, you are going to fall.

Living against the grain of reality hurts everyone. So why do we do it?

JESUS AS OUR HEAD

One reason it's natural to ignore this concept of headship is that using the word "head" sounds kind of weird. When people do talk about the concept, many tend to substitute the word "leader" or "authority" for "head," but this substitution causes confusion in both marriage and the church. Leadership and authority are part of headship, but these terms are not synonymous with the biblical word *head*. As we noted in Chapter 4, we see women leading in various ways and exercising delegated authority throughout Scripture. But they are never called the *head* of men.

So what's the difference? To understand headship, we look to Christ for our example, as he is not only the head of men but also the head of the church.

> And He put all things in subjection under His feet, and gave Him as *head* over all things to the church, which is His body, the fullness of Him who fills all in all. (Ephesians 1:22–23, NASB)
>
> . . . we will grow to become in every respect the mature body of him who is the *head*, that is, Christ. From him the whole body, joined and held together by every supporting ligament, grows and builds itself up in love, as each part does its work. (Ephesians 4:15b–16)

Christ is also called the head (Greek: *kephale*) cornerstone (*gonia*):

> The stone that the builders rejected has become the cornerstone [*kephalen gonias*]. (1 Peter 2:7b)
>
> Haven't you read this passage of Scripture: "The stone the builders rejected has become the cornerstone [*kephalen gonias*]?" (Mark 12:10)

What is a cornerstone? And why would "head" be used with it?

A cornerstone is the first stone set in a stone foundation, with the other stones in the structure set in place around it. When referring to the "head cornerstone," the Bible is referring to this first stone set in a foundation—the stone that all other stones will be aligned with as they are set. This cornerstone ensures that the walls are stable, straight, and strong. What a beautiful image! The idea in Ephesians 5:22–24 is that what Christ does as a head cornerstone for the church, men should do for women.

In Ephesians 2:19–22, Paul fleshes out this metaphor, noting that Christ bears the weight of the building, creates a solid foundation, and ensures that each stone can fulfill its potential as we are joined together to become a spiritual house, a holy priesthood, for God.

> So then you are no longer strangers and aliens, but you are fellow citizens with the saints, and are of God's household, having been built on the foundation of the apostles and prophets, Christ Jesus Himself being the cornerstone, in whom the whole building, being fitted together, is growing into a holy temple in the Lord, in whom you also are being built together into a dwelling of God in the Spirit. (Ephesians 2:19–22, NASB)

Peter elaborates on the idea of Christ as the head cornerstone with us being built around him as fellow "living stones."

> Come to him, a living stone, though rejected by mortals yet chosen and precious in God's sight, and like living stones, let yourselves be built into a spiritual house, to be a holy priesthood, to offer spiritual sacrifices acceptable to God through Jesus Christ. For it stands in scripture: "See, I am laying in Zion a stone, a cornerstone chosen and precious; and whoever believes in him will not be put to shame." To you then who believe, he is precious; but for those who do not believe, "The stone that the builders rejected has become the very head of the corner." (1 Peter 2:4–7, NRSV)

With Christ as our archetype for headship, we can see that it isn't about domineering authority, at least about worldly notions of it. But does headship have *anything* to do with authority? Yes: Christ is the head of the church, and all authority in heaven and on earth was given to him by God (Matthew 28:18).

Christ's headship is exercised with authority, but it is strikingly different from worldly authority that so often exercises itself through privilege and tyranny. John A. Cuddleback offers an excellent description of Christlike authority in his article, "Authority and the Gift of Fatherhood":

> To recover an understanding of authority (which we must do to recover an understanding of fatherhood and of manhood), we must overcome misconceptions about it, perhaps most of all this one: that authority always "comes between" persons, rather than grounding the most intimate of loving relationships.
>
> Authority is the power to give direction to another person precisely because *of a responsibility to care for that person*. Real authority is always a way of taking care of people—to be a cause of their proper growth and development. . . . Authority, in its primary form, is precisely an act of love.[69]

Jesus exercised his authority with this kind of caring-via-responsibility power in both bold *and* gentle ways.

BOLD AND GENTLE HEADSHIP

When it was almost time for the Jewish Passover, Jesus made a whip out of cords, drove all the people and animals from the temple courts, scattered the coins of the money changers, and overturned their tables (Mark 11, John 2). In his excellent article, "Jesus Turns the Tables," Jonathan Parnell notes that although commerce in the temple *was* a problem, that wasn't the only thing, or even the *main* thing, Jesus was addressing by exercising his authority. Parnell explains:

> The real fiasco was how out of sync Israel's worship was with the great end-times vision Isaiah had prophesied—the new age that Jesus had come to inaugurate. . . .

69. Italics mine; John A. Cuddleback, "Authority and the Gift of Fatherhood," Institute for Family Studies, June 15, 2022, www.ifstudies.org/blog/authority-and-the-gift-of-fatherhood (accessed October 19, 2022).

> The context of Isaiah 56 tells us more. According to Isaiah's vision, eunuchs would keep God's covenant (Isaiah 56:4), and foreigners would join themselves to him (Isaiah 56:6), and the outcasts would be gathered with his people (Isaiah 56:8). But Jesus approached a temple pulsing with buying and selling. The court of the Gentiles, the place designed all along for foreigners to congregate, for the nations to seek the Lord, was overrun with opportunists trying to turn a profit. And the Jewish leaders had let this happen.
>
> Their economic drive, and their false security in the temple as an emblem of blessing (Jeremiah 7:3–11), had crowded out space for the nations to draw near, and therefore Jesus was driving them out. The great sadness of this scene wasn't so much the rows of product and price-gouging, but that all this left no room for the Gentiles and outcasts to come to God.[70]

Jesus' bold authority made space for people to come to God.

Jesus also exercised his authority with gentleness and care, placing his hands on little children and praying for them (Matthew 19:13–14), healing the sick, feeding the crowds (Matthew 14:13–21; 15:29–39; Mark 8:1–3), teaching men *and* women (Luke 10:38–42; Mark 4:34), and more.

If we use the term *head* in our marriages and in church, we must use it as Christ demonstrates: as a shepherd cares for sheep. Fierce when facing the enemy and gentle when tending the flock, our Lord is the standard for this concept called *head.*

What does headship mean for men today? It means using your authority to give direction because of a love relationship. It means taking responsibility for those in your care. It means making space for people to flourish and fulfill their God-given potential.

As we move to the specific evidence in the New Testament of what it means to be male and female, we will see this concept of headship serve as the backdrop of

70. Jonathan Parnell, "Jesus Turns the Tables," Desiring God, March 30, 2015, www.desiringgod.org/articles/jesus-turns-the-tables (accessed October 19, 2022).

many of these passages. There is much more to be said about this theme of headship in the Bible (Greek: kephale*). As we proceed, let's keep in mind this fundamental biblical portrait of headship as bold and gentle and fiercely intent on others' good.*

6

WHAT'S UP WITH HEAD COVERINGS IN 1 CORINTHIANS 11?

RICHARD OSTER, RENÉE WEBB SPROLES

This will be an in-depth chapter where we examine what 1 Corinthians 11 teaches about men and women in the church. Although we are soft complementarians, along the way we will be engaging with books from a couple of thinkers with more egalitarian leanings: John Mark Hicks's Women Serving God: My Journey in Understanding Their Story *and Scot McKnight's* Blue Parakeet: Rethinking How You Read the Bible. *We chose these two men because they are influential in the circles of Renew.org leaders, and they serve as common examples of the posture many are taking today.*

Our culture is putting tremendous pressure on church leaders and churches to explain in more egalitarian ways what the Bible teaches regarding church leadership. Cultural pressures regarding these sometimes-confusing passages compel us to pause and give such questions solid focus.

When we get to passages like 1 Corinthians 11 and 14 or 1 Timothy 2, Paul has in mind the biblical narrative—what we have called the "circumstantial evidence" regarding men and women found throughout the Bible, particularly in Genesis. He writes with an assumption that the audience has some sort of grasp of the grand story of Scripture, giving a shorthand explanation of the relationship between men and women, as it applies to more particular and direct teaching. In 1 Corinthians, Paul addresses how men and women participate in the assembled church and focuses on the gendered ways we do that with the larger scriptural backdrop in view.

To help us with this chapter, I (Renée) sat down with Dr. Richard Oster, professor at Harding School of Theology for over forty years and a published expert on the Roman veil practices in 1 Corinthians 11 and ancient Ephesus (1 Timothy 2). Rick also pointed us to an excellent resource that the leaders of the church he attends created after extensive study with Rick and others, including their senior minister, Rodney Plunket, PhD. It is called "Study With the Shepherds—Women and Men Serving the Church," which we use extensively with permission.[71] *When quoted, we will reference it as SWS.*

Oster: I'd like to say something before we begin this conversation. The epistles we have in the New Testament are what scholars call occasional, which means 1 Corinthians was written to the church regarding Corinth, Galatians was written to the churches of Galatia, and so on. And that doesn't detract one bit from their authority, their inspiration, or their belonging in the canon of Scripture. However, it does mean that we should start by trying to understand the issues that are in those letters, to understand why Paul or Peter or John wrote them. Step one of good hermeneutics is to determine what the original authors meant in their letters, and I think Scot McKnight and John Mark Hicks would agree with this.

The issue is—and this is where I begin to disagree with Hicks and McKnight—that the Bible doesn't tell us what parts of these letters are cultural. It's not like Paul said in his letter to the church in Philippi, "I'm going to put a little note here, and these things are cultural." Or to the Corinthians, "Okay men and women, these three sections are just cultural." Culture and the problems arising from churches living in culture are responsible for *everything* and *every letter* in the New Testament.

The 1 Corinthians 15 passage offers a good example of something crucial to the Christian faith and practice, which Scripture addresses due to a situation. We don't have Chapter 15 simply because Paul said, "I want to share some wonderful theology about the resurrection." We have that chapter because there were specific, occasional problems coming from some

71. The Church of Christ at White Station, Memphis, Tennessee. You can find the entire "Study with the Shepherds: Women and Men Serving the Church" at www.cocws.org/about-us/women-and-men-serving-the-church.

Christians in Corinth who didn't understand the resurrection. They didn't get it. This is the same reason we have 1 Corinthians 13. Some Christians at the church of Corinth didn't understand spiritual gifts within their religious and cultural setting.

So we must be careful when we say, "Well, this is just something that's temporal and cultural, and this over here is eternal because it's not connected to anything situational in the letter." Those conclusions can be arbitrary, reflecting more of what our own pet theological interests are, rather than based on pure exegesis.

Sproles: That's a great point. I don't see many books or articles questioning if what Paul wrote about the resurrection in 1 Corinthians 15 was cultural. Likewise, there aren't many people saying that the spiritual gifts listed by Paul in 1 Corinthians 13 were tied to ancient culture and, therefore, not relevant to us today.

But gender?

That's a big issue in North America, so we tend to stop short when we read what the apostle Paul wrote about men and women. Now let's move to the passage at hand so we can determine what Paul meant about head coverings and the relationship between men and women at the Corinthian church.

> *Every man who prays or prophesies with his head covered dishonors his head. But every woman who prays or prophesies with her head uncovered dishonors her head. (1 Corinthians 11:4–5a)*

Q. Some scholars suggest that 1 Corinthians 11 is filled with problems, reflecting an intricate relationship between culture, theology, and church practices in the first century about which we have significant uncertainties. Is this passage truly difficult to understand?

Oster: I hope to show you that it actually isn't so hard to understand. Consider the following passage from "Study With the Shepherds" (SWS):

In SWS: The following interpretation of 1 Corinthians 11:2–16 is informed by a historical reconstruction of the relevant context. This reconstruction is based on hard evidence regarding the wearing of head coverings in the first century. Some question the value and validity of historical reconstructions for the purpose of interpreting Scripture. However, we base our ability to replace the "holy kiss" (commanded in Romans 16:16; 1 Corinthians 16:20; 2 Corinthians 13:12; 1 Thessalonians 5:26) or "kiss of love" (commanded in 1 Peter 5:14) with a handshake by means of a historical reconstruction indicating the first-century meaning of the holy kiss or kiss of love corresponds more to a handshake in our culture than it does to a kiss.

The Corinthian assemblies were made up of believers from different cultural backgrounds. Roman Christians and non-Roman Christians brought different head covering customs into the early church. Since the use of head coverings related to authority and submission for at least some in the Corinthian church and for Paul, he had to give them clear instructions regarding covering the head while speaking in the church's assembly.

The Roman view: The wearing of devotional head coverings was the norm for Roman women and men and amounted to a religious law. This affected the way both women and men were viewed when speaking in the Corinthian church. Many, if not all, Roman Christians would have considered it irreverent when women or men took an active role without covering their heads. See images below that display the Romans' use of head coverings in worship settings and in depictions through which they conveyed their religious reverence.

The non-Roman view: Non-Romans did not possess that "religious law." As a result, it is almost certain that those whose backgrounds were Greek, Egyptian, Asian, German, etc., did not have their heads covered when taking a leading role in the assembly.

Greek authors, for example, actually state how strange the practice of the Romans seemed to them. Greeks distinguished themselves by their speech and education; but Romans by what they wore, especially in worship settings.[72] Consequently, when Roman men took a leading role in the church's

72. Richard Oster, "When Men Wore Veils to Worship: The Historical Context of 1 Corinthians 11.4," *New Testament Studies*, vol. 34 (1988), 494, quoted in Ben Witherington III, *Conflict and Community in Corinth: A Socio-Rhetorical Commentary on 1 and 2 Corinthians* (Eerdmans, 1995), 234.

assembly with their heads covered, the non-Romans viewed that as odd; and Paul, and almost certainly others, viewed it as an affront to the biblical doctrine of headship. When women did not cover their heads while praying or prophesying, it appeared to Paul and almost certainly to others that they were not honoring the biblical doctrine of headship.

To keep this in perspective, covering the head was not the general social attire for either Romans or non-Romans.

The head covering issue only applied when taking an active role in a worship assembly. Ancient altar reliefs portray Roman pagan worship in which the only person in the procession with a head covering, whether male or female, is the one officiating a specific act of worship at the moment. Outside of these settings, Roman men typically uncovered their heads in the presence of others, especially among social superiors. This was also true for some of the more well-to-do women.[73] This helps us place limits on the application of the text. It is not referring to what women or men should wear in public or even in worship assemblies generally. In 1 Corinthians 11:2–16, Paul's instructions only apply to persons who are praying or prophesying in the assembly.

Also relevant to this question is the awareness that not all women in the Greco-Roman world of Paul's time were accustomed to living lives publicly secluded from social and religious activities or being kept from participation and leadership in religious priesthoods. On both the first (Acts 13:50) and second (Acts 17:12) missionary journeys, Paul encounters "women of high standing." These were women of wealth and civic significance. In Paul's time and world, there were women who held high civic offices and even served as priestesses and high priestesses in various religions, even the emperor cult. It is certainly possible historically that some women of high standing and wealth (like those addressed in 1 Timothy 2:9) felt constrained by the gender understandings affirmed by Paul and, therefore, preferred not to cover their heads.

73. Oster, "When Men Wore Veils to Worship," 235.

Put simply, Paul required the men not to cover their heads when they spoke in the assembly; and he required the women to cover their heads. Those requirements were implemented to resolve confusion regarding the church's posture relative to the biblical doctrine of headship. In conclusion, we see that both men and women spoke in the church's assemblies.

Q. Some question the meaning of head (*kephale*), noting that it is sometimes literal and sometimes metaphorical, and calling it one of the thornier problems in the passage. Is it a metaphor for authority or rank; or a metaphor for source or origin?

Oster: I believe a straightforward reading of the text, along with the archeological evidence we will soon consider, reveal that *kephale* (head) denotes authority. First, interpreting "head" to mean "source" creates all kinds of Christological problems. In 1 Corinthians 15:28, Paul says that Christ will be in eternal submission to God, the Father. Second, taking *kephale* (head) to mean source contradicts most of the imagery in the New Testament. Anyone in the first century who heard the phrase "father and son,"—a recurring image in the New Testament to describe the relationship between God and Jesus— is not going to think "source." They're going to think authority.

It seems like special pleading to take Paul's assertion that "the head of Christ is God" to mean "the source of Christ is God."[74]

Q. Some translations use "husband" and "wife" instead of "man" and "woman." Is Paul addressing husbands and wives, specifically, or men and women, generally?

In SWS: Paul is addressing both men and women. Traditionally, discussions of this passage have focused solely on women. Some argue that Paul mentioned head coverings for males hypothetically to round out the argument but that only the women's conduct was in question. While there are some references exclusive to women (11:6, 10, 13), the most natural reading suggests Paul is addressing both genders. Most references are to both genders

74. "Special pleading" is argument in which the speaker deliberately ignores aspects that are unfavorable to their point of view.

in chapter 11 (11:3, 4–5, 7, 8–9, 11–12, 14–15), and in each case where men and women are paired, men are mentioned first.

A case can be made from the Greek words used (*gyne* for women/wives and *aner* for men/husbands) that husbands and wives are the sole concern here. The terms can mean women/men in general, but when paired, often mean wife/husband. Because of this, translators must be careful to determine the meaning based on context. They must be consistent, however, which is a problem with the RSV translation that alternates between translating *gyne* as "women" in some occurrences and "wives" in others.

The best understanding is that the text refers to men and women generally, which would certainly encompass husbands and wives in the assembly, but not exclusively. This fits better with 11:11–12, which refers to the origins of men and women. It would also help explain why Paul said "the head of the woman is the man" with nothing in the context to single out a marriage relationship. Note that Paul refers more commonly to every woman (11:5) or a woman (11:6, 10, 13, 15) without any indication of marital status just as he does not limit his instruction to married men but to every man (11:3, 4) or a man (11:7, 14). As Witherington writes, "The argument is not about family relations but about praying and prophesying in public worship."[75]

Q. Some suggest that we cannot be sure whether the covering on a woman's head is referring to a veil or long hair, and whether some kind of sexual impropriety or impiety is in view here. Do you agree?

Oster: No. There is clear archeological evidence of what is going on here regarding veils and what they mean.

Julius Caesar founded Corinth as a Roman colony in 44 BC, right before he was assassinated. The purpose of a colony is to reflect, in a concentrated form, the language, law, religion, and values of the capital city: in this case, Rome. Roman civilization had particular religious practices, and we can easily find them in archeology and ancient literature. So if we look at the evidence, we can visualize what Paul is talking about here.

75. Witherington III, *Conflict and Community in Corinth*, 235.

In SWS: We know Roman men wore head coverings when they prayed or prophesied in any religious service. While operating without that information, scholars commonly suggested that Paul mentioned men here solely to be even-handed because his real concern was the importance of head coverings for women. Now we have ancient texts and other archeological remains that reveal devotional head coverings were the norm for Roman males as well as females, as described in the quotation below:

> The Roman psyche had a special interest, if not fixation, with proper apparel, proper for both secular and sacred occasions. . . . It is not difficult to imagine the tenacity displayed by those of Roman heritage regarding the nature and propriety of head coverings during prayer and prophecy. . . . Certain Roman sacerdotal officials constantly kept their heads covered . . . [and] the small group of Vestal Virgins customarily covered [their heads] . . . while performing their sacerdotal functions. [Even more common was the] garment used in private as well as public devotional acts such as prayer, sacrifice, and prophecy that was typically referred to by the phrase *capite velato*. This gesture consisted of pulling part of one's garment or toga over the back of the head and then forward until it approached or covered the ears. . . . It is this widely disseminated devotional gesture, used by both permanent Roman clergy and by officiating laymen, that provides the matrix of the devotional apparel mentioned in 1 Corinthians 11:4. . . . The conventionality of this Roman practice is attested by Greek and Latin texts, monuments, coins, and statuary remains, all reflecting Roman devotional patterns and mores in both the western and eastern regions of the empire. . . . Evidence shows the pervasive association of this gesture with significant political rulers, with official and public priestly liturgies, and with devotional expressions of the common people.[76]

See the following images reflecting the Roman head-covering practice.

76. Oster, "When Men Wore Veils to Worship," 481–505.

[Bas relief from Arch of Marcus Aurelius showing sacrifice. User: MatthiasKabel / CC BY-SA (https://creativecommons.org/licenses/by-sa/3.0)]

In this image, Roman Emperor Marcus Aurelius is wearing a head covering while engaging in a religious ritual, the offering of a sacrifice. Note that the others present are not wearing a head covering; only the one who is actively involved in the offering wears a veil.

[Pompeii_Temple_of_Vespasian_altar_close-up. Wmpearl. Public domain.]

Again, what you see here is that the man specifically involved in the act of worship has a head covering. The people who are doing the accompaniment are not covered, and the people who are watching are not covered.

[CaesarAugustusPontiusMaximus. RyanFreisling at English Wikipedia. Public Domain.]

This is the Emperor Augustus attired as *capite velato* since he is participating in a religious ceremony. Missing from his right hand was the bowl used in religious ceremonies. The term for this bowl (*phialē*) is found about a dozen times in the book of Revelation.

Oster: Paul is not telling everyone to wear a head covering when they're in a worship service; he's talking about the men and women who are praying and prophesying. And that's what you see in the statuary, coins, and friezes. The people who are specifically involved in those acts of worship are covered, demonstrating submissiveness, respect, and awe in the presence of the deity. This was pervasive throughout the entire Roman empire. From the Tigris to the Thames, this is how a Roman would worship, and the Romans stood alone in this unisex practice of head coverings. Both men and women covered their heads as they worshiped.

Q. Why would some scholars believe that this passage is about sexual propriety, not authority?

Oster: They could very well be quoting someone who doesn't know any better. No scholar knows everything. We each have our areas of expertise, so we must be careful whom we reference for interpretations. The archeological evidence contradicts this interpretation. If wearing veils was about sexual propriety, why would men wear one?

This is not the kind of covering you put on when you go shopping at the Agora. This is not the kind of covering you wear when you come into a sacred building or into the assembly. This is a covering for praying and prophesying. It's worn only during those two acts. Pagans also wore them while performing sacrifices, but Christians no longer had the need for sacrifices.

So this archeological material gives us a visual example of what that would look like. The veiled men and women are the people who were actually involved in worship. The other people who were in the assembly in a secondary way, participating and observing, don't cover themselves. This would be true of the pagan temple worship, as well as the church of God in Corinth. At Corinth, not everyone is praying or prophesying, simultaneously and out loud; it's just the men and women with uncovered and covered heads, respectively.

Q. So are you saying that Paul is making a distinction between a unisex Roman practice in worship and a Christian one that reflects an eternal order between God the Father, Christ, men, and women?

Oster: Yes. Paul is addressing a situation where men's heads are covered and women's heads are uncovered. And what does Paul say?

He says it's a dishonor. It's communicating, visually and culturally, a misunderstanding of this headship relationship in verse 3, where Paul lays a theological foundation for his instructions on head coverings: "But I want you to realize that the head of every man is Christ, and the head of the woman is man, and the head of Christ is God" (1 Corinthians 11:3).

The Corinthian church was culturally mixed. The Greeks, the Jews, the Egyptians, and the people in Asia Minor did not have this practice. It was unique to Roman worship. The Roman Empire encompassed many geographical locations, each with its own religious norms, practices, and mores. The Romans are in charge, and there are Romans in this Corinthian church, so Paul is sorting out how to get them on board with everyone else so that they reflect the truth about headship and authority in relationships.

Q. So you believe that this a theological issue rather than a cultural one, of men and women worshiping and interacting in ways that reflect an eternal truth. Right?

Oster: Yes. I think what is bothering Paul is that the women have their head coverings off, while the men simultaneously have their heads covered in the assembly. This is sending the wrong message; it looks like the men are in submission to the women. But the eternal truths are laid out at the beginning of chapter 11.

In SWS: In 1 Corinthians 11:3, Paul uses the term "head" (Greek: *kephale*) to describe the relationship of God to Christ, Christ to man, and man to woman. Paul's point is that the relationship between man and woman corresponds in some way to the relationship between Christ and men and the relationship between God and Christ. Certainly, some things contained in sacred texts are cultural, but when Paul explicitly connects the headship of men to the headship of God and the headship of Christ, he makes clear that male headship is not subject to change as culture changes. In this sense, Paul is applying a universal principle of headship to a specific, cultural issue (head coverings) in the Corinthian church. First Corinthians 11:3 expresses the spiritual reality that women are to express submission to men just as Christ does to God. A specific way this was to be displayed in Corinth was the wearing of head coverings.

In 1 Corinthians 11:7–8, Paul writes, "man . . . is the image and glory of God; but woman is the glory of man. For man was not made from woman, but woman from man. Neither was man created for woman, but woman for man." Paul clearly connects the principle of male headship all the way back to creation. That connection rules out the possibility of headship being just a cultural issue of Paul's time that can be ignored today.

Paul also ensures this headship is not to be understood in any authoritarian or dominating sense.

Adam needed help, thus "woman for man" (11:9), and "woman is not independent of man or man independent of woman" (11:11). In addition, all men owe their existence to women (11:12). Through these words, Paul teaches interdependency and mutuality; men and women stand in need of each other.

Paul also presents the argument from nature (11:13–15). He argues that we know by nature that what one has on the head can be gender-distinguishing. He knew his Corinthian readers would acknowledge that if they woke up one day and all women were bald and all men had long hair, something would not be right with the universe. Paul is using that awareness to help his readers recognize that head coverings also can serve as means of distinguishing between women and men.

At the conclusion of 1 Corinthians 11:2–16, Paul conveys his awareness that some may not agree with his instruction. So he warns against anyone being contentious and affirms his teaching as universal practice for all churches (11:16).

Q. Who would want to argue about it?

Oster: The Roman Christians, of course. Paul is telling them that the dominant values of the Roman Empire, their worldview, is wrong. The Roman Christians are going to argue and be contentious about that. So Paul basically says, *All I can say is that we have no other custom than this, and all the churches of God feel the same way about it.*

And remember, Paul's language is not nearly as strong in this instruction as it is in the coming passage on the Lord's Supper. The Roman Christians aren't likely intending to be rebellious about head coverings; they just grew up in a culture where we know, from the evidence, that head covering in worship was a gender-neutral issue. It was a unisex practice.

Another historical point that helps us understand what the original readers of this letter would have heard is that the Corinthian church is a missional church. There is no one who grew up in a Christian home. The oldest convert, when Paul writes 1 Corinthians, is five years old. It's a church filled with immature Christians. Paul starts this section of the letter off gently by saying, "I want to commend you. . . ." He just wants this issue of head coverings while praying and prophesying fixed. And his reasoning is theological: There is an order to creation. Women praying with uncovered heads while men pray with covered heads is not showing proper respect for headship.

Q. Is there any explicit distinction between assemblies within 1 Corinthians 11–14?

In SWS: Yes. [1 Corinthians 11] does pertain to the assembly as noted above and as additionally supported in the points below.

The phrase "I praise you" in 11:2 connects to the phrase "I do not praise you" in 11:17. Paul employs these phrases to connect 11:2–16 to 11:17–34. In this way, he makes clear that these two passages are discussing activities that are somehow related.

Since 1 Corinthians 11:2–16 discusses the use of head coverings and 11:17–34 discusses the Lord's Supper, how are these passages related?

First Corinthians 11:17–34 refers to the Lord's Supper observance in the context of believers assembled for worship. We know that because in 11:18 Paul writes, "when you come together as a church" (NIV). The Greek word for "church" here is *ekklesia*, which literally means "assembly." If both the praying and prophesying in 1 Corinthians 11:1ff and the Lord's Supper observance in verses 17ff are not occurring in the context of believers assembled for worship, then the verbal connection Paul makes is bewildering at best and misleading at worst.

First Corinthians 11:2 is the beginning of a three-part section (11:2–14:40). It is beyond dispute that part two (11:17–34) and part three (Chapters 12–14) address activities taking place in the assembly. To view part one as addressing an activity taking place outside the assembly is to ignore the verbal connection it has with part two (noted above) and the fact that it precedes and is connected to two sections, which unquestionably address activities taking place within the assembly.

The prophesying of 14:1–40 took place "when the whole church comes together" (14:23), which suggests that the prophesying of 11:2–16 was in the same context. Certainly, prophecies were common in a variety of settings outside the assembly, but in 1 Corinthians 12–14 Paul is referring to the exercise of communicative spiritual gifts in the assembly.

Even in Christian circles, women probably would not have had much, if any, occasion to minister to men in "one-on-one" settings, since these encounters would be easily misinterpreted within the gender restrictions of that culture. Since the wearing of head coverings by women was to show submission to men, they would not have been worn when men were not present. Therefore, the only setting in which they would have been needed was the corporate worship assembly.

The reference to angels being concerned about gender-specific behavior (11:10) makes best sense when seen as analogous to Jewish beliefs about the role of angels in public worship.

In 11:16, Paul refers to the practice of other "churches," which favors a reference to the gathered assembly. As noted above, the word "church" translates *ekklesia* which means "assembly." If it does not have that meaning in 11:16, it would be the only exception in thirteen occurrences of this term in Chapters 11–14:12

Q. So if we agree that women were praying and prophesying in the assembly, and can still do so, what roles are prohibited for women, if any?

In SWS: The prohibited role is one of an authoritative teacher who guides the congregation in faith and practice.

This fundamental difference between prophet and teacher is evident in the Old Testament distinction between prophet and the teaching office of priests. Contrary to popular misconceptions, the Old Testament priesthood did not consist of only butchering animals and offering grain and animal sacrifices but also teaching. In the Old Testament, it was not the duty of prophets to regularly provide instruction based upon Scripture; that was the duty of the priests. Note the teaching duties of priests referred to in these diverse Old Testament texts (all in the NRSV translation):

- 2 Kings 17:27 – "Then the king of Assyria commanded, 'Send there one of the priests whom you carried away from there; let him go and live there, and teach them the law of the god of the land.'"
- 2 Chronicles 15:3 – "For a long time Israel was without the true God, and without a teaching priest, and without law."
- 2 Chronicles 19:8 – "In Jerusalem also, Jehoshaphat appointed some of the Levites, priests and heads of Israelite families to administer the law of the LORD and to settle disputes. And they lived in Jerusalem."
- 2 Chronicles 31:4 – "He ordered the people living in Jerusalem to give the portion due the priests and Levites so they could devote themselves to the Law of the LORD."
- Deuteronomy 17:18 – "When he takes the throne of his kingdom, he is to write for himself on a scroll a copy of this law, taken from that of the priests, who are Levites."
- Deuteronomy 31:9 – "So Moses wrote down this law and gave it to the priests, the sons of Levi, who carried the ark of the covenant of the LORD, and to all the elders of Israel."
- Jeremiah 2:8 – "The priests did not ask, 'Where is the LORD?' Those who deal with the law did not know me; the leaders rebelled against me. The prophets prophesied by Baal, following worthless idols."
- Jeremiah 18:18 – "They said, 'Come, let's make plans against Jeremiah; for the teaching of the law by the priest will not be lost, nor will counsel from the wise, nor the word from the prophets. So come, let's attack him with our tongues and pay no attention to anything he says.'"
- Ezekiel 7:26 – "Calamity upon calamity will come, and rumor upon rumor. They will try to get a vision from the prophet; the teaching of the law by the priest will be lost, as will the counsel of the elders."
- Ezekiel 22:26 – "Its priests have done violence to my teaching and have profaned my holy things; they have made no distinction between

the holy and the common, neither have they taught the difference between the unclean and the clean. . . ."

- Ezekiel 44:24 – "'In any dispute, the priests are to serve as judges and decide it according to my ordinances. They are to keep my laws and my decrees for all my appointed feasts, and they are to keep my Sabbaths holy.'"
- Micah 3:11 – "Its rulers give judgment for a bribe, its priests teach for a price, its prophets give oracles for money. . . ."
- Haggai 2:11 – "This is what the LORD Almighty says: 'Ask the priests what the law says. . . .'"
- Malachi 2:7 – "For the lips of a priest ought to preserve knowledge, and from his mouth men should seek instruction—because he is the messenger of the LORD Almighty."
- Ezra 7:12 – "Artaxerxes, king of kings, To Ezra the priest, a teacher of the Law of the God of heaven: Greetings."
- Ezra 7:21 – "Now I, King Artaxerxes, order all the treasurers of Trans-Euphrates to provide with diligence whatever Ezra the priest, a teacher of the Law of the God of heaven, may ask of you. . . ."

In Old Testament Scripture, the priest was always male, never female.

In the New Testament, teaching and prophecy are identified as different ministries and gifts in the early church:

- Acts 13:1 – "In the church at Antioch there were prophets and teachers: Barnabas, Simeon called Niger, Lucius of Cyrene, Manaen (who had been brought up with Herod the tetrarch) and Saul."
- 1 Corinthians 12:28 – "And in the church God has appointed first of all apostles, second prophets, third teachers, then workers of miracles."
- 1 Corinthians 12:29 – "Are all apostles? Are all prophets? Are all teachers? Do all work miracles?"
- 1 Corinthians 14:6 – ". . . if I come to you speaking in tongues, how will I benefit you unless I speak to you in some revelation or knowledge or prophecy or teaching?"
- Ephesians 4:11 – "It was he who gave some to be apostles, some to be prophets, some to be evangelists, and some to be pastors and teachers."

- 2 Peter 2:1 – "But false prophets also arose among the people, just as there will be false teachers among you, who will secretly bring in destructive opinions."

There were essential differences between the role of the prophet and the role of the teacher.

Prophecy seems to be a direct giving of messages to current situations and could encompass ethical exhortation, encouragement, etc. The purpose, intent, or function of prophecy in that setting was strengthening, encouraging, comforting, and edifying the body (cf. 1 Corinthians 14:3–4). Women did prophesy in the church assemblies at Corinth.

Q. Some conclude that because women prophesied in the church at Corinth with God's sanction and gifting, they can also preach because prophesying is more substantive than teaching or preaching. Is that an appropriate conclusion?

In SWS: The issue of women teaching and preaching is more complex. In part, the complexity arises from the New Testament texts themselves. 1 Timothy 2:12 states, "I permit no woman to teach or to have authority over a man; she is to keep silent." However, there are other passages where women teach. For example, Acts 18:26 reports, "He [Apollos] began to speak boldly in the synagogue; but when Priscilla and Aquila heard him, they took him aside and explained the Way of God to him more accurately." Priscilla is actually listed first here as she is in four out of the six occurrences of her and her husband's name in the New Testament. Many scholars view this placement as a way of indicating that Priscilla possessed or demonstrated some type of superiority relative to Aquila.

Evidence supporting that viewpoint is the example of a woman named Julia Severa, who also lived in the first century. When married to a man named Servenius Capito, who was from a family of high distinction, her name is always listed second when paired with his. He died sometime after AD 63, and Julia Severa married Tyrronius Rapon, who was from a much less distinguished family. When Julia's name is paired with Tyrronius's name, her name is always first.[77] However, what is most relevant to our study is in the case of Priscilla and Aquila, a woman is involved in teaching a man, so some level or type of teaching must be within the realm of women's engagement in ministry.

Additionally, in Philippians 4:2–3 we read of two women, Euodia and Syntyche, in the congregation at Philippi. According to Paul, these two women "struggled beside me in the work of the gospel, together with Clement and the rest of my coworkers, whose names are in the book of life." Clearly, these two women helped Paul in his work as a missionary.

However, Scripture describes a level of "Ministry of the Word" (Acts 6:2–4; cf. Luke 1:2) that is tantamount to guiding specific congregations in their faith and practice. In the New Testament, this role is filled only by males, most notably by Timothy in Ephesus and Titus in Crete, who were to "command and teach. . . with all authority" (Titus 2:15). These men had the duties to "preach. . . reprove, rebuke, and exhort with complete patience and teaching" (2 Timothy 4:2) and were to do so in a formative way that established the order (Titus 1:5) of proper behavior in the church (1 Timothy 3:15). They were to declare sound teaching (Titus 2:1, 15), remind people of their duties (1 Timothy 3:15; Titus 3:1), insist on the truth of Scripture (Titus 3:8), warn divisive persons (Titus 3:10), and rebuke false teachers (Titus 1:13) as gently as possible (2 Timothy 2:25) while being ready to take it to the level of battle if necessary (1 Timothy 1:18). While others within the church could read Scripture, publicly exhort, and teach (1 Timothy 4:13), the teaching of Timothy and Titus carried the weight of command (1 Timothy 4:11) and authority (Titus 2:15) even to the extent of charging and entrusting others to teach (2 Timothy 2:2; 1 Timothy 1:3). The closest equivalent to the role of Timothy and Titus in today's churches would be the preacher, who is something more akin to the "pastor-teacher" from Ephesians 4:11.

It is also clear from Scripture that the apostles fulfilled a similar Ministry of the Word (Acts 6:2–4) and that elders served many of the same functions (Acts 20:28–31). We also see evidence that "the council of elders laid

77. William Mitchell Ramsay, *The Cities and Bishoprics of Phrygia* (Oxford: Clarendon Press, 1897), 639.

hands on" (appointed) people like Timothy and Titus to join in this aspect of their work (1 Timothy 4:15) even to the extent of appointing elders in their contexts (Titus 1:5). Collectively, these men are the ones who "lead" (Hebrews 13:7, 17, Greek: *Hegoumenois*) and "keep watch over" the congregation, primarily as they "speak the word of God" (Hebrews 13:7). It is the men who function as shepherds and overseers and are tasked with watching the flock and protecting it from error (Acts 20:28–31). Elders serve this function, alongside the ministers of the Word (Acts 6:2–4) whom "the body of elders have laid hands on" (appointed) to "command and teach" the church as a whole (1 Timothy 4:11–14), sometimes correctively (2 Timothy 4:2). These are the ones who "lead" (Hebrews 13:7, 17, Greek: *Hegoumenois*) the congregation.

As in Paul's time, many kinds of teaching involving both men and women take place in congregations today. However, Scripture also indicates that the roles of elder (1 Timothy 3:1–7; Titus 1:5–9) and those who fulfill the Ministry of the Word by communicating authoritative teaching to the congregation (e.g., preacher, Titus 2:15) are reserved for men.

Q. Are all up-front roles in the assembly—e.g., leading prayer or songs, leading a communion devotional, etc.—part of the same category that should be reserved for men because of the biblical doctrine of headship?

In SWS: The relevant biblical texts indicate women can serve in these up-front roles. What needs to be understood is that biblical headship always involves leading, but much of what today is referred to as leading is often not something the New Testament church would have viewed as the exercising of headship.

We should distinguish the biblical definition of the term "headship" from the contemporary meaning of the term "leadership." While there is debate as to the exact meaning of "head" (Greek: *kephale*) in the New Testament, the most natural reading suggests first in order, chief, prominent, or having authority over.

In contemporary culture, "leadership" is used to refer to many activities that are not within the scope of headship as understood in Scripture. We must adhere to a more biblical understanding of "headship" and contrast it with the contemporary meaning of "leadership." If we do not, we will be controlled by various modern understandings and subjective views like the ones governing current understandings of baptism. Believers should not allow later ideas about baptism to dictate what the New Testament actually meant by that term. Problems are created when later English meanings are substituted for the original meanings of scriptural terms.

We must not let modern meanings of the terms "leadership" or "leading" define New Testament headship. Currently, the idea of "leadership" is used to refer to many activities that are not within the scope of headship as presented in Scripture. For example, 1 Corinthians 11:2–16 makes clear that speaking does not always equal headship because Paul does not object to women's speaking in that passage, which clearly affirms the biblical doctrine of headship.

From early in the Old Testament onwards, God used female "leaders," as described in some detail in the previous sections. Please be reminded of the Old Testament's presentations of the roles of Miriam, Deborah, and Huldah. In the New Testament, be reminded of the roles of women like Phoebe the *diakonos* and *prostatis* in Romans 16:1–2, Prisca the "fellow worker" in Romans 16:3, and Mary, Tryphaena, Tryphosa, and Persis who "worked hard in the Lord" in Romans 16:6, 12. In addition, we have seen that women were praying and prophesying in the assemblies in Corinth, and Paul affirms this vocal participation as long as the biblical doctrine of headship is displayed. And yet that same apostle Paul, in 1 Corinthians 11:2–16, refers to the story of creation in Genesis to establish that man is the head of woman.

Today, the primary person commissioned to fulfill the Ministry of the Word role is referred to as our "pulpit minister"; this designation is problematic because others often speak from the pulpit during the assembly to make announcements, offer communion devotionals, etc. Headship is not intrinsic to every role performed from the platform we call the "pulpit." Scripture reveals speaking roles for women in the assembly; and speaking roles in our assemblies are generally best accomplished from the platform.

Since God established the principle of headship at creation, and yet God has placed women in positions of leadership, not all instances of female leadership violate the biblical doctrine of headship, else God has acted inconsistently with his own order. Therefore, in the ministries and worship services of the church, the leadership gifts of women are to be employed in ways that conform to the examples in Scripture, ways that do not violate the biblical doctrine of headship.

In this chapter, we learned that Paul's instructions in 1 Corinthians 11 on head coverings were based in the biblical principle of headship. In an assembly in which Roman men kept their heads covered while praying and prophesying and non-Roman women kept their heads uncovered, the biblical order of headship was visibly undermined. Paul wanted to prevent this confusion and to point people to the timeless principle of headship. In the next chapter, we will look at another passage meant to address gender issues within the church: 1 Corinthians 14.

7

WHY MUST WOMEN STAY SILENT IN 1 CORINTHIANS 14?

RICHARD OSTER, BOBBY HARRINGTON, RENÉE WEBB SPROLES

This is another in-depth chapter where we examine what the Word of God teaches about men and women in the church. In this conversation, Dr. Bobby Harrington will further clarify the translation of the word (head), and then Dr. Rick Oster will help us understand what's going on in 1 Corinthians 14.

> *"Women should remain silent in the churches. They are not allowed to speak, but must be in submission, as the law says." (1 Corinthians 14:34)*

Harrington: Before Rick Oster delves further into the concept of headship, let me point out that his description of "veils" in 1 Corinthians 11 is not some fringe interpretation of scholarship on veils. It is seminal. As Preston Massey pointed out in the *Journal of Biblical Literature* in 2018, "Oster anticipated the discussion of male head coverings by a margin of over twenty-five years."[78]

One more thing before Rick's comments. Some scholars eschew male leadership when it comes to translating "head," by pointing to statements from church leaders in the 300s and later who had a "Nicene Trinitarian theology." Some of these church leaders argued that submission in the Trinity will

78. Preston Massey, "Veiling among Men in Roman Corinth: 1 Corinthians 11:4 and the Potential Problem of East Meeting West," *Journal of Biblical Literature* (2018): 501–517.

not exist in eternity, and that, therefore, it is inconsistent to see "head" as implying the authority of God the Father over the Son (see below).

It is also pointed out that there are early church leaders who, in discussing the Trinity, understood "head" as "source"; their quotes in a Trinitarian context are then used to interpret *headship* as described in the New Testament, and ultimately cast a shadow on the ecumenical consensus of the early church that God calls men to a special Christlike leadership in the church and in the home.

We want to be careful when we quote ancient sources, including someone like Photius, the Patriarch of Constantinople, as an authority on this point. He lived approximately 800 years after the apostle Paul and is not a good guide on the meaning of a word from Paul's time. It is not as though church creeds and Patristic sources are unhelpful; they are. But it is helpful to clarify that while we value Patristic resources, we at Renew.org reaffirm that Scripture is our ultimate and final authority.

AUTHORITY IN THE TRINITY?

Oster: Regarding the Nicene Council, I very much appreciate the need in the fourth-century church to oppose the errors of the Arians with their false understanding of Christ. I do not, however, therefore elevate those documents to such a level of significance that they become the normative lens for interpreting Scripture on any topic. If this is my understanding of the Nicene Creed, how much less authoritative are ecclesiastical documents written by individual church fathers penned in some cases half a millennium after Nicea. Even when ancient authors are extremely significant or perhaps even a joy to read, they still fall far beneath the standard of being sacred writings.

Turning to Scripture, Paul teaches that Christ will be subordinate to the Father for all eternity, and rightfully so since this eternal posture of submission (*hypotassō*) best captures the heart of the relationship between God the Father and the Son.

> Then the end will come, when he hands over the kingdom to God the Father after he has destroyed all dominion, authority and power. (1 Corinthians 15:24)
>
> When he has done this, then the Son himself will be made subject to him who put everything under him, so that God may be all in all. (1 Corinthians 15:28)

Paul's language of "Father" and "Son" did not arise in the New Testament from some centuries-later mystical argot about the Trinity. There is a picture of the triune God in the New Testament, although most New Testament scholars acknowledge that the ideas and wording of later Trinitarianism are not found in the New Testament. Regarding the language of the "Father" and the "Son," these terms and this facet of the triune God stem explicitly from the Royal (Davidic) Covenant that Jesus fulfilled as the royal heir of David, and not from obscure metaphysical language of later centuries. As a reading of the New Testament makes clear, this Davidic covenant is one of the most important covenants in the Jewish scriptures (2 Samuel 7:4–17, delivered by the prophet Nathan) and one of the most pervasive in the New Testament. The most relevant part of Nathan's message reads:

> When your days are over and you rest with your ancestors, I will raise up your offspring to succeed you, your own flesh and blood, and I will establish his kingdom. He is the one who will build a house for my Name, and I will establish the throne of his kingdom forever. I will be his father, and he will be my son. When he does wrong, I will punish him with a rod wielded by men, with floggings inflicted by human hands. But my love will never be taken away from him, as I took it away from Saul, whom I removed from before you. Your house and your kingdom will endure forever before me; your throne will be established forever. (2 Samuel 7:12–16)

This is the foundation for numerous Psalms about the Royal Covenant and God's anointed and obedient king. Repeatedly, the writings and sermons of the New Testament teach that Jesus of Nazareth is the last heir of David's covenant, raised and enthroned to sit next to YHWH with the task of conquering enemies. All of this is the fulfillment of Psalm 110:1: "The LORD [YHWH] says to my Lord [the King]: 'Sit at my right hand, until I make your enemies your footstool.'"

In Paul's brief description of this in 1 Corinthians 15, he writes that when the end of the earth arrives, "He [Jesus Christ] hands over the kingdom to God the Father after he has destroyed all dominion, authority and power" (1 Corinthians 15:24b). This has been the millennia-long task of the obedient Davidic Christ (Anointed King), made clear at his enthronement in the first century by the teaching of Psalm 110:1 and Psalm 8:6 (among others). This is not peripheral teaching about who Jesus is, but is foundational to the first Petrine sermon in Acts 2 and the first Pauline sermon in Acts 13. Many New Testament scholars point out that Psalm 110:1 is either quoted or alluded to in the New Testament more than any other psalm. Usually phrases like "at his right hand" or "under his feet/footstool" are clear indications that Psalm 110 is in mind.

Psalm 2 is another Davidic psalm that plays a clear role in the New Testament. For example, when both of the terms *Lord* and *Anointed* (Christ) occur together as in Luke 2:11 ("Today in the town of David a Savior has been born to you; he is the Messiah, the Lord") and Acts 2:36 ("Therefore let all Israel be assured of this: God has made this Jesus, whom you crucified, both Lord and Messiah"), it resonates with the testimony of Psalm 2:2: "The kings of the earth rise up and the rulers band together against the LORD and against his anointed [Greek: *chrīstós*]." The plot of the story mentioned in Acts 4:25–26 is found in Psalm 2.

In addition, "You are my Son; today I have become your father" is taken from Psalm 2:7 and applied to Jesus more than once in the New Testament (Acts 13:33; Hebrews 1:5; 5:5). This demonstrates again that the Scriptures read by Jesus and the apostles are where one should look for guidance about terms like "Son" and "begotten" when considering the submissive and obedient Davidic King Jesus whom YHWH called to his throne. A final connection between Psalm 2 and the New Testament is the Davidic King's submission to YHWH's directive to break to pieces rebellious nations like a potter's vessel (Psalm 2:9; Revelation 2:26–27; 12:5; 19:15).

SILENCING WOMEN IN 1 CORINTHIANS 14

Harrington: Dr. Rick Oster pointed us to an excellent resource that the leaders of the church he attends created after extensive study with Rick and others, including their senior minister, Rodney Plunket, PhD. It is called a *Study with the Shepherds: Women and Men Serving the Church.* As stated in a previous chapter, we use this document extensively with permission. When quoted, we will reference it as SWS.

Oster: Let me remind everyone that when you plant the gospel in a pagan culture for the first time, almost everybody's a new Christian. Nobody grew up in a Christian home. Nobody. The number of truths that would have to be taught is staggering. Nobody's at the fifty-yard line; everybody's starting at zero except for those who came over from the synagogue. That's what is happening at Corinth. Most of the Corinthians' problems stem from their pagan background.

The reason the American church is in such trouble is that we can't even see the way the church is being assimilated to our own cultural values and away from biblical truth. One of those truths is that God is the Creator of men and women, and that in his role as Creator, he gets to set the definitions and categories for them. People who continually listen to culture for its categories and paradigms will find themselves out of step with what Scripture says is true.

Sproles: At the same time, we want to be sensitive to where we've come from, especially within Restoration Movement churches (many Renew.org churches are a part of this tribe). As John Mark Hicks points out in his book, *Women Serving God: My Journey in Understanding Their Story in the Bible*, there have been many Christian men who have argued that women were unfit for public life, having been designed solely for domesticity. Others believed that women should be prohibited from practicing medicine, law, and politics, and should even be denied the right to vote. In my own experience growing up, I never saw a woman participate in public ways in the assembly.

I am grateful that those are not the prevailing attitudes toward women today. I am grateful for those who wrestled with these passages of Scripture to make sense of the fullness of what God says about men and women. I am grateful for those who had the courage to contradict, correct, and instruct men in their wrong attitudes toward women.

And yet, I am concerned. I agree with Dr. Oster that the American church is quickly assimilating to the culture around us in terms of gender and sexuality. Just this week, an online discussion of gender roles and the church was shut down because offering a soft complementarian viewpoint, as opposed to a fully egalitarian one, was considered harmful and toxic toward women.

What I find in Scripture about how men and women should interact in marriage and in the family of God is good news. I am grateful for this opportunity through Renew.org to discuss such an important and emotionally charged topic; if we stop talking to one another, if we stop studying and searching for the truth, if we say it's just too difficult to understand, then we are defeated.

Oster: And let me say that there will likely be people who are going to push back against this who are sort of populist and say, "You know, why do we have to know any background at all to know the Bible? Can't we just read it and obey? My grandmother didn't know anything about all this. Are you saying she's not going to heaven?" Of course I'm not saying that. My grandmother had a sixth-grade education and was a kind and godly woman. I'm not talking about who gets into heaven by understanding these issues.

I am talking about people who are trying to be responsible teachers, people who are talking about these issues. If we're going to talk about these things and try to interact with what Scripture says in context, then we need to be as well-versed as we can regarding what was going on in the day and age in which Paul wrote. Like it or not, Jesus did not come back during the Roman Empire, which means the church since then must put forth some effort to learn about antiquity to have translations of the Bible in our language. So we must spend time learning about the ancient world.

Sproles: That's a great point. Let's get started.

Q. Why does Paul say the women should keep silent in the assembly in 1 Corinthians 14 when in chapter 11 it is clear that women are speaking and Paul does not disapprove?

Oster: Because Scripture does not contradict itself, serious students must view both chapter 11 and chapter 14 as theologically consistent one with the other.

In SWS: Since we believe in the inspiration of Scripture and affirm the resulting commitment to sound principles of biblical interpretation, we cannot say chapter 14 trumps chapter 11 or that chapter 11 trumps chapter 14. . . . We cannot ignore 1 Corinthians 11:2–16, which reveals women are praying and prophesying in the assembly. . . [and] we cannot ignore 1 Corinthians 14:34–35 in which Paul states women should remain silent in the assembly.

The challenge for every student of the Word is to step back from a given text and review it in its entirety. With this in mind, it seems the structure of 1 Corinthians 11–14 reveals that the problems addressed in these four chapters all relate to the assembly.

- 1 Corinthians 11:2–16 addresses problems associated with praying and prophesying in the assembly.
- 1 Corinthians 11:17–34 addresses problems associated with the Lord's Supper in the assembly.
- 1 Corinthians 12–14 addresses problems associated with spiritual gifts in the assembly.

This same commitment to consistency in interpretation makes it difficult to regard 1 Corinthians 11:2–16 as about non-assembly occurrences of praying and prophesying while knowing that 11:17–34 is about the assembly.

Q. Okay, so let's take a broader look at this whole chapter for a moment. Can you help us understand what is happening in 1 Corinthians 14?

Oster: First Corinthians 14 is part of a three-chapter block of information (chapters 12–14), and the focus is spiritual gifts (1 Corinthians 12:1). All of 1 Corinthians 14 is about spiritual gifts, except for verses 34–35, which we'll talk about later. Paul is addressing the use of spiritual gifts in an orderly way in the assembly; he ends by insisting upon it in verse 40.

Q. So what is going on in particular?

In SWS: In 1 Corinthians 14:26–33, Paul silences tongues speakers and prophets with no gender references. First Corinthians 14:34's instructions to women run parallel to Paul's instructions to the other two groups. All three sets of instructions use an imperative form of the same Greek verb (*sigaō*) for "be silent."

- The first occurrence (14:28) is employed to command a tongues speaker to be silent when no interpreter is present.
- The second occurrence (14:30) is employed to command a prophet to be silent when another prophet receives a revelation.
- The third occurrence (14:34) is employed to command women to be silent instead of being vocally disruptive.

Each of these commands calls upon a different group within the assembly to cease certain types of audible disruptions. Therefore, the instructions in 14:34 do not constitute a universal prohibition of women speaking in the worship assembly; instead, just like the two preceding "be silent" commands, the command in 14:34 is intended only to call for silence relative to vocal disruptions.

Oster: Yes. In the first two instances, no one understands the imperative "be silent" to mean the people can't say anything. It's understood that anytime they're violating this particular area, they have to stop speaking. The only reason they're told to be quiet is that they are being disruptive and straying from what God expects for the assembly to accomplish in terms of edification, instruction, and concern for others.

Q. So in 1 Corinthians 14 Paul is talking about order in the assembly when exercising spiritual gifts. What would you say to someone who believes it's clear that "silent" means "silent"—for all women, for all reasons, and for all time in the assembled church?

Oster: When correcting tongues speakers, prophets, and women, Paul uses the same Greek verb *sigaō*, which means be quiet, or be silent. As I mentioned before, no one understands the first two instances of the imperative "be silent" to mean the people can't say anything ever. Additionally, we have good reason to believe, from the wording Paul uses, that this is a particular problem with some married women.

In SWS: Paul says the women should ask their questions of "their husbands" at home. The Greek word translated as "husbands" is *andras* (plural accusative of *aner*), a word that can mean either "men" or "husbands." However, the two-word Greek phrase, translated here as "their own husbands" (NIV), occurs five other times in the New Testament where it always refers to a husband or husbands. It should be translated and understood the same way here.

This reference to "their own husbands" in 14:35 is most naturally interpreted as an indication that the women Paul is addressing in 1 Corinthians 14:34–35 are all married. Some resist that interpretation, but to interpret it any other way creates a problem.

We know there were unmarried women in the Corinthian church (see 1 Corinthians 7). If Paul is viewed here to be telling all women to be silent, he is giving only the married ones a means of appropriately seeking the information he indicates is legitimate for them to seek; they are just not to seek it by asking interrupting questions during the assembly.

Are we to conclude that the unmarried women had no questions or that Paul wasn't concerned about their questions? In line with the previous two "be silent" exhortations, it is far more likely Paul is only addressing all or some of the married women because they are the ones guilty of creating vocal disturbances.

Therefore, this command is not addressing all the Christian women in Corinth but only the married women or, more likely, some group of married women. In light of the context, he does that because only they are creating disorder comparable to that created by tongue speakers without interpreters and prophets who speak simultaneously rather than one-at-a-time. The disorder appears to be the asking of interrupting questions during the assembly. Paul commands them to quit; instead, they are to ask their husbands when they get home. Even if 1 Corinthians 11:2–16 were not part of 1 Corinthians, 1 Corinthians 14:34–35 would still be best interpreted as a passage applicable only to married women.

So in these verses, Paul is not prohibiting women from ever speaking in the assembly. He is commanding them to quit creating disorder by vocal disruptions. Why does he do that in 1 Corinthians 14:34–35? Because the purpose of this section is to bring order to the Corinthian assemblies.

Q. So must wives always learn from their husbands at home?

In SWS: No. Paul is not saying wives can only learn from their husbands at home. He is saying if they cannot participate in the assembly in an orderly way, then they need to take their inquiries home. It is as if Paul is saying, "Don't learn so loudly in the church!"

Paul uses this same kind of construction in 11:34a: "If anyone is hungry, let him eat at home, lest you come together for judgment" (NKJV). He does not mean no one should eat at the Lord's Supper or that it is wrong to be hungry when one gathers in church; his point is that it is better to eat at home than to disrupt the Christian community by the way one eats at church.

In 14:34, Paul commands some or all married women to be silent in church to stop them from asking interrupting questions that bring shame upon them and others.

Q. The concluding clause in 14:35 is, "For it is shameful for a woman to speak in church." Could this clause be Paul's way of revealing that the silence of women applies to the entire assembly?

In SWS: Acts 18:1ff reports Paul's planting of this church and living and teaching in Corinth for a year-and-a-half. What explanation could possibly be offered for that church now having women praying and prophesying (as reported in 1 Corinthians 11:2ff) and being vocal in some other way (as reported in 1 Corinthians 14:34–35) and not already knowing that women speaking at all was "shameful"? If Paul had indeed taught them that any speaking by a female was shameful and they were ignoring it, why does he not remind them of that in 1 Corinthians 11? Why does he make the discussion in 1 Corinthians 11:2ff all about headship and head coverings and never mention it was shameful for women to be vocal at all? Why wait until 1 Corinthians 14, and why say it in a clause following an exhortation only addressed to married women?

The answer to these questions is clear. In 1 Corinthians 14:34–35, Paul is instructing all or some of the married women to stop their shameful behavior of disruptive speaking in the assembly. He is not prohibiting these women or any other women from ever speaking in the assembly. The larger context reveals that Paul's intent in this final clause of 14:35 is to report that "it is shameful for a woman to speak in church" as these women are speaking. They are speaking non-submissively and disruptively.

Q. So to interpret the "keep quiet" mandate as a prohibition of women ever speaking in the assembly requires us to ignore the actual context and content of these verses?

Oster: Yes. Paul is saying that the way some of the women are interacting with some of the men is dishonoring male headship. If they wanted to learn something, those particular women needed to be quiet and wait until they got home to ask their husbands, because they obviously didn't know how to learn correctly, in an orderly way.

In SWS: Paul's message in verses 34–35 is that women must act that way just like the corrected tongues speakers and prophets must act in that way (14:27–33).

To argue that Paul in 1 Corinthians 14:34–35 is commanding all women to be silent at all times in all the church's assemblies in a section of 1 Corinthians explicitly correcting disorder in the assembly requires us to believe that anytime women speak they are disorderly.

Q. 1 Corinthians 14:34–35 is not found in the same place in all the ancient Greek manuscripts, and some scholars say someone other than Paul added it later. Is that true?

In SWS: It is true that in some ancient Greek manuscripts, the passage located in our English Bibles at 1 Corinthians 14:34–35 is found after what we have in verse 40. However, no ancient manuscripts are absent of this material. Therefore, these verses should be regarded as authentic.

[In verse 34], women are told to keep silent in the congregations. Here we have some women who are acting in ways that are contrary to how the assembly is supposed to be conducted. We know from earlier in the book, clearly they can pray and prophesy, and because we have the word *ekklesia* 1 Corinthians 11:16, we must take seriously the fact that this is in an assembly. Now, we see, once again, the same kind of tenor, the same implications of the verb "be silent" as in the previous two occurrences.

Q. Is there any way for us to know what Paul is talking about when he says, "They must be in submission as the law says"?

Oster: Yes. Let's address the law first and then move to the idea of submission. Paul is not the first in Scripture to use the term *law* [Greek: *nomos*] to refer to materials other than those preserved in the books of Exodus through Deuteronomy, or to materials specifically related to priestly activities set forth at Sinai. My purpose is not to look at the context or exegesis of each of these separate verses, but rather to demonstrate that it was a well-known convention at the time of Jesus and the early church to use the term *law* [*nomos*] to refer to a lot more than Sinai materials or the literature of Exodus through Deuteronomy.

- John 10:34 – Jesus asked, "Is it not written in your Law [*nomos*], 'I have said you are gods'?" This quotation ("I said, you are gods") is from Psalm 82:6.
- John 15:25 – Jesus said, "But this is to fulfill what is written in their Law [*nomos*]: 'They hated me without reason.'" This quotation ("They hated me without a cause") is from Psalm 69:4.
- Galatians 4:21–22 – Writing to his opponents, Paul says, "Tell me, you who want to be under the law [*nomos*], are you not aware of what the law [*nomos*] says? For it is written that Abraham had two sons, one by the slave woman and the other by the free woman." The Law

[*nomos*] that Paul cites is a summary from Genesis 16 regarding Sarah and Hagar, an episode many generations prior to Mt. Sinai.

- Romans 3:19 – Paul concludes a Scripture-based argument with these words: "Now we know that whatever the law [*nomos*] says, it says to those who are under the law [*nomos*], so that every mouth may be silenced and the whole world held accountable to God." The several Scriptures Paul cited in Romans 3:10–18 that demonstrate "whatever the law [*nomos*] says" are from the Psalms and the prophets, not from the Law of Moses.
- 1 Corinthians 14:21 – Paul writes, "In the Law [*nomos*] it is written, 'With other tongues and through the lips of foreigners I will speak to this people, but even they will not listen to me, says the Lord.'" These words that Paul cites are a direct quotation from the prophet Isaiah, chapter 28:11–12.

Regarding your question, no modern interpreter of Paul should be astonished that he would use the term "law" to refer to the creation story. Both Jesus and Paul in other places used "law" to refer to non-Pentateuchal Scripture. As the above Scriptures demonstrate, "law" was easily used to refer to the Psalms and the prophets. Significantly, it is shown above that "law" is also used in reference to stories in Genesis.

Jesus and Paul, by our standards, were pretty free in their use of the term. In any case, it certainly proves beyond any doubt that in 1 Corinthians 14:34, Paul could easily be referring to the creation story by his use of the term "law" [*nomos*].

In SWS: Because Paul grounds male headship in the creation narrative (Genesis 1–3) . . . just as he does in 1 Corinthians 11:7–9 and 1 Timothy 2:11–15 . . . it is all but certain he is grounding the submission of women in that same narrative here.

Q. What would you say to someone who thinks that since 1 Corinthians 14 addresses disorderly women, they may fully exercise their spiritual gifts as long as they aren't disruptive in church?

Sproles: It is important to recognize that spiritual gifts are not the only measuring stick for service in the body of Christ, as many egalitarians assert. In the exercise of spiritual gifts, gender must be taken into account. Paul continually points us to the creation account to remind us of this. Elisabeth Elliott (a missionary and wife of martyred missionary Jim Elliot) noted that even though she had better gifts than most men for being a pastor—knowing the Bible in several languages, expositing it with much experience, attaining maturity through suffering, and so on—there were biblical parameters for their use.

Harrington: I would like to add one concluding thought to this chapter. Within the boundaries of our shared faith statement at Renew.org, there are some of us who arrive at the same conclusions, but by different paths.

For example, another reason Paul might have asked for silence from the women is that the elders are judging prophecies in 1 Corinthians 14:29. That is, they are judging truth from heresy, which was a task of the elders of the synagogue in Jewish worship. Therefore, Paul grounds his command for women to be silent at this time in the service in the principle of submission found in the law, which, as Oster pointed out earlier, is the Old Testament in general and the order of creation in particular (Genesis 2), as he did in 1 Corinthians 11. This, too, is consistent with how Paul points to the law to back up his principle.

This evaluation of prophecy would be reserved for godly male leadership, including the public teachers and elders, as described in 1 Timothy 2 and 3. Paul makes the argument for godly male leadership explicit in 1 Timothy 2:12–14, where the teaching/authority role is only for men, which is the subject of our next chapter.

Next, we move to 1 Timothy 2 for a discussion with Rick Oster, Bobby Harrington, and Daniel McCoy on "authoritative teaching" and what that means for today.

8

DOES GOD ALLOW WOMEN PREACHERS IN 1 TIMOTHY 2?

RICHARD OSTER, BOBBY HARRINGTON, RENÉE WEBB SPROLES, DANIEL MCCOY

This is another in-depth chapter where we examine what the Word of God teaches about men and women in the church, turning our attention to the important teaching of 1 Timothy 2.

We will continue to engage with John Mark Hicks's Women Serving God: My Journey in Understanding Their Story *and Scot McKnight's* Blue Parakeet: Rethinking How You Read the Bible. *We chose these two men because they are influential in the circles of Renew.org leaders, and they serve as common examples of the posture many are taking today. We continue to make use of a church position paper created by Rodney Plunket, PhD, and others. This paper utilized Rick Oster's input and is referred to as SWS below.*[79]

At Renew.org, we believe the New Testament teaches that the lead teacher/preacher role in the gathered church and the elder/overseer role are for qualified men. While our next chapter will focus on the elder/overseer role, this chapter will focus on the teacher/preacher role in the gathered church. The text of 1 Timothy 2:11–15 will be our focus:

79. The church position paper (SWS) is called, *Study with the Shepherds—Women and Men Serving the Church*, which was created by the Church of Christ at White Station, where Rick Oster and his wife Sandy have attended for over a decade.

> A woman should learn in quietness and full submission. I do not permit a woman to teach or to assume authority over a man; she must be quiet. For Adam was formed first, then Eve. And Adam was not the one deceived; it was the woman who was deceived and became a sinner. But women will be saved through childbearing—if they continue in faith, love and holiness with propriety. (1 Timothy 2:11–15)

Q. In *Women Serving God*, John Mark Hicks says that "*there is significant uncertainty about the meaning and application of this text*" (163, italics his). Do you agree?

Oster: There is disagreement about the meaning and application, but I don't think it stems from uncertainty. I think it is primarily because we live in a world where egalitarian notions of humanity dominate. I think we can, with some historical and cultural background, determine what is happening here.

Q. Hicks says that besides 1 Timothy 2:12, "*. . . no other text explicitly identifies a gender boundary in the exercise of the Spirit's gifts*" (116, italics his). Do you agree?

Oster: No. We have just seen in 1 Corinthians 11 where boundaries are drawn regarding veils when praying and prophesying in the assembly. Paul's reasoning is grounded in the creation narrative, as we see in 1 Corinthians 11:7–10. And in 1 Corinthians 14, Paul is saying that male headship is being dishonored by the way some of the women are interacting with some of the men. If they wanted to learn something, those particular women had to be quiet and wait until they got home to ask their husbands, because they didn't know how to learn in a submissive, orderly way.

Q. In Part 6 of Hicks's book, titled "My Firewall," Hicks notes that he used to believe 1 Timothy 2:8–15 was "a *timeless, and universal command*" (163, italics his), but that he now believes Paul is really addressing "*a local situation with a temporary prohibition for a specific problem*" (165, italics his). Which is it?

Sproles: Bobby Harrington recommended a resource that was really helpful for me when thinking through this question. It's Kathy Keller's *Jesus, Justice,* *and Gender Roles*. In it, she notes that "everything that Paul (or any other biblical author) wrote was to a specific group of people with a specific situation in view. . . . In compiling the canon, it was a presupposition that God's truth was applicable to the church throughout history."

Moreover, 1 Timothy, out of all of Paul's letters, could be seen as a "church planting manual—how to set up a church in an organized way."[80] Andreas Köstenberger and Thomas Schreiner also point out that Paul "had functioned as a missionary and church planter for so many years, he likely had a general vision of how churches should be structured. Hence, his instructions were not entirely situational but reflected the pattern of governance that he expected to exist in his churches."[81] Indeed, if we claim that Paul's instructions to specific situations do not apply to the church today, most of the New Testament would be irrelevant. The goal, then, is to find out what Paul is saying in this particular historical and cultural context and how we can obey his teaching today.

Oster: I agree. As I mentioned in an early conversation, the epistles we have in the New Testament are what scholars call "occasional," which means 1 Corinthians was written to the church regarding Corinth, Galatians was written to the churches of Galatia, and so on. And that doesn't detract one bit from their authority, from their inspiration, or from the fact that they belong in the canon of Scripture. However, it does mean that our starting point is to try to understand the issues in those letters, to understand why Paul or Peter or John wrote them.

Q. Does 1 Timothy 2:8 restrict women from praying in the assembly?

In SWS: Some point to 1 Timothy 2:8–15, where men were asked to pray, supposedly just men, not women, as effectively a prohibition against women praying in the assembly. However, the purpose of 1 Timothy 2 is not to give instruction on who gets to pray and who does not. The purpose is to effect "peaceful and quiet lives in all godliness and holiness" (2:2). The men in Ephesus (Timothy is in Ephesus at this time) had been sidetracked from

80. See Kathy Keller, *Jesus, Justice, and Gender Roles* (Grand Rapids: Zondervan, 2012), 24.
81. See Andreas J. Köstenberger and Thomas R. Schreiner, *Women in the Church 3rd Edition: An Interpretation & Application of 1 Timothy 2:9–15* (Wheaton: Crossway, 2016), 167.

this witness by their inability to pray without "anger and disputing" (2:8). Paul's instruction seeks to re-establish this witness, not by restricting prayer to men, but by addressing the specific issue with the prayers these men were offering alongside their quarreling.

Q. With that in mind, let's set the stage for this discussion. What is going on in 1 Timothy 2:8–15?

In SWS: The arrangement of 1 Timothy 2 provides much interpretive assistance. This chapter begins by encouraging that prayers be made for all people and those who rule over them (2:1) so that believers may live "peaceful and quiet [Greek: *hesuchia*] lives in all godliness and holiness" (2:2, cf. 2 Thessalonians 3:11–12). The pursuit of "peaceful and quiet lives in all godliness and holiness" is Paul's main interest in 1 Timothy 2. That main interest leads Paul to promote three applications of that main interest. Each application is introduced by "therefore" in 2:8–15:

- The men must not pray with "anger and disputing" (2:8).
- The women must not tarnish their witness through immodest dress or adornment (2:9–10).
- The women must not tarnish their witness through authoritative teaching (2:11–15).

1 Timothy 2:12 clearly states, "I permit no woman to teach or to have authority over a man; she is to keep silent." However. . . Acts 18:26 also clearly states, "He [Apollos] began to speak boldly in the synagogue; but when Priscilla and Aquila heard him, they took him aside and explained the Way of God to him more accurately." Priscilla is a woman, and she is certainly part of explaining the Way of God to a man, Apollos. In Philippians 4:2–3 we read that there were two women named Euodia and Syntyche in the congregation at Philippi who "struggled beside me in the work of the gospel, together with Clement and the rest of my co-workers, whose names are in the book of life." It is clear these two women helped Paul in his ministry of the gospel.

It is worth noting that 1 Timothy 2 shares with 1 Corinthians 11:2–16 and 1 Corinthians 14:34–35 a conviction that the creation narrative is the ground for the biblical doctrine of headship. This is an important conviction of Paul's, and it is very significant that it is present in all three texts that relate to the roles of women in the church.

Oster: The relationship of the church to the outside world is crucial at every stage of its growth in the first century. There are a lot of rich truths leading up to 1 Timothy 2:8–15, and they highlight the fact that Christians need to live peaceful and godly lives. The stakes are high because God wants all men to be saved and to come to a knowledge of the truth (1 Timothy 2:3–4).

So Paul wants church members to behave themselves.

First, he addresses the men. When they pray, they should lift holy hands. This is a common posture for prayer mentioned in the Old Testament (Psalms 28:2; 63:4; 141:2; Lamentations 2:19; 3:41; Isaiah 1:15). It's also documented in the statuary and iconography of the ancient world: pagans did this. And Paul says the life of piety for God's people cannot just be outward acts. This is clear if you know the prophets of the Old Testament (Isaiah 1:10–15; 58:1–14; 66:1–4; Hosea 6:4–6; Amos 5:21–27; Jeremiah 7:1–11; Malachi 1:6–14) and Jesus (Matthew 5:23–24; 6:1–8; 23:23–24) too. Paul says they need to have a heart and a tranquil life that's not consumed with anger and quarreling. That's the word to men.

(Left) An Ephesian woman, Cominia Junia, of the second century AD who has raised hands in prayer at worship; note that she also has her head covered in worship. (Right) A boy praying with raised hands, taken in the Altes Museum in Berlin. Photos property of Dr. Rick Oster.

Then he turns to the women, who are clearly women of wealth, and tells them that their dress and demeanor are affecting their witness to a world in need of salvation.

> I also want the women to dress modestly, with decency and propriety, adorning themselves, not with elaborate hairstyles or gold or pearls or expensive clothes, but with good deeds, appropriate for women who profess to worship God. A woman should learn in quietness and full submission. I do not permit a woman to teach or to assume authority over a man; she must be quiet. For Adam was formed first, then Eve. And Adam was not the one deceived; it was the woman who was deceived and became a sinner. (1 Timothy 2:9–14)

Q. Hicks says the exact nature of the problem with these women and their attire are uncertain. Were they "high-minded, aggressive, and seductive"? Were they recent converts from the Artemis cult? Were they

"spreading false teaching and seducing men" (169)? What can we know about this portion of 1 Timothy 2?

Oster: We have clues from the text as to what is happening. We know there are instructions for those in the church who are wealthy, especially in 1 Timothy 6. In the Roman world, there was not a big middle class, economically. This indicates that there are people from that small group in Ephesus, and generally in the Roman Empire, who had wealth.

Now, these women who have the kind of wealth presupposed by the description in verse 9 are obviously going to be women who have had educational opportunities. They had tutors if their parents wanted them to have tutors. They were being groomed to be married off, at a young age perhaps, into other aristocratic, wealthy families, maybe even some families connected to senatorial families in Rome. At the least, they would have been from a high class of families in the Roman province of Asia. The family values of these women's upbringing were more akin, to paraphrase Jesus, to "the rulers from among the rich and famous who knew how to lord it over others, and their great ones exercise authority over others" (Matthew 20:25) than to the Pauline teachings about submissiveness (1 Timothy 2:11) in this area of teaching.

These women with braided hair, gold, pearls, and costly attire need to adorn themselves with modesty and self-control, which is a fruit of the Spirit. The typical church member couldn't have costly attire. This was directed to a very small percentage of the church members in Ephesus, unless it was a demographically peculiar church.

Q. Let's talk about the Artemis cult. Hicks makes much of this cult in his suggestion that these commands are not timeless. Here is a section from Hicks's book:

> The generic woman ("a woman") encouraged to learn and forbidden to teach in [1 Timothy] 2:11–12 belongs to the group identified in 2:9–10. Some women (including widows), who dressed immodestly and pursued sensuality through drawing attention to themselves, were going from house church to house church practicing their astrology

> and magic as well as promoting myths. For example, the Artemis cult promoted seduction, sexual fulfillment, and safe childbearing, and the clothing described here reflects the practices of women in the Artemis cult (Hoag). They apparently had some success and were overpowering men in some way, which may have resulted in quarreling among the men. Paul wants to stop this. Therefore, he insists the women submit to the gospel by learning the mystery of godliness. Women should not teach until they learn sound doctrine. Consequently, Paul forbids *these women* (not every woman)—the women of 2:9–10—from teaching and overpowering men with their influence.
>
> In other words, 1 Timothy 2:12 *is not a timeless principle but a specific application of the gospel story* in the context of women who were teaching false doctrine, just as the prohibition against wearing gold and pearls was an *application* rather than a statement of a timeless principle. Read that sentence again; it is an important one.[82]

Oster: Unfortunately, John Mark Hicks's presentation of the Artemis cult is a distortion. He draws on Hoag's work and Hoag's fruitful imagination, creating a synthesis of the Ephesian Artemis with the Egyptian goddess Isis (introducing all types of archaic Egyptian mythology that was not a part of the "faith and practice" of the religion of the Ephesian Artemis).[83] Time and time again, Hoag's work is woven from repeated possibilities rather than probabilities. When reading this imaginative reconstruction, one is reminded why the term "Parallelomania" was coined long ago to describe how authors perceive apparent similarities and construct parallels and analogies without historical basis.

The truth of the matter is, sexual seduction and erotic themes were simply not a part of the Ephesian Artemis cult. At the same time, there is a lot we do not know about the backgrounds to the problems of 1 Timothy (Hoag is not even certain whether 1 Timothy is Pauline), but that uncertainty, in my judgment, is better than an alternative view based upon a speculative

82. John Mark Hicks, *Women Serving God: My Journey in Understanding Their Story in the Bible* (2020), 191.
83. Gary Hoag, *Wealth in Ancient Ephesus and the First Letter to Timothy: Fresh Insights from Ephesiaca by Xenophon of Ephesus* (Winona Lake, IN: Eisenbrauns, 2015).

synthesis. The apostle Paul, whose spiritual guidance I read in other letters, would not be so kind to believers as Paul is to the women in 1 Timothy who, according to John Mark, are participants in idolatry, sexual immorality, and (pagan) mythology.

Harrington: The historical and cultural background issues can be confusing for those of us who hear different scholars saying different things. This is why we asked Rick Oster to help us with these conversations. He has a widely respected archaeological and historical specialization on the veils in 1 Corinthians 11 and on life in ancient Ephesus. In fact, his academic focus has been on ancient Ephesus (starting with his postdoctoral fellowship).

So I would also like to point out another important item that he helped me and others to understand. Sometimes commentators will say there is a unique situation with the Artemis cult in Ephesus, making it the basis of a *unique* injunction on women in 1 Timothy 2. But the Artemis cult was not unique to Ephesus. There were Ephesian Artemis temples (and cults) throughout the ancient world. This is demonstrated not just by archaeology but also by the Word of God in Acts 19:27. In this verse, Luke quotes Demetrius, the silversmith in Ephesus, as referring to the temple of the great goddess Artemis, saying that the goddess "is worshiped throughout the province of Asia and the world." Oster points to numerous cities in the ancient world where this cult thrived.[84] For example, a friend gave me the following picture of the ruins of an Artemis Temple from the ancient city of Sardis. This may be the temple of Artemis to which the ancients referred in their inscriptions.

84. Richard Oster, "The Ephesian Artemis 'Whom All Asia and the World Worship' (Acts 19:27): Representative Epigraphical Testimony to *Aptemix Ephesia Outside Ephesosos*" in *Texts and Studies: Contributions to Biblical and Patristic Literature*, edited by D.C. Parker & D.G.K. Taylor, Volume 4, Transmission and Reception: New Testament Text-Critical and Exegetical Studies, edited by J.W. Childers and D.C. Parker (Piscataway, NJ: Gorgias Press, 2006).

Q. So when Paul says, "Let a woman learn quietly with all submissiveness" (1 Timothy 2:11), what is he talking about?

Oster: When there are people of wealth and aristocratic heritage who are in a household filled with slaves, in a city like Ephesus, or the Roman province of Asia, they are the upper crust. A term like *submissiveness* is not what comes to mind as a way of life. These wealthy women would have been expected to be submissive to their parents, but in general, the tenor and tone of being submissive would have been foreign to them.

The "quiet" in this passage is like a quiet spirit. Paul is describing a quietness of demeanor (a common meaning of the relevant Greek term in the New Testament) rather than silence. The Greek word here is *hesuchia* and not *sigaō*, which is the word used in 1 Corinthians 14 to tell the disruptive wives to stop talking. Instead, it's a totally different word. *Hesuchia* has to do with the tranquility mentioned in the opening part of the chapter.

Paul is admonishing these women to learn quietly in the church. And the word *quietly* here certainly resonates with what we saw in the opening verses of the chapter about praying that the government would allow the church to live quiet lives. And by the way, these rich women would likely know some of those government officials they should be praying for in verses 1 and 2.

In SWS: Paul characterizes these women as idle, going about from house to house, busybodies who talk nonsense, and say things they ought not to say (1 Timothy 5:13). In 2 Timothy 3:7, Paul also reveals they are "always learning but never able to come to a knowledge of the truth." If these women are to mature in the faith, it is clear their posture must change to one more conducive to learning. That is what Paul is seeking to bring about through his fellow minister, Timothy.

One point of special note comes from William Mounce's *Pastoral Epistles, Word Biblical Commentary*: ". . . Paul here, in contrast to segments of Judaism that prohibited women from learning, asserts the ability and value of women's education, that they should be students of God's ways. . . ."[85] However, they were to learn in quietness and full submission.

Q. Hicks says the text doesn't say to whom or to what women are to submit. What do you think?

Oster: Just like we saw in 1 Corinthians 11 and then in 1 Corinthians 14, we have a theological argument here based upon the creation story and primogeniture.

It's an appeal to the law, and in this case, it has to do with the priority of the creation of Adam. "For Adam was formed first, then Eve" (1 Timothy 2:13). This is the third time Paul is addressing the issue of how women can participate in the community, and he's putting some boundaries on that. This perspective is ingrained in Paul's thinking.

Primogeniture is even assumed in places like Samuel's selection of a king from Jesse's family in 1 Samuel 16:1–13. When Samuel goes to anoint the new king over God's people, he immediately believes that God has chosen Eliab since Eliab is Jesse's firstborn son (1 Chronicles 2:13; 1 Samuel 16:6). Samuel is operating from a worldview of primogeniture, until YHWH informs him that he has chosen David, the youngest son, by looking at his heart (1 Samuel 16:7).

For people like Paul, being firstborn or first created meant that this person had special privileges and responsibilities in leadership. Why would Paul have inserted this reason unless he had a worldview where the priority of birth meant a leadership authority? As far as Paul is concerned, it's

85. William D. Mounce, *Pastoral Epistles, Word Biblical Commentary* (Nashville: Thomas Nelson, Inc., 2000), 119.

embedded in the DNA of creation, but the world in Paul's day and our day doesn't get its understanding from the creation account. However, it's pretty important that we, as Christians, should get our understanding from the creation account.

Q. Let's discuss that. *Authenteo*, the word Paul uses for authority, is used only this one time in Scripture. How do you understand "to teach or to have authority over a man" (1 Timothy 2:12)? What is Paul prohibiting?

In SWS: Likely, it means that Paul permits no woman to serve in the role of authoritative teacher. Most of the questions generated by this passage about women's role in the assembly relate to the phrase that women are not to "have authority over" a man. The phrase "have authority over" is translated many different ways, including "exercise authority," "assume authority," or "usurp authority." This particular word (Greek: *authentein*) is not used in any other passage of Scripture, so we are not entirely sure how it should be translated. It likely means that women should not be in the teaching role. However, we must remember that teaching in the early church was not what it is today. "Teaching" was a spiritual gift and office (see Ephesians 4:11) for the expounding and applying of Scripture. These authoritative teachers functioned very much like priests and rabbis. This teaching is a form of congregational leadership. In 1 Timothy 2:12, therefore, Paul is likely declaring that women cannot serve in that role.

It is helpful at this point in the study to be reminded of Acts 18:26: "He [Apollos] began to speak boldly in the synagogue; but when Priscilla and Aquila heard him, they took him aside and explained the Way of God to him more accurately." Priscilla is a woman, and she is certainly part of explaining the Way of God to a man, Apollos. To place the name of Priscilla before her husband's name may actually indicate that Priscilla was the more engaged of the couple as they did that. Since we seek to include all relevant passages when determining our faith and practice, it is important that this one not be forgotten. Clearly, women are to serve in some teaching responsibilities. They are gifted to do so, and Acts 18:26 displays the value of their using that gift.

Oster: I believe this word for authority has to do with theological education in the context of the church. I understand "teacher" here to be what we would call the preacher of a church, someone who is assigned the task of giving theological teaching, leadership, and guidance to a congregation.

Sproles: Hicks (and others) make much out of *authenteo*, as if we cannot be sure what Paul is saying because of its singular use here, *or* that he must mean something very different than what a plain reading of this verse suggests ("I do not permit a woman to teach or to assume authority over a man"). I love a good word study as much as anyone, but when scholars tell average readers that they cannot be sure what the Bible is saying, they undermine our confidence to read and obey God's Word. So when a word is used just once in the Bible, we simply move to extra-biblical writings to get clarity.

Authenteo, while not used anywhere else in Scripture, was used in extra-biblical writings centuries before 1 Timothy was written. I recommend Andreas Köstenberger and Thomas Schreiner's book, *Women in the Church: An Analysis and Application of 1 Timothy 2:9–15,* to help understand this word:

> Its first occurrence in surviving Greek literature is dated to the first century BC, not long before Paul used it, and for centuries after that its recorded uses are quite rare. In fact, until the official recognition of Christianity under Constantine in the year 312, the verb appears in only a handful of places, most of them in obscure nonliterary sources. No doubt part of the reason for this paucity of attestation is that *authenteo* was considered a colloquial word, so that writers with literary pretensions avoided it.
>
> The initial uses of *authenteo* indicate the "rather specific meaning [of] 'kin-murderer,' someone guilty of killing his or her own flesh and blood." Much later (in the first century BC), *authenteo* is found meaning "not 'murderer' but 'master,' and it seems to have belonged to the colloquial."[86]

86. Andreas Köstenberger and Thomas R. Schreiner, *Women in the Church: An Analysis and Application of 1 Timothy 2:9-15*, 2nd edition (Grand Rapids: Baker Academic, 2015), 68.

Some scholars think these two different definitions for *authenteo* indicate that it's a homonym: one word with two meanings. Whether it is or not, we can safely assume that *authenteo* has to do with authority or mastery of some kind.

And with all the ways Hicks noted women serving God in Scripture—as prophets, judges, teachers, heralds, Levitical singers, sages, etc.—we do *not* see an exception to the rule when it comes to priests and rabbis. That would be equivalent to a senior pastor or preacher in today's context.

Q. Hicks and McKnight suggest that these women were following their unchaste culture and teaching unorthodox ideas (*Blue Parakeet*, 254). Hicks concludes, "The problem with some women in Ephesus was not that they were teaching per se, but that they were promoting ungodliness. They spread the ideas of a different doctrine. Their dress, behaviors, and words brandished that ungodliness. Paul responded with the gospel. He denied the women of 1 Timothy 2:9–10 an opportunity to teach, not because women are too emotional, inherently gullible, or simply because they are women. On the contrary, he denied them opportunity because they did not understand and practice godliness. . . . They had been deceived by others" (205–206).

McCoy & Harrington: McKnight is right to point out that some of the young women in the Ephesian church were vulnerable to significant temptations: sexual desire, gossip, and even leaving the faith (1 Timothy 5:11–15). Yet these young widows are set in contrast to older, godly widows in the congregation; such a woman is said to "put her hope in God and continues night and day to pray and to ask God for help" (5:5b), and she "is devoting herself to all kinds of good deeds" (5:10b).

If Paul had in mind only to prevent the especially vulnerable women from public teaching and exercising authority over men (2:11–13), then why did he make his statement about women in general, and not about the especially vulnerable ones? And, again, why did Paul ground his statement in the created order itself (2:13)?

As for the idea that these Ephesian women must have been teaching unorthodox ideas, it's true that some of the younger widows had become "idlers . . . busybodies who talk nonsense, saying things they ought not to" (5:13b). One could try to construe "saying what they should not" to mean that they were teaching untrue doctrines. But the truth is, the false teachers in Ephesus that Paul mentioned were all men, not women (1 Timothy 1:19–20; 2 Timothy 2:17–18; Acts 20:30).

Oster: Yes. To be clear, if these Ephesian women were teaching the idolatrous ideas that John Mark imagines, the apostle Paul would not be nearly as gentle with them as he is. He would say, "You all are idolators, and God killed people like you in the wilderness." You'd have something in 1 Timothy 2 like you have in 1 Corinthians 10:6–13. This would be idolatry. As I was reading this material of John Mark's, I thought he painted these women in 1 Timothy to be the most sinister, evil women in the Ephesian church. I know he's tried to liberate them in a sense, but his path to get there is overdone.

If these women were false teachers, if they were promoting pagan myths, Paul wouldn't say don't let them teach men. He would say don't let these heretical women teach anybody. They shouldn't teach children. They shouldn't teach women. They shouldn't teach men. They should be turned over to Satan and kicked out of the church. Why would Paul say just don't teach men?

In SWS: Paul's concern here about women teaching men is not designed only to address a situation in which some women are teaching false doctrine. If Paul were concerned that some Ephesian women were teaching falsely, then he would have said these women cannot teach anyone. Obviously, Paul is just as concerned to protect women from false teaching as he is to protect men from false teaching. So Paul's statement here is not about what a woman might teach; it is about the fact of her teaching at all. In the context of 1 Timothy 2, that means she should not be permitted to serve in the authoritative teacher role comparable to priests in the Old Testament.

Q. And the reason given for the prohibition is twofold: "For Adam was formed first, then Eve; and Adam was not deceived, but the woman

was deceived and became a transgressor" (1 Timothy 2:13–14). Hicks says that there is ambiguity in Paul's reasoning. Can you help us understand that?

Sproles: Adam fails to go first, to exercise authority in the garden, and Paul is concerned that the order of creation be upheld. The point is not that the woman is more easily deceived. *She was in a position to be deceived because she heard the command secondhand from Adam.*

Paul is saying that God's order of headship is in jeopardy when men are not in the position given to Adam: guarding the boundaries. He is telling them not to re-enact what happened in the Fall. And to further clarify his point, he follows this up with instructions to men about being elders in chapter 3.

Thanks to Alastair Roberts for noting that there are poetic reversals of the original theme of deception (the serpent deceiving the woman), where the woman deceives the serpent. The point in these stories is that the woman is getting her revenge. If the woman had not been deceived, that would not make sense.

- Jochebed, the midwives, and Miriam all work to thwart the serpent, Pharoah, who is killing baby boys (Numbers 26:59; Exodus 1:17; Exodus 2:7).
- Michael protects David against the serpent, Saul (1 Samuel 19:11).
- Ruth lies at the feet of Boaz to rescue her and Naomi from the serpent of extreme poverty (Ruth 3).
- Esther protects the Jews against the serpent, Haman (Esther 7:3–4).
- Rahab protects the Jews against the men of Jericho (Joshua 2:1–11).
- And in Revelation, the woman clothed with the sun evades the dragon, who then makes war on the rest of her offspring (Revelation 12).

So in 1 Corinthians 11 and 14, and now in 1 Timothy 2, Paul is arguing that the garden order must be maintained in the new creation. This is not something we can leave behind. It didn't happen after the Fall. It was established from the beginning.

Many egalitarians say that there is no hint of authority or order in the creation account before sin entered the world. Hicks says again and again that authority in these texts is inferred, not explicit, and then explains them away by saying Scripture points toward mutually submissive deference and unity. This reminds me of parents creating house rules like, "Don't hit your sister." Then, when the child gets in trouble for hitting his *brother*, he claims that the principle was only inferred and not explicit.

I would say that Hicks goes even further, though, because complementary authority structures are explicitly found throughout Scripture—from governments and families to the tabernacle, temple, and churches. Only those of us living in a culture where authority is viewed as suspect at best and evil at worst would have a hard time seeing authority as for our good, as needed structure, as a way to create order.

The inspired, biblical writers have coherency and cogency, and this reference to the Genesis account of creation comes up again and again. Paul and others continually explain passages in the Old Testament, making the Bible the best explanation for itself. To be clear, the New Testament regularly sees itself as interpreting the Old Testament—hundreds of times. So when Paul says that Adam was formed first to explain why women should refrain from authoritative teaching over men, this naturally points us to the creation account and the idea of primogeniture, which describes the special rights and responsibilities of the firstborn.

Hicks would insist, however, "Whatever we say about its universal or restricted application, nowhere in Scripture is the principle of primogeniture explicitly explained and then applied to the relationship between men and women as a transcultural norm. It is simply *assumed* that Adams's temporal priority *entails a primogeniture principle* that gives Adam authority over Eve. *That is an inference*" (195, italics his). This seems to ignore exactly what Paul is doing here. Thomas Schreiner notes the following transcendent norms from creation:[87]

---

87. Thomas Schreiner, "Paul and Gender: A Review Article," *Themelios*, www.thegospelcoalition.org/themelios/article/paul-and-gender-a-review-article/ (accessed October 19, 2022).

- Jesus appeals to creation to support the notion that marriage is between one man and one woman for life (Matthew 19:3–12).
- Paul grounds his argument against same-sex relations in creation (Romans 1:26–27).
- And he says that marriage and eating all foods are good because of creation (1 Corinthians 10:25–26; 1 Timothy 4:1–5).

We should not wonder what is happening when Paul tells women they cannot assume authoritative teaching over men. Yet again, the reason given is the creation order in Genesis 2.

McCoy & Harrington: Wayne Grudem lists ten arguments showing there was indeed male headship before the Fall. The Fall didn't create gender distinctions and roles; rather, the Fall distorted those roles into ugly power plays. Here are Grudem's ten arguments:[88]

- The order: Adam was created first, then Eve (note the sequence in Genesis 2:7 and 2:18–23; 1 Timothy 2:13).
- The representation: Adam, not Eve, had a special role in representing the human race (1 Corinthians 15:22, 45–49; Romans 5:12–21).
- The naming of woman: Adam named Eve; Eve did not name Adam (Genesis 2:23).
- The naming of the human race: God named the human race "Man," not "Woman" (Genesis 5:2).
- The primary accountability: God called Adam to account first after the Fall (Genesis 3:9).
- The purpose: Eve was created as a helper for Adam, not Adam as a helper for Eve (Genesis 2:18; 1 Corinthians 11:9).
- The conflict: The curse brought a distortion of previous roles, not the introduction of new roles (Genesis 3:16).
- The restoration: Salvation in Christ in the New Testament reaffirms the creation order (Colossians 3:18–19).

88. Wayne Grudem, *Evangelical Feminism & Biblical Truth: An Analysis of More than 100 Disputed Questions* (Wheaton: Crossway, 2012), 109.

- The mystery: Marriage from the beginning of creation was a picture of the relationship between Christ and the church (Ephesians 5:32–33).
- The parallel with the Trinity: The equality, differences, and unity between men and women reflect the equality, differences, and unity in the Trinity (1 Corinthians 11:3).

A serious look at those verses will demonstrate that the Fall in Genesis 3 didn't create Adam's headship; rather, it corrupted it. Unfortunately, on his way back to the oneness of creation, McKnight gets too fixated on Genesis 3:16b ("Your desire will be for your husband, and he will rule over you"). In so doing, he misses the many instances of Adam's God-given headship that predate the Fall.

We ought not ignore this feature of the created order; contrary to Hicks's and McKnight's assertions, it was Adam's headship to which Paul appealed in discussing gender roles for the New Testament church (e.g., 1 Timothy 2:13).

The truth, however, is that it is more than just egalitarians (or "full participationists") who get stuck in Genesis 3:16. This side of Eden, it is only natural for all of us to seek to dominate rather than serve each other. The power plays of Genesis 3:16 are fitting descriptions of many ugly realities we can find in our marriages and churches.

And here we arrive at an important truth: nobody naturally tends toward the kind of biblical, sacrificial headship described throughout the Bible. Do people thirst for power? Absolutely. But as both head of the church and submissive Son of God, it is Jesus who teaches us what actual headship and submission look like. None of it looks like the ugly power plays in Genesis 3:16, which come so naturally to us humans.

With sacrificial biblical norms—rather than selfish power plays—as the standard, we believe men and women can flourish in marriage and in the church.

Sproles: It's also worth noting that Hicks says the only certainties about this portion of Scripture involve chronology. While I disagree that it's the *only* certainty we can have in this text, I agree that chronology does, indeed, matter to Paul. Primogeniture (Adam being born first) is the logic behind his argument forbidding authoritative teaching by women.

Oster: We should also note that teaching is not prophecy. When we look at 1 Corinthians 12, Acts 13, and other passages, we see people being teachers and prophets, which are not the same two offices. There is the gift of teaching and the gift of prophecy. As I mentioned earlier, in the Old Testament God commissioned the priests as teachers of Israel. A common misunderstanding many Christians have is that the priests were just butchering livestock. They did that, but one of the main tasks of the priests in the Old Testament was to teach Israel the law of God. The way people were to know about Mosaic Law, the ethics, and the ceremonial guidelines was from the priests. All of the priests had to be males. You had female prophetesses in the Old Testament. You didn't have female teachers. The teachers were men. The teachers were priests.

Q. So may a woman ever speak to the congregation in a teaching role?

Harrington: This is a point that needs clarifying for our Renew Network churches.

There are respected leaders in Renew.org who understand that Paul is prohibiting a woman from having any church-recognized teaching authority over men in 1 Timothy 2. Yet, in keeping with this perspective, they believe that a woman can give a message to the church on occasion, if it is under the explicit direction of the elders and not as the main preacher-teacher. That is, a woman may be a special guest speaker, like a missionary or a subject expert. These leaders think the prohibition in 1 Timothy 2 is only about authoritative teaching. But there are differences in our network on this point.

Sproles: So those who allow a woman to address the congregation on occasion would hold a variation of the soft complementarian view, similar to that of John Frame and Craig Blomberg. This position leaves the door open for special, one-off occasions where the elders agree to allow a woman to speak. Frame says, "As unofficial teachers, women have as much right and obligation as anybody to edify their fellow believers, whether men, women, or children. . . . She is not forbidden to teach, or even to teach men; she is only forbidden to occupy the special office [in 1 Timothy 2:12]. . . . May she stand behind the pulpit as she exhorts the congregation from the Word of God? Scripture does not forbid that."[89]

This view is totally foreign to my experience growing up in the Churches of Christ, where there were heated discussions of whether fathers could be in the room when their daughters prayed or read Scripture; and where women were forbidden to pray with men or dismissed from teaching boys once they were baptized. This rigid complementarianism is not only a wrong application of what we find in Scripture, but it also strips men of the strong help of women as described in the creation account.

Harrington: I respect the position of those who will let a woman preach on occasion. But I personally believe—and I am joined by many other Renew Network leaders and churches on this point—that it is prudent for the main preacher/teacher to facilitate an interview. This format can provide the full expression of a woman's perspective, but under authority, as this text teaches. Of course, it can also be an interview by another one of the male teaching ministers or an elder.

When a woman preaches to the gathered church, the medium is, itself, a message. No matter her topic, the first message is that women may assume teaching authority over men. I believe it is more in step with the spirit of male teaching-authority envisioned in 1 Timothy 2 for women to speak in an interview format. Again, not all Renew Network leaders believe as I do on this point, while we all uphold the view that the main preacher/teacher role in the gathered church is reserved for qualified males.

Q. What in the world could Paul be talking about when he writes, "Yet she will be saved through childbearing—if they continue in faith and love and holiness, with self-control" (1 Timothy 2:15)?

Oster: Paul believes, as most cultures throughout human history have believed, that childbearing is the normal experience of women. It is uniquely

89. John Frame, *The Doctrine of the Christian Life* (Phillipsburg: Presbyterian and Reformed, 2010), 639.

female. And for most of human history, childbearing has been considered a noble undertaking. The opening chapters of Genesis teach that the creation of families and the bearing of children are noble.

I think Paul is pointing to what the norm would be, what God has called women to do, and that is to bear children in the context of a marriage. Paul is not writing things about every couple on the planet. He's not describing the birth practices of every woman who will ever live. That is not what Scripture does. It's not written to anticipate every exception or personal autobiographical issue you can bring to it. And God's laws are not constructed based on exceptions. The way it works, if you read Scripture, is that God gives, depending on the circumstance, general plans, expectations, laws, warning, etc., and knows, as we do, that the contingencies of life and history will bring forth exceptions. God lays down his laws, and then there can be exceptions.

Sproles: Andreas Köstenberger notes that there are different meanings of the word for salvation *(sōzō)* throughout the New Testament. Looking at them gives us some much-needed clarity for this verse.

There is a sense of salvation *(sōzō)* in a lowercase "s" way. It means "to be healed," "to be made whole," "to get well." The Gospels are rife with examples of *sōzō* as ultimate salvation. Köstenberger writes, "Thus the woman who sought to receive physical healing from Jesus thought, 'If I just touch his garments, I shall get well'" (Mark 5:28 par.).[90] This kind of physical healing doesn't seem to fit with women being saved through childbearing.

Moving to Paul's writing, we find a capital "S" type of salvation, which is achieved through Christ alone. Köstenberger again: "In the vast majority of [Paul's] instances, the expression refers to spiritual (religious) salvation. Romans 5:9 may serve as an example: 'Much more then, having now been justified by his [Christ's] blood, we shall be saved from the wrath of

90. Andreas Köstenberger, "Saved Through Childbearing? A Fresh Look at 1 Timothy 2:15 Points to Protection from Satan's Deception." This essay is a summary of the author's argument in "Ascertaining Women's God-Ordained Roles: An Interpretation of 1 Timothy 2:15," *Bulletin of Biblical Research* 7 (1997): 1–38. www.s3.amazonaws.com/5mt.bf.org/2017/10/12-Saved-Through-Childbearing.pdf (accessed October 19, 2022).

God through him.'"[91] This meaning conflicts with 1 Timothy 2:15, because if women can save themselves through childbearing, then salvation is not through Christ alone.

But there is another sense of salvation in a lowercase "s" way, which is an escape from danger achieved through protection from physical or spiritual harm.

- "How do you know, wife, whether you will save your husband? Or, how do you know, husband, whether you will save your wife?" (1 Corinthians 7:16).
- "Watch your life and doctrine closely. Persevere in them, because if you do, you will save both yourself and your hearers" (1 Timothy 4:16).
- "The Lord will rescue me from every evil attack and will bring me safely to his heavenly kingdom" (2 Timothy 4:18a).

In the first two examples, we don't understand Paul to be saying that a spouse can ultimately save their marital partner or that Timothy can provide salvation to his hearers. God does the saving, not humans.

> A better solution involves the recognition that being "kept safe" from harm or danger is a perfectly legitimate meaning for the Greek term *sōzō*. In that case, Timothy is merely said to help keep his hearers safe from the dangers of succumbing to false teaching in their beliefs and practical life application. . . .
>
> What do we learn from all of this? Simply put: that *sōzō*, the term in the passive frequently rendered "be saved," may in certain contexts denote a person's physical or spiritual preservation from danger or harm.[92]

Childbearing is a lowercase "s" kind of salvation.

91. Köstenberger, "Saved Through Childbearing?"
92. Köstenberger, "Saved Through Childbearing?"

> Eve, Paul implies, was not kept safe at the Fall; she was deceived. Why? Because she left her proper domain under her husband's care. What happened as a result? She became an easy prey for Satan. How can women under Timothy's charge (and in churches everywhere) avoid repeating the same mistake? By "childbearing," that is, by adhering to their God-ordained calling, including a focus on marriage, family, and the home. 1 Timothy 2:15 thus turns out to be Paul's prescription for women as a lesson learned from the scenario of the Fall described in the preceding verse.[93]

When a woman bears a child, she is participating in the particular, unique role of women as we exercise our dominion over the earth and help to fill it (Genesis 1:26–28).

Q. Surely you aren't saying that all women must stay home and have children and let the men do all the leading?

Sproles: No. We're not. Many thanks to Alastair Roberts who gives us further clarity here. In an interview on the *Homefires* podcast, he points out that in these verses Paul is connecting Eve with her daughters. Eve fell into deception, and now her daughters are tempted to repeat her sin in various ways, but they should take hold of the promise given to Eve.[94]

"And I will put enmity between you and the woman, and between your offspring and hers; he will crush your head, and you will strike his heel" (Genesis 3:15). The serpent will bruise the heel of the woman's children but he, the Christ, will bruise the serpent's head.

This Genesis account is the first of many of God's salvation stories that begin with babies.

- The baby Moses preceded the exodus of Israel (Exodus 2).
- The baby Samuel became a great prophet in Israel (1 Samuel 1).
- The baby Obed was born to Ruth, in a climax of a redemption story for her and Naomi (Ruth 4).

---

93. Köstenberger, "Saved Through Childbearing?"
94. Roberts, "The Dance of the Sexes."

- The baby John was born to Elizabeth, who was very old (Luke 1:5–25).
- And, of course, the baby Jesus, the promised Messiah, was born of Mary (Luke 1:26–38).

God's way of telling the story is one where women receive a prominent role at pivotal points, precisely because childbearing carries the weight of the promise in Genesis 3: Woman will bear the seed and protect the seed.

So when Paul calls women to bear children, he's not just saying, "Women stay at home and have babies and stay out of the public square." He's saying that *she* will be saved if *they* (women) continue. He's connecting women with the great promise of the gospel and with Eve. The seed of the woman will crush the serpent's head, and Eve's daughters will also be part of the salvation story if they live out this calling. Paul is describing the normal experience of women, yes, but he's also elevating childbearing.[95]

Putting all of this together, Paul is saying that the order of creation is not abandoned in the covenant. Rather, there is a renewed declaration of the order of creation within the context of Christ's work. The order is *restored*, not overcome or rejected.

Oster: One more thought before we close: I think it's important that we not let our culture guide how we understand these things. I have heard some argue that if a woman is more theologically mature than a man, she should be the preacher. But if you look at the Davidic King in the Old Testament, clearly Isaiah was theologically more mature than King Ahaz in the eighth century. However, that did not mean that Isaiah could become the Davidic King. God has an order of things, and things are set up by covenants and by creation. That's the way we follow them.

I think it's because of democratic values rather than divine values that we start making arguments about a person who is more qualified based on their performance rather than based on God's call or God's arrangement of things in creation.

95. Roberts, "The Dance of the Sexes."

Sproles: That seems to be exactly what Hicks and other scholars are arguing. It appears that they cannot imagine a good God creating an order, a structure, or an arrangement, for men and women—at least one that isn't jettisoned by the church as we seek to live out new creation right now. To be clear, Hicks says:

> The future envisions men and women—however that differentiation is maintained and to whatever purpose—gathered around the throne without hierarchy sharing in the praise of God as each gives voice to their gratitude and awe before God. Each one will bring a hymn, a testimony, a praise, or whatever it might be before the throne of God as we worship and serve together throughout eternity. . . . The assemblies of Christ—the churches of Christ—worship in the eschatological assembly according to the order of the new creation and not according to the disorder of the present evil age.[96]

Of course, disorder will not exist in the new creation, but what about the existence of order or structure now? Thomas Schreiner notes,

> The eschatology isn't here yet, and there are dimensions of the new creation that don't apply now. For instance, marriage exists in the present age but in the eschatology, marriage as an institution will be dissolved (Matthew 22:30). Some of the orders and structures of the present age won't exist when the age to come is consummated. Certainly, when the end comes, there will be no need for elders, pastors, and overseers. Life in the new creation—life in the world to come—isn't necessarily continuous with the structures and practices of the present time. Appealing to eschatology doesn't resolve the matter definitely.[97]

I agree with Hicks that we should "honor all the gifts God has given to women," but I disagree with how he makes gifting *the only measurement* for

96. Hicks, *Women Serving God*, 159.
97. Thomas Schreiner, "Paul and Gender: A Review Article," *Themelios* 43, no. 2, www.thegospelcoalition.org/themelios/article/paul-and-gender-a-review-article/.

full participation when Paul points to an order in creation that limits the role of preacher and elder to men.[98]

In our modern Western culture, the idea that every role in the church isn't open to both sexes, or that a husband and wife would have different roles and responsibilities in relating to one another, seems wildly unjust and even illogical. Kathy Keller would have us remember, however, "Justice, in the end, is whatever God decrees. So whether or not you are able to see justice in divinely created gender roles depends largely on how much trust you have in God's character. Shall not the judge of all the earth do right? Can we define justice as something other than God's design? Using what as our guide? What do we know that he doesn't know?"[99]

As the book of Isaiah (40:13–15) reminds us mortals:

> Who can fathom the Spirit of the LORD,
> or instruct the LORD as his counselor?
> Whom did the LORD consult to enlighten him,
> and who taught him the right way?
> Who was it that taught him knowledge,
> or showed him the path of understanding?
> Surely the nations are like a drop in a bucket;
> they are regarded as dust on the scales;
> he weighs the islands as though they were fine dust.

As redeemed humanity, we get to live out these principles—of headship and strong help, of order—in a way that's good for men and women. Because of our sinfulness, it's not good and beautiful when people who do not have the Spirit of God try to do this.

In a fallen world, unredeemed humans don't have access to true repentance, forgiveness, restoration, and the Spirit of God, who gives us wisdom and guides us in holiness. Acting like interchangeable humans is a safeguard among unredeemed humanity. But inside Christian marriage and inside the church, we get to act out reality as it should be. We get the honor of putting

98. Hicks, *Women Serving God*, 206.
99. Kathy Keller, *Jesus, Justice, and Gender Roles*, 38.

God's beautiful order on display. And it really is good for us. However, instead of seeing this as good news, we can get pulled along by the current of our culture and think, *No, no. This is unfair. It can't possibly be right. We have to look like the world.*

It has helped to ask myself, *What good thing is God up to here? Why did he create two genders instead of a unisex human? Why did he create an order for relating to one another?*

When I see in the creation narrative that God created headship, order, submission, love, and sacrifice between the sexes, and when I see these concepts explained even further by Jesus, Paul, Peter, and others in the New Testament, I cannot call them merely situational. I must trust that God has my best interests in mind for my marriage and the church. I must trust his justice and his judgment more than my own. I must try my best to obey. And obedience, Jesus notes, brings its own understanding (John 8:31).

In the next chapter, we will explore the concept of church elders and ask whether gender should have any bearing on who becomes a church elder.

9

CAN WOMEN BE ELDERS?

BOBBY HARRINGTON, DANIEL MCCOY, GARY JOHNSON, JIM ESTEP, DAVID ROADCUP, RICHARD OSTER, RENÉE WEBB SPROLES

"If you want something said, ask a man; if you want something done, ask a woman."
—Margaret Thatcher

"Women have discovered that they cannot rely on men's chivalry to give them justice."
—Helen Keller

"It's time to see what I can do, to test the limits and break through, no right, no wrong, no rules for me; I'm free."
—Disney's Elsa from the movie *Frozen*

These sentiments are a glimpse into our cultural moment. Are there actually "rules" we should follow in the church when it comes to gender? With so many churches in decline in the West, wouldn't prudence suggest that anyone who is qualified should be elders, men or women? And isn't it practical, logical, and fair to place all men and women in any and every role according to their gifts?

We will seek to answer these questions and more in this chapter, exploring what Scripture says about the role of elders. We want to take the opportunity to discuss this important topic about which many thoughtful Renew.org readers have questions.

Renew.org believes that New Testament norms teach that the lead minister/pastor role in the gathered church, as well as the elder role, are for qualified men. In discussing eldership, we were grateful to be able to talk with Gary Johnson, David Roadcup, and Jim Estep of e2: effective elders.[100] *E2 is a ministry that equips elders to serve the local congregation by providing practical training, relevant resources, and authentic relationships. Gary, David, and Jim have helped many churches build biblical and effective elder teams. We also spoke to Dr. Rick Oster, a professor at Harding School of Theology for over forty years and an expert on ancient Ephesus.*

Q. Are there any preliminaries to be aware of as we begin this discussion of elders?

Harrington: I think the best mindset is one grounded in Jesus and his teachings throughout Scripture. So, first and foremost, headship in God's church is more about being a servant of others than anything else. Jesus puts it plainly for us:

> Jesus called them together and said, "You know that the rulers of the Gentiles lord it over them, and their high officials exercise authority over them. Not so with you. Instead, whoever wants to become great among you must be your servant, and whoever wants to be first must be your slave—just as the Son of Man did not come to be served, but to serve, and to give his life as a ransom for many." (Matthew 20:25–28)

We start by thinking about elders as chief servants.

Second, we start with a background mindset culminating from previous chapters, that God called qualified men to special headship roles in God's church and family. Without going into all we have already discussed, it is important to note how the norms of Scripture show that men are given unique headship responsibilities that transcend culture. Here is a summary of some of these responsibilities:

100. For more information on e2: effective elders, see e2elders.org.

- Adam was created first (1 Timothy 2:13), and Eve was created as his strong helper (Genesis 2).
- The role of Old Testament priests was created by God for males only (even though there were female priests in surrounding cultures), and these priests were given a special teaching role in Israel.
- Jesus picked only men to be his twelve apostles.
- In the marriage relationship, the husband has a Christlike headship role as a servant leader, which entails authority (Colossians 3:18–19; 1 Peter 3:1–6; Ephesians 5:21–33).
- In the Christian gatherings, boundaries are established to uphold male headship in the church when women pray and prophesy (1 Corinthians 11) and during disruptions (1 Corinthians 14).
- First Timothy 2:11–15 teaches that in the gathered church, women are not to teach or exercise authority over men.

We at Renew.org are committed to making disciples of Jesus in a way that is both faithful to Scripture and effective to culture. With this in mind, we want to handle the issue of gender and church ministry in a way that steers between the extremes of progressivism and rigid traditionalism. The chapters leading up to this one have described a biblical path that avoids these unbiblical extremes. We seek to continue on that path in this chapter, which explores what the Bible says about elders/shepherds/overseers.

Q. Why is this discussion about gender and the Bible so critical? Can't we just agree to disagree?

Johnson: We have noticed at e2 that when a church decides to embrace egalitarianism, they have made some pretty significant decisions prior to that: decisions about what kind of authority Scripture has and about their hermeneutical process. (Egalitarians believe that men and women have interchangeable roles in the home and in the church when it comes to leadership.)

I have lived in Indianapolis for decades, and I remember one morning when I went out to the mailbox to get the paper, the headline was "Disciples Table Jesus." The Disciples of Christ headquarters are here in Indianapolis, and every two years they hold their annual convention. That year the discussion was about Jesus: Is he the only way to be saved? At the end of the week, *they could not even decide that Jesus alone saves.*

How did they get there?

Well, the Disciples of Christ had jettisoned belief in the inspiration, infallibility, and inerrancy of Scripture years before. Once they took that giant step, it became easy for them to embrace egalitarianism and then homosexuality, and finally they were unable to come to a consensus on the exclusivity of Jesus as Lord and Savior.

Sproles: Yes, how you arrive at a position can be as important as the position itself. That's why I am glad e2 is here. You are a boots-on-the-ground kind of organization and can see how we are all tempted to use the culture around us to define things like *equality* and *gender* before then trying to locate them in Scripture. You also see the fallout that happens when we do that, too.

Estep: Yes, in one of our books for elders, we have a section titled "Can Women be Elders?" where we outline the hermeneutical gymnastics that people must use when trying to vault around a passage and make it sound like they are actually dealing with it. Typically, they'll take a passage from Galatians or Colossians and use it to trump the whole of Scripture. As Renée said, many arguments assert that gender boundaries are merely cultural, or influenced by cultural pressure, and that's incorrect. You're laying modern ideas of equality and gender on the text that simply are not there.

On the other hand, we want to be careful to note that we are not saying women can't be elders because they are inferior to men. That's not what we're saying at all. That's bad Christian thinking and bad biblical reasoning.

Q. So which passages in Scripture talk about elders?

Johnson: Of course, my mind immediately goes to the pastoral epistles: Titus 1 and 1 Timothy 3. Yet it's important to understand that the word *elder* runs through Scripture like a golden thread from the opening pages to its conclusion. Exodus 3:15–17 is an important passage because it's the first time elders are mentioned in the Bible.

> God also said to Moses, "Say to the Israelites, 'The Lord, the God of your fathers—the God of Abraham, the God of Isaac and the God of Jacob—has sent me to you.' This is my name forever, the name you shall call me from generation to generation. Go, assemble the elders of Israel and say to them, 'The Lord, the God of your fathers—the God of Abraham, Isaac and Jacob—appeared to me and said: I have watched over you and have seen what has been done to you in Egypt. And I have promised to bring you up out of your misery in Egypt into the land of the Canaanites, Hittites, Amorites, Perizzites, Hivites and Jebusites—a land flowing with milk and honey.'"

Notice that God told Moses to go back to Egypt and gather the elders. This was when Israel was enslaved in Egypt, and already, early on in Israel's history as a nation, men were called to that role. And I want to point out here that I use the word *role* intentionally. At e2 we never speak of the elder *office.* It is a *role of responsibility.* The passages that speak of elders in the New Testament are patterned after this role of elders watching over the people of God in the Old Testament.

There are many more passages that talk about elders. In Acts 15, Paul, Barnabas, and Peter return to Jerusalem to meet with the apostles and elders. In Acts 20, Paul turns in his letter of resignation to the Ephesian elders. Even in Revelation 4, 5, and 7, we see elders around the throne of God. From Exodus to Revelation, this idea of elders, of shepherds, permeates Scripture.

When we are coaching elders, we tell them that their name is described using three distinctive Greek words: *presbuteros* (elder)*, episkopos* (bishop), and *poimen* (pastor).

Q. When it comes to the description of elders in 1 Timothy and Titus, are these more a checklist or a character profile? What should churches do with these texts since they overlap but are not identical?

Oster: You are right to point out that the lists are not identical. Perhaps seeing them more as character profiles was a response, a sort of pushback, because people were using those lists in a mechanistic way, without really being concerned about the virtuous nature of the man or looking at the overall tenor of his life to see if it was virtuous. There is some merit to this approach that seeks to get beyond a checklist.

We need to keep in mind that the first converts Paul had were Jews and Gentiles who were under the shadow of the synagogue. However, as Christianity grew, more and more Gentiles filled the church. A person nurtured by the pagan culture wouldn't bring anything to the table in terms of shepherding the church. New converts would not have an understanding of who God is or a clear sense of biblical morality. The impulse might have been to say, "This person has wealth," or, "This person has status," and therefore make them an elder for the church. But you can find these crucial character attributes of elders in the Old Testament, the Sermon on the Mount, and Peter and Paul's writings. It's important that the church, then and now, insists upon these characteristics.

Estep: I have seen churches produce lists of the qualifications with little boxes to check off, based on Titus 1 and 1 Timothy 3. However, we believe that making a checklist is inadequate. There's a phrase in 1 Timothy 3:7a that says, "He must also have a good reputation with outsiders." This points me to the man's overall behavior. By what behaviors is he characterized? These men are not only going to be approved by the church but should also be recognized as moral leaders in the community. So I encourage churches to look at these passages and ask things like, *Are they not given to much wine? Are they known as a one-woman man? Are they generally self-controlled and gentle?* while keeping in mind their reputation in the community.

Q. But how do we know these passages are gender specific? Couldn't they also be describing women? Why or why not?

Oster: It seems simplistic to say, but these passages are addressed to men: "Whoever aspires to be an overseer desires a noble task" (1 Timothy 3:1b).

Sproles: Additionally, the preceding verses in 1 Timothy 2 were specifically prohibiting women from authoritative teaching over men based on creation order. That was the third time Paul addressed the issue of how women can participate in the community (1 Corinthians 11 and 14; 1 Timothy 2), and he's drawing boundary lines based on creation order.

We get even further clarity regarding the prohibition of women having teaching authority over men when we note that Paul moves immediately into an explanation of elders—those who would have the authoritative role previously mentioned. In many churches today, this would also include the role of senior pastor, who would be responsible for delivering the authoritative teaching on a regular basis to the church.

Harrington: Dr. Thomas Schreiner, one of the best New Testament scholars of our time, has some helpful perspectives on this question. He explains that the elder holds an office that requires two qualities that are not required of deacons:

> First, elders must have an ability to teach biblical truth and correct deviant teaching (1 Timothy 3:2; 5:17; Titus 1:9). Second, they must have gifts of leadership (1 Timothy 3:4–5; 5:17; Titus 1:7). And remarkably, teaching and exercising authority over men is the very thing disallowed for women in 1 Timothy 2:12. Women therefore may serve as deacons because the diaconal office is one of serving, not leading. Deacons don't teach and exercise authority, but rather help in the church's ministry.[101]

Roadcup: As to why these passages are solely describing men, I think it's really God's plan more than anything else. Thirty years ago when I was struggling with the issue of women elders, I was taking a class with Louis Foster at Cincinnati Christian University on the Pastoral Epistles. One day after class I asked him, "Where are you on the issue of women serving as elders?" And he said that he was a complementarian. For him it boiled down to Scripture very clearly showing that men should be the protective covering for women and the church. Basically, he said, women can do anything men can do except usurp authority over men (1 Timothy 2:11–12).

Women can do many things in the church—whether it's leading a ministry team, music program, youth program, women's ministry, or whatever it is—but they do them under the love, care, protection, and management of

101. Thomas Schreiner, "Does the Bible Support Female Deacons? Yes," *The Gospel Coalition*, February 19, 2019, www.thegospelcoalition.org/article/bible-support-female-deacons-yes/ (accessed October 19, 2022).

the elder team. Men are to provide the protection, oversight, blessing, and encouragement. Why? Because it's God's good plan.

Johnson: It goes back to the creation order in Genesis 2. Women do have the gift of leadership; there's no doubt about it. In Romans 12:6–8, Paul talks about different spiritual gifts. He says if your gift is leadership, then govern diligently. We have brilliant women in our churches all across America, and we need to leverage their gifts. However, we must honor the boundary lines drawn in Scripture. There is just one thing a woman cannot do in the local church: she cannot be an elder who preaches (1 Timothy 5; 1 Peter 5). It is our belief that an elder is to bring the doctrinal teaching of the church; this falls under the purview of a spiritual man called of God to serve as a humble overseer of the body of Christ.

Q. Since managing one's own family well is one of the qualifications for elders, is there a relationship between the role of an elder in church and the role of a husband in the home?

Harrington: I have heard these two concepts connected, that male eldership should reflect the home where the husband is the head in the husband-wife relationship, loving and caring for her; and that his children obey him with proper respect. So you have this characteristic of doing well in managing your family as a backdrop for being qualified to be an elder. First Timothy 3:4–5 says,

> He must manage his own family well and see that his children obey him, and he must do so in a manner worthy of full respect. (If anyone does not know how to manage his own family, how can he take care of God's church?)

Johnson: Absolutely. I have been a preacher for forty years, so I have performed many weddings. When it comes to the exchange of rings, before the bride puts the ring on the groom's finger, I say to the husband, "You listen to me. She is going to declare you to be her husband in the name of God the Father, Son, and Holy Spirit. This word *husband* comes from an old English word, *husbonda*, which means a "band around the house." And it's your obligation in the sight of God and all these witnesses to keep your marriage and your family intact." And then I'll say to all the men in the room, "We are all going to be held accountable by God for keeping our families intact. That's what this ring means." So men must manage their households. If you cannot do that for the people under your roof, how can you possibly do that for the house of God—the people of God?

Estep: I was actually speaking at a church on this very subject and after my presentation, a woman came up to me and said, "Are you telling me that a woman, just because she's a woman, cannot be an elder? Why is it that men only can be elders?" I was trying to give her an answer and this eight-year-old girl walked up and said, "It's easy. They're the daddies of the church." And on the whole, that makes sense. You see that in 1 Timothy 3, the daddies of the home—the servant leaders in the family—are tied to a qualification for the role of elder.

Q. Are there other clues in Scripture that show us an elder should be male?

Estep: Within the description of the bishop, the overseer, there are phrases that I cannot see applying to a woman. "Husband of one wife" is not original to Paul. It is a phrase used in Greco-Roman literature. On epitaphs, it's somewhat of a title that depicts a very faithful person. In fact, in some parts of Roman and Greek culture, that phrase is used for someone who was a widower who never remarried and then died. It's found on their tombstone, and there is a female equivalent to it: "the wife of one husband." Both titles were available to Paul, but he chose only "the husband of one wife" when describing the role of an elder.

In fact, we see the phrase "wife of one husband" a few chapters later in 1 Timothy 5, when Paul is talking about which women should receive financial support from the church. If he meant for the role of elder to be open to women, why didn't he use the equivalent phrase "wife of one husband" in 1 Timothy 3? Once again, this points to the role being exclusive to men.

The phrase "not a brawler" also seems masculine. That is, he should not have the reputation of someone who likes to get into a good fist fight. It just doesn't seem to fit women. Men, not women, are known to brawl.

Johnson: I'm also thinking of Acts 20:28–31 when Paul meets with the elders of Ephesus:

> Keep watch over yourselves and all the flock of which the Holy Spirit has made you overseers. Be shepherds of the church of God, which he bought with his own blood. I know that after I leave, savage wolves will come in among you and will not spare the flock. Even from your own number men will arise and distort the truth in order to draw away disciples after them. So be on your guard! Remember that for three years I never stopped warning each of you night and day with tears.

Do women protect against savage wolves? I believe that language is a strong indication that this is a role to which only men are called.

So we have the backdrop of Scripture, going back to the creation story, with Adam's headship. Then we have male servant leadership in the home explicitly tied to the role of elder in 1 Timothy 3. And then you have the gender-specific description of the role as a whole. They all point to the role of elder being for only men.

Sproles: And if the idea of a role being unavailable to women on the basis of our sex makes some of us uncomfortable, that's okay. This discussion was really difficult for me in years past, in part because my worldview had been informed more by the legal system of our country than by Scripture. The idea of having one standard outside the church and one standard inside the church seemed unjust, but it's more nuanced than that. Let me try to explain.

Most of us have lived our entire lives under the Civil Rights Act of 1964, which, besides ending segregation, banned employment discrimination based on race, color, religion, sex, or national origin. This was a much-needed piece of Civil Rights legislation for our nation. In all civilizations, in all cultures, in all periods of history, men and women have regularly failed to honor one another as God intended. We've hurt each other in countless ways. (Margaret Atwood summed up this conflict when she said, "Men are afraid that women will laugh at them. Women are afraid that men will kill them.") But the world doesn't have the final answer for this problem. God does. We turn to Scripture to see how God intended for us to live together, and it is in a complementary way. In a fallen world, placing men and women in positions regardless of sex is a necessary protection.

Mary Steward Van Leeuwen collected C.S. Lewis's writings on gender in her book *A Sword between the Sexes?: C.S. Lewis and the Gender Debates.* She writes, "In his 1948 essay arguing against opening up the Anglican priesthood to women, C.S. Lewis declared that woman are 'no less capable than men of piety, zeal, learning and whatever else seems necessary for the pastoral office.'"[102] When addressing the idea of women representing God at the altar, Lewis noted:

> The innovators are really implying that sex is something superficial, irrelevant to the spiritual life. To say that men and women are equally eligible for a certain profession is to say that for the purposes of that profession their sex is irrelevant. . . . This may be inevitable for our secular life. But in our Christian life we must return to reality. . . . The kind of equality which implies that the equals are interchangeable (like counters or identical machines) is, among humans, a legal fiction. It may be a useful legal fiction. But in church we turn our back on fictions. One of the ends for which sex was created was to symbolize to us the hidden things of God. One of the functions of human marriage is to express the nature of the union between Christ and the Church.[103]

We know from Scripture that, within the broad scope of spiritual gifts for men and women, there *are* particular roles for the sexes in marriage and in church. Acting as if men and women are interchangeable is a safeguard among unredeemed humanity; but as redeemed humanity, as the church of the living God, we get to live out reality as it should be, symbolizing the "hidden things of God" within our genders. Christians have the honor of putting God's beautiful design on display.

---

102. See Mary Steward Van Leeuwen, *A Sword between the Sexes?: C.S. Lewis and the Gender Debates* (Grand Rapids: BrazosPress, 2010), 48.
103. Van Leeuwen, *A Sword between the Sexes?*, 49.

In Ephesians 5, while calling for mutual submission between a husband and wife, Paul also requires wives to respect their husbands and husbands to love their wives. (In those verses, we can see the fears that Margaret Atwood so keenly observed being addressed. Wives respect husbands. Husbands love wives.) Those are particular duties for the sexes.

When describing the ways men and women can build up the body of Christ and serve in the assembly, Paul notes that *one role* is exclusively available for men: that of authoritative teacher, which we have noted is an elder or a senior pastor.

Q. What's the main argument for women elders?

Oster: There is often the cultural argument to which Renée alluded. We tend to think that because we have prominent women in our modern, Western society, this was not also true in Paul's day. In Paul's day and age, you have women who are very prominent in society. Here are three passages that demonstrate this:

- Acts 13:50 – "God fearing women of high standing. . . in the city" stirred up persecution for Paul and Barnabas.
- Acts 17:4 – In Thessalonica "quite a few prominent women" were persuaded to believe the gospel.
- Acts 17:12 – In Berea "a number of prominent Greek women" believed the gospel along with the men.

So we have three texts in Acts, and with the advent of archeology, we have discovered inscriptions that shed light on these prominent women. Greek literature did not talk much about women, but once we found these inscriptions, we found out that, in fact, there were many women who were prominent in the society in Paul's time. They didn't hold political office, but they had all kinds of leading roles that they played in society: religious roles, civic roles, benefactors, heads of organizations, high priestesses of things like the emperor cult, donating money for public buildings. They were really prominent in society. Acts had already told us that, but with archeology we get to flesh that out. Many people think that in Paul's day, women were all kept in the kitchen or confined to special rooms in the house. But that's really an unfortunate misunderstanding of the life of women in Paul's world.

So this argument—in the modern world we have women who are advanced in society, so we can no longer hold to the biblical standard, to Paul's instructions—isn't true. To be clear, women were not as advanced in the ancient world as they are now. But, of course, women weren't as advanced in America before 1920, when they were guaranteed the right to vote, yet they were active in public life and even held prestigious positions in society. So to say that women are now advanced and therefore should be elders is not a valid argument. Women were advanced and qualified in Paul's day as well, but he notes that this is a position for men only.

It would not have been a stretch for Paul to include women elders, yet he does not. In fact, there was a book published several years ago by a feminist scholar who gathered up some synagogue inscriptions from the second and third centuries AD that show there were women elders in some synagogues. She was using this evidence to prove that the early church must have had women elders. But I would say it suggests the opposite: the fact that there were not women elders in the early church shows that it was intentional.

Johnson: We could also add from Paul's world Acts 16. He met Lydia at the river in Philippi, and she was a dealer in purple cloth. This was *her* business. She wasn't relegated to the supply room, and a few verses later, after she was immersed into the faith, the church met in her home. Paul stayed in *her* home.

In Acts 12, we see the church meeting in the home of John Mark's mother. It was large enough to have a prayer meeting to pray for Peter's survival when he was arrested by Herod. So we find many instances in Scripture where women of substance had financial leadership, were esteemed, and were of high standing. It's unequivocal.

Q. What's an argument made from Scripture for women elders?

Johnson: I'd say 99 percent of the time people go to Galatians 3:28, which says there is no male or female. "There is neither Jew nor Gentile, neither slave nor free, nor is there male and female, for you are all one in Christ Jesus" (Galatians 3:28).

Oster: It strikes me as a peculiar hermeneutic when you take a verse like Galatians 3:28, which exegetically and contextually is not talking about the topic that we're interested in, and use it to undermine a text that we *are* interested in. Galatians 3:28 is talking about who can be saved but it is used to undermine 1 Corinthians 11 and 14 and 1 Timothy 2, which are explicitly about the roles and ministries of women in the church. It's the most unsound kind of exegetical and hermeneutical method. It's pseudo-scholarship.

Harrington: Even people like N.T. Wright, Scot McKnight, and Ben Witherington are doing that, and they are highly regarded scholars.

Oster: I know that's what they're doing, and I wish they wouldn't. The social forces and theological pressures are strong for people to do that. However, I believe that they would not tolerate that kind of exegetical method on other topics.

Estep: And when you consider that Galatians and 1 Corinthians were written at almost the same time, that means Paul would be writing two different positions on the sexes almost simultaneously. We should seek harmony between the texts rather than saying that one trumps the other. Also, 1 Timothy, Titus, and 1 Peter were written *later*. So if it really was Paul's intention to take an egalitarian view in Galatians and Colossians, why would he paint a contrary picture of church leadership twenty years later? When you look at the chronology of when they were written, that interpretation doesn't make sense.

McCoy: I agree. People like to make the argument that the trajectory of Scripture is toward Galatians 3. For example, in his many references to Galatians 3:28 in *Blue Parakeet*, Scot McKnight presents it as if it's the culminating verse of Scripture, the new reality to which the entire trajectory of Scripture points. This verse gives him a lot of mileage for his oneness-otherness-oneness method of seeing the Bible's story. And, if we're talking about *whom God saves*, then they're right; Galatians 3:28 is a perfect summary of beautiful news: there are no ethnic, social, economic, or gender hurdles for our redemption by the Son (Galatians 4:5), our adoption by the Father (Galatians 4:5), or our indwelling by the Spirit (Galatians 4:6). Praise God! Yet Galatians predates a lot of the discussions about church roles, and church roles are not even the focus of Galatians 3. If the trajectory of Scripture is toward ever-greater egalitarianism, then why was Galatians written *before*, for example, 1 Timothy 2–3?

Sproles: I'll add that many egalitarians see the big picture "trajectory" of the canon as men and women becoming interchangeable according to their gifts or talents. Disregarding the circumstantial evidence for complementarity in almost every book of the Bible, they point to texts like Galatians 3:28 and insist that gender roles or complementarity has been erased by Jesus. The problem is that Paul isn't talking about gender roles or headship in Galatians. He's emphasizing that Greeks, women, and slaves are equal to Jews, men, and the free in particular ways:

- In justification by faith
- In freedom from their bondage to legalism
- In their status as children of God
- In their reality as clothed with Christ
- In their possession by Christ
- In their status as heirs to the promises to Abraham

Glaringly absent is any reference to gender roles or headship—except to mention a *Father* who provides his firstborn *son* with a cosmic inheritance.[104] Galatians 3:28 not only fails to demonstrate an egalitarian argument, but it also actually suggests the opposite.

Our sex does not determine if we are sons of God any more than our ethnicity (Jew or Greek) or our worldly status (slave or free) do. Whoever becomes clothed with Christ keeps their embodied identities as male or female even as each is *equally granted the status of an heir of God*. And there is a masculinity that is so perfect and complete that both men and women are symbolized

104. Jeff Robinson, "Many Evangelicals Unwittingly Live as Feminists, Moore Says," *Baptist Press,* November 28, 2005, www.baptistpress.com/resource-library/news/many-evangelicals-unwittingly-live-as-feminists-moore-says/ (accessed October 19, 2022).

as feminine in relationship to it. Of course, I'm talking about Christ and the church.

There is a big-picture trajectory in Scripture, but that trajectory leads toward redeemed complementarity: the headship of men and strong help of women.

Q. When you see churches that have women elders, are there any consequences you have observed?

Estep: Well, the thing I want to know when I talk to someone in a church with women elders is how they got there. One of the biggest concerns I have is when you are no longer using a sound hermeneutic to interpret Scripture, what is there to stop you from bringing a cultural view of sexuality and applying it to Scripture? Or, as Gary mentioned, bringing a universalist view of salvation that allows you to question the exclusivity of Christ as Savior? The problem is you lose your brakes.

People undermine the authority of Scripture by circumventing a text's meaning. They do "eisegesis" (putting your meaning *into* the text) instead of "exegesis" (pulling the meaning *out of* the text). If you can do that with one passage, you can do it with all.

Sproles: I read Tim Keller's *The Reason for God: Belief in an Age of Skepticism* several years ago, and one passage has stuck with me ever since. It actually sparked my attempt to make sense of the whole of Scripture in terms of sex and gender.

> To stay away from Christianity because part of the Bible's teaching is offensive to you assumes that if there is a God he wouldn't have any views that upset you. Does that belief make sense?
>
> Now, what happens if you eliminate anything from the Bible that offends your sensibility and crosses your will? If you pick and choose what you want to believe and reject the rest, how will you ever have a God who can contradict you? You won't! You'll have. . . a God, essentially, of your own making, and not a God with whom you can have a relationship and genuine interaction. Only if your God can say things that outrage you and make you struggle (as in real friendship

> or marriage!) will you know that you have gotten hold of a real God and not a figment of your imagination. So an authoritative Bible is not the enemy of a personal relationship with God. It is the precondition for it.[105]

Q. Has e2 ever helped a church who had women elders to change that position?

Johnson: Yes. It was a church that was part of the Disciples of Christ, and they eventually came out of that denomination. It really was a journey back to the Word of God. When I helped them articulate their vision, mission, and core values, they identified Scriptural authority as a core value. At that point, I was able to have the discussion about egalitarianism. (They didn't have any idea what that word meant, even though they were practicing it.)

I took them back to the Bible and said, "Alright, if you're going to say, 'We honor biblical authority,' do you or do you not?" There were a few people who didn't want to make a change to male servant leadership, but after almost three years, the congregation officially began practicing what Scripture describes. They have become far healthier as a church and are doing exceptionally well. We know that healthy things grow, and that is happening in that church.

At e2 we help churches understand how to live out God's design in a practical way. It's like Tinkertoys, Lincoln Logs, and LEGO sets. They all come with instructions, and if you're going to build what's on the cover of the box, you must follow the instructions. Similarly, we have the Bible, the Word of God, and we can see how he intended to build his church. Are we going to build the church according to his instructions? If we do, then we'll be under God's blessing.

We are practitioners who help elders who have a day job, who farm, who run a business, who lead a corporate office, or who teach in a classroom. We're going to help these elders connect the dots in an easy-to-understand way so that they can build the local church according to what we find in Scripture.

105. See Tim Keller, *The Reason for God: Belief in an Age of Skepticism* (New York: Riverhead Books, Penguin Group, 2008), 116, 118.

Sproles: I really appreciate that approach, because Jesus tells us that obedience brings its own understanding (John 8:31). Anyone who has raised children knows that preschoolers must obey many things for their own good, for their health and safety, before they understand them. I believe we should bring the same humility to the Scriptures. In the end, we must ask ourselves if we're going to allow our personal beliefs to contradict Scripture, or if we are going to allow Scripture to contradict us. If I pick and choose what I like from the Bible and discard the parts I don't like, it becomes no different than any self-help book on the shelves at Barnes & Noble. However, Scripture is much more powerful than any other book. It is "God-breathed and is useful for teaching, rebuking, correcting and training in righteousness" that we may be complete and equipped for every good work (2 Timothy 3:16–17).

Q. How do you respond to the perception that an all-male eldership is about preserving power or misogyny?

Roadcup: In my mind, it's very much a cultural issue that we're getting hammered by. There is a perception among some that men have their boot heel on the women in the church. So I believe we must return to Scripture to remind ourselves that elders are shepherds, fathers, and men who love, protect, and care for women. We really want to live out what we find in Scripture, and that kind of misogyny or power grab is not found there.

Johnson: In our culture, we think of authority as vertical. In business, you have a board of directors. They hire a CEO, who hires a CFO, a COO, etc. Vertical, positional authority is rooted in power. We do not find that in Scripture. If you look at Philippians 2:1–10, Paul explains how we should interact with one another.

> Therefore if you have any encouragement from being united with Christ, if any comfort from his love, if any common sharing in the Spirit, if any tenderness and compassion, then make my joy complete by being like-minded, having the same love, being one in spirit and of one mind. Do nothing out of selfish ambition or vain conceit. Rather, in humility value others above yourselves, not looking to your own interests but each of you to the interests of the others. In your relationships with one another, have the same mindset as Christ Jesus:

> Who, being in very nature God, did not consider equality with God something to be used to his own advantage; rather, he made himself nothing by taking the very nature of a servant, being made in human likeness. And being found in appearance as a man, he humbled himself by becoming obedient to death—even death on a cross! Therefore God exalted him to the highest place and gave him the name that is above every name, that at the name of Jesus every knee should bow, in heaven and on earth and under the earth, and every tongue acknowledge that Jesus Christ is Lord, to the glory of God the Father.

Paul says that when there is conflict in the church, each of you should look not only to your own interests but also to the interests of others. And then he notes that Jesus relinquished his positional authority. What did he do? He put on flesh and came into our neighborhood, so to speak. He humbled himself and became obedient to death. So when people complain that we're misogynistic or making a power play because we believe elders must be male, that's not the picture of an elder. We take the world's notion of vertical, positional power and turn it on its side.

The flow chart of a local church should be flat and fluid. You push authority with responsibility into people's lives like we see in Acts 6, where the apostles said to choose seven men among you known to be full of the Holy Spirit and wisdom, giving them the responsibility and authority to feed the Greek-speaking widows. Lay your hands on them and delegate that authority to them.

Elders do not sit in chairs of oppressive authority. We must have a servant heart like Jesus. So when someone claims that we're just chauvinists seeking all kinds of power over women, that's not even close. It's not found in Scripture.

Sproles: Each of us here knows the Bible has been used incorrectly to totally silence women. But if we say that we changed our minds about headship because we met some really talented women who are just as able to preach as men, then all we're repenting of is misogyny. It just shows that our views were based on a faulty view of men and women, not based on what the

Bible actually says. Nowhere does Scripture say that women are less able or capable to be an elder or rabbi. And the kind of skepticism that asks question after question after question—making us think we can't be sure what it means to be a man or a woman or what roles they may have in marriage or the church—is unhelpful, undermining our confidence in the Scripture.

The truth that is revealed in Scripture overrides my opinion, my inclinations, or what I wish were so. I don't get to sing like Elsa in the popular Disney movie *Frozen*, "No right, no wrong, no rules for me, I'm free."

When we connect all of the important roles women play in the New Testament church with our all-important work of making disciples, the New Testament picture is not one of restricting women at all. Rather, the picture of elders and authoritative teachers is one of empowering women and men for "works of service, so that the body of Christ may be built up until we all reach unity in the faith and in the knowledge of the Son of God and become mature, attaining to the whole measure of the fullness of Christ" (Ephesians 4:12–13).

We never want to adopt the false view that the truly important and gifted people are the main preacher-teacher and elders. At their root, their jobs are to equip the rest of the church to serve God in countless ministries that are vitally important in the eyes of God—including the most crucial job any of us could have: making disciples.

Q. How can biblical eldership steer us away from the notion that it's about power and control?

Roadcup: Gary kind of answered that in the previous question, but I can add that elders should be living examples of the kind of servant leadership we've discussed. They should be in the lobby on Sunday mornings, shaking people's hands and connecting with people. They should respect and love the women of the church, empowering them to use their spiritual gifts to their fullest potential so that they can bless the body of Christ. In this way, people can come to the church and see for themselves the opposite of power and control. They'll see empowerment and freedom to exercise spiritual gifts. But again, this would be under the love and care of the elder team.

Q. So in practical terms, how can elders empower the spiritual mothers of the church to fulfill their calling to serve the church?

Johnson: It's essential that we, as elders, discover what everybody's spiritual gift is. In 1 Peter 4:10 we are told, "Each of you should use whatever gift you have received to serve others, as faithful stewards of God's grace in its various forms." If a woman's gift is leadership, then we should look for a way that she can lead in an area of her passion. For example, if a woman has a heart of mercy and encouragement as well as leadership, the elders could delegate the authority to develop a ministry, perhaps to shut-ins or a nursing home. She could deploy that ministry and develop it as she works under the oversight of the elders. They are her covering and protection.

Roadcup: There was a woman in a church that I served, and she and her husband were close friends to me and my wife. She began going to a nursing home to visit friends, and they asked her if she would bring some videos of Bible stories. They'd wheel all the residents to the solarium, and she would show the videos. The residents began asking her questions after the video, and she was nervous answering them at first. But she grew in this gifting. Fast-forward two years later, and she has a hundred women in a Bible class every Sunday morning, teaching them in a dynamic way.

And I thought to myself, *Well, here's Judy, who was nervous about answering a few questions, and now look at her up there! She's leading all these women to be better wives and mothers and followers of Jesus.* That's what elders do with women in the church. So it's the opposite of oppression; it's empowerment. It's protecting and affirming who they are.

Johnson: Again, this is a flat and fluid model of leadership. So if we know our people, love them, and empower them to lead in an area of responsibility, we're not lording it over them. We're not keeping them under our thumbs. This is an environment where people want to stay; it creates incredible health not only in the church staff but throughout the church. It becomes a place where people are highly regarded and valued.

How church is set up is one thing. But does God's Word give transcultural gender-specific "roles" to be lived out in homes in the twenty-first century? We now turn to the Bible's gender-specific instructions for husbands and wives to explore whether they should still apply in families today.

10

WHAT ABOUT HUSBANDS AND WIVES?

RICHARD OSTER, RENÉE WEBB SPROLES

Talk of "gender roles" in the context of marriage might strike some people as old-fashioned and even oppressive, especially if they have been wielded to gain and maintain power. Yet as disciples of Jesus, it's more important that we ask what the Bible teaches about these matters than asking how we naturally feel about them. So this chapter focuses on gender and marriage.

In the New Testament, we see the role of singleness honored and elevated, since the unmarried disciple of Jesus has a uniquely undivided focus on the things of the Lord (1 Corinthians 7:32–35). However, a discussion of gender within the context of marriage is important because the Bible elevates this institution as much more than merely a social construct as many today believe. It is part of the creation order involving the two-part sexuality of humankind (Genesis 1:27; 2:18), and Jesus affirmed this foundational truth (Matthew 19:4–5).

I am talking once again with Dr. Richard Oster, a professor at Harding School of Theology for over forty years and an expert on ancient Ephesus, as we work through these key passages on gender and marriage: Ephesians 5:22–33, Colossians 3:18–21, and 1 Peter 3:1–7.

Sproles: Before we begin, I'd like to lay some groundwork for our discussion.

Contrary to what modern Western culture believes, marriage is not fundamentally about two consenting adults who think they have found their soulmate. Contrary to what some rigid complementarians believe, marriage is not fundamentally about women submitting and men leading. And contrary to what some egalitarians believe, marriage is not a partnership with interchangeable roles.

The apostle Paul says that marriage is fundamentally about representing Christ and his church to the world. Husbands represent Christ and wives represent his church. And so, the greatest danger to a marriage is the unrepentant sin inside of a husband or a wife that distorts this picture. Especially the sin that says *my will be done* instead of *thy will be done.*

Imagine the freedom of living in a marriage where the husband and wife say *no* to selfish desires so that they can say *yes* to one another. Where a man says *yes* to showing the world how Christ loves his church. Where a woman says *yes* to showing the world how the church responds to Christ's initiating, sacrificial love.

So let's get started by looking back in time at ancient marriages.

Q. What did ancient cultures think about marriage, family, and household management?

Oster: Historical context is important. The household imperatives in Ephesians 5:22–33 look far more like the way Greeks and Hellenistic Jews talked about household codes than the way the Old Testament talks about it. This shouldn't surprise us because Paul wasn't writing to anybody who lived in the time of Moses and the prophets. Paul was writing to people who lived in Greek and Roman cities in Western Asia Minor, and he was writing in ways that were familiar to them.

For centuries before the advent of Christianity, the Greek and Roman civilizations had a good grasp on the significance of the home and family. They valued organization and rule in the home because they understood that without properly functioning homes and marriages, civilization would not continue. There would be chaos.

Sproles: That's helpful to know, because I think many of us tend to think of ancient cultures as primitive and less advanced than we are. Consciously or unconsciously, we have what C.S. Lewis called "chronological snobbery."

Uncritically accepting "the intellectual climate of our own age" as superior, we have trouble seeing our own blind spots and assumptions. Instead, we should allow the "breezes of the centuries" to blow through our minds by exposing ourselves to ideas from the past. Then, we'll gain a helpful vantage point from which to see our present-day views more clearly.[106]

In truth, all cultures assign meaning to things, and because sinful humans are stamped with the image of God, each civilization will get some things right and some things wrong. How beautiful and encouraging that God's eternal Word can affirm and correct all cultures throughout history (2 Timothy 3:16). It sounds like, for parts of their history, the Greeks and Romans rightly valued order in the home.

Oster: I do think that the Greeks and Romans were perhaps more advanced than we are in terms of understanding the importance of marriage and families. Certainly, they demonstrated that they were able to continue for many centuries as a civilization. We haven't demonstrated that yet. We'll just have to wait and see if American civilization can continue amidst the collapse of families.

So when these pagan cultures talked about the home, they recognized the three relationships that Paul mentions: husbands and wives, parents and children, masters and slaves. Even so, we must remember that before there were Hebrews, before there were Greeks and Romans, before there were Christians, marriage was arranged by God as demonstrated in the opening chapters of Genesis. God is concerned about the stability of homes and marriages of everybody on the planet.

Although Paul doesn't write letters to non-Christians, he does have congregants, in 1 Corinthians 7 for example, who are married to non-Christians, and he is concerned that these are happy marriages. He wants them to have harmonious, productive, meaningful marriages. It would be an error for modern Christians to think that God is only concerned with Christian marriages or that Scripture has something to say only to people who follow Christ.

106. Art Lindsey, "C.S. Lewis on Chronological Snobbery," C.S. Lewis Institute, Spring 2003, www.cslewisinstitute.org/webfm_send/47 (accessed October 19, 2022).

Q. So the Ephesians would likely have had high regard for order in marriage, family, and households. But surely their marriages were very different from ours in modern culture?

Oster: In any society, there is great diversity in marriage. If you looked at a large congregation today and could see into the hearts of people, you would find some marriages that are robust and healthy and some that descend into dysfunction, even violence. There would be catastrophes and train wrecks as well as loving, strong partnerships.

There is a scholar named Plutarch who gives us an interesting window into marriage in the ancient world. He was a younger contemporary of Paul's protégé Timothy and was a priest, philosopher, and voluminous author. In one of his essays, he gave advice to a young bride and groom. Scholars note that Plutarch's categorization of marriages helps us understand what at least some pagans thought about marriage:

- There are people who marry for economic advantage. That is, they want to get ahead in life and choose a spouse who they think will help them attain the good life they desire in terms of wealth, status, and children. They're like an army with different soldiers working together in a unit.
- There are people who merely live together, but there's no intimate relationship. They share a bed; they cohabit.
- Then, there is an ultimate kind of marriage. Like a mixing of two liquids, some marriages are an intimate union where all things are shared; all things are in common.

And we see all three types of these relationships in the modern world.

We also find sepulcher monuments, tombstones, and things pertaining to ancient burials where some beautiful sentiments are expressed by the living spouse about the deceased. Now, some modern scholars are very cynical about them and don't really believe it. I choose to believe that these men and women wouldn't have wasted their money, putting all that in stone, if they didn't at least believe some of it. Perhaps some of it was perfunctory, but I don't think all of it was self-serving or artificial. In fact, one of the longest personal inscriptions (as opposed to a government inscription) that we have is from a man on behalf of his dead wife in the first century BC. They were both pagan and married more than forty years. It's line after line of his admiration and love for her:

> Uncommon are marriages which last so long, brought to an end by death, not broken apart by divorce; for it was our happy lot that it should be prolonged to the 41st year without estrangement. Would that our venerable association had been dissolved by something happening to me rather than to you, by which it would have been fairer that I as the older surrendered to fate!
>
> As for your domestic virtues, loyalty (to our marriage), obedience, courteousness, easy good-nature, your assiduous wool-working, reverence (for the gods) without superstition, attire not designed for attracting attention, modest refinement—what need have I to make mention of these? Why should I speak of your love for your own, your devotion to your family, since you have treated with equal honor my mother and your own parents, and provided for her the same peace (in retirement) as for your own family; and other virtues too many to count you possess in common with all other married women who cherish a good name.
>
> Distinctive of you are these features which I am declaring, and very few women have met with similar circumstances so that they should suffer such experiences and manifest such achievements, matters which the Fortune of women has taken care to ensure are seldom their lot.[107]

Sproles: What you're telling me is that ancient marriages were varied in their quality, just as they are now. There were beautiful, intimate marriages; there were partnerships; there were platonic relationships with no passion or intimacy; and, of course, there were really bad marriages.

---

107. English translation from Greg H.R. Horsley, "A More than Perfect Wife," *New Documents Illustrating Early Christianity* 3, no. 8 (1983): 34.

What Paul is teaching in Ephesians 5 about wives and husbands would address each of these situations. Chronological snobbery leads us to believe that these instructions for marriages, families, and households are outmoded or patriarchal.

We live in a modern, Western culture where sex is considered everything on the one hand (you can't live a full life without it) and nothing on the other (it's just an appetite to be sated, like hunger). Equality for men and women has come to mean sameness, marriage has become disposable, and divorce ravages families. In this culture, it is tempting to assume that Paul was wrong about how men and women should behave inside their marriages.

Marriage gives men a place to direct their sexual, physical, and emotional energies in positive ways. Marriage not only benefits a man's family, but it also blesses his community. As Katy Faust and Stacy Manning note, "When a father leaves, stability often leaves with him and the risk of childhood traumas that lie at the heart of so many of our social problems skyrockets."[108]

Our culture disagrees.

According to our post-Christian culture, marriage is the cherry on top of an already-great life. It is for two people who love each other, whether that's two men or two women, or a man and a woman. The state's marriage license has become a stamp of approval to validate an emotional bond between consenting adults.[109] Marriage should fulfill you emotionally, financially, physically, and sexually. But at the same time, a marriage shouldn't ask *too* much of you. And if your romantic or sexual desires change, waver, or lead you somewhere else? Well then, you get a no-fault divorce.

Living in decadent America, we should not be surprised that the Bible's teaching on sex, marriage, and gender seems odd, outdated, irrelevant, or worse. Self-absorbed sexuality and do-it-yourself forms of family are some of our culture's idols, and Scripture contradicts the teaching we receive through TV, movies, magazines, and social media.

108. Faust and Manning, *Them Before Us*.
109. For more on this thinking, see Chapter 4 ("Marriage Matters") in *Them Before Us*, especially pages 72–73.

Now let's look at the big picture of Ephesians before drilling down on chapter 5.

Q. Is there a format to Paul's letter to the Ephesians that would help us understand how the instructions for husbands and wives fit into the letter?

Oster: Yes. Ephesians is laid out in an interesting fashion. It has forty-one imperatives, and forty of those are in chapters 4, 5, and 6. So the first three chapters are where the indicative material lies. That is, chapters 1, 2, and 3 are where we find the statements about what God has done and is doing for Christians. This lays a theological foundation for what's to come in the second half of the letter.

In chapters 4, 5, and 6, Paul spells out the life to which God has called us, and that always requires imperatives. It's never self-evident to God's people what they should do. That's why, once God gathered a people in the exodus, it was necessary to have the Ten Commandments. It's delusional to imagine that the people of God are going to somehow know what to do simply based on an experience of redemption. So Paul writes these three chapters with a series of imperatives for the Ephesian churches.

The imperative I want us to talk about is in Ephesians 5:18, which says to "be filled with the Spirit." So I'd like to start with verse 18 for this discussion.

> Do not get drunk on wine, which leads to debauchery. Instead, be filled with the Spirit, speaking to one another with psalms, hymns, and songs from the Spirit. Sing and make music from your heart to the Lord, always giving thanks to God the Father for everything, in the name of our Lord Jesus Christ.
>
> Submit to one another out of reverence for Christ.
>
> Wives, submit yourselves to your own husbands as you do to the Lord. For the husband is the head of the wife as Christ is the head of the church, his body, of which he is the Savior. Now as the church submits to Christ, so also wives should submit to their husbands in everything.

> Husbands, love your wives, just as Christ loved the church and gave himself up for her to make her holy, cleansing her by the washing with water through the word, and to present her to himself as a radiant church, without stain or wrinkle or any other blemish, but holy and blameless. In this same way, husbands ought to love their wives as their own bodies. He who loves his wife loves himself. After all, no one ever hated their own body, but they feed and care for their body, just as Christ does the church—for we are members of his body. "For this reason a man will leave his father and mother and be united to his wife, and the two will become one flesh." This is a profound mystery—but I am talking about Christ and the church. However, each one of you also must love his wife as he loves himself, and the wife must respect her husband. (Ephesians 5:18–33)

There are four participles that follow the command to "be filled with the Spirit,"—four simple clauses that elaborate on what Paul means. These imperatives don't exhaust this topic, to be sure, but in the context of the epistle, this is what Paul has in mind:

- Speaking to one another in psalms, hymns, and spiritual songs
- Praising God in our hearts
- Giving thanks always to God
- Submitting to one another out of reverence for Christ

It's that fourth one, submission, in verse 21, where there is so much conversation and disagreement. In Greek, verse 22 literally says, "Wives to their own husbands as to the Lord." So, to get the word "submit," we must go back to verse 21. When scholars put verse 21 with verses 18–20 and make a break before verse 22, they create confusion. Verse 21 is a connecting verse, sort of a hinge connecting the two sections. "Submitting to one another out of reverence for Christ" is the fourth area where being Spirit-led is demonstrated, and Paul gives three examples from the household:

- husbands and wives
- parents and children
- masters and slaves

Q. In complementarian circles, the shorthand for the dynamic in Ephesians 5 between husbands and wives often gets reduced to "*wives submit; husbands lead.*" Is this the best summary of the male-female relationship?

Sproles: No. It's an overly simplistic summary of what we find in Ephesians 5. Paul calls for submission to one another in the marriage relationship in verse 21, and then he lays out particular commands.

"Wives submit and respect and husbands submit and love" is a more accurate shorthand; we see that in Colossians 3 as well.

Author and Gospel Coalition contributor Rebecca McLaughlin notes:

> Ephesians 5 sticks like a burr in our 21st-century, Western ears. But we must not misread it as justifying "traditional" gender roles. The text doesn't say the husband is the one whose needs come first and whose comfort is paramount.
>
> In fact, Ephesians 5 is a withering critique of traditional gender roles, in its original context and today. In the drama of marriage, the wife's needs come first, and the husband's drive to prioritize himself is cut down with the axe of the gospel. . . .
>
> And it's a daily challenge to remember what I'm called to in this gospel drama, and to notice opportunities to submit to my husband as to the Lord—not because I'm naturally more or less submissive, or because he is naturally more or less loving, but because Jesus submitted to the cross for me.
>
> My marriage isn't ultimately about me and my husband, any more than Romeo and Juliet is about the actors playing the title roles. My marriage is about reflecting Jesus and his church.[110]

Q. So how should we understand submission in these verses?

110. Rebecca McLaughlin, "Confessions of a Reluctant Complementarian," *The Gospel Coalition*, September 13, 2018, www.thegospelcoalition.org/article/confessions-reluctant-complementarian/ (accessed October 19, 2022).

Oster: "Submitting to one another out of reverence for Christ" is to be understood in all three relationships mentioned here.

Some scholars say Paul's initial plan to show mutuality sort of unravels after the first demonstration between husbands and wives, that Paul couldn't carry forth what he said he was going to do. These scholars are smart enough to know that, in the first-century context, no one in their right mind would have a mutuality understanding of children and parents or slaves and masters—where, for example, the masters are going to become the servant for the day. So these scholars think that mutuality works in the first instance and not in the second and third.

However, I am going to tell you my understanding of how this consistently works. With these three pairs of relationships, we can make a chart:

Husbands	Wives
Parents	Children
Masters	Slaves

The people in the left-hand column are the ones in Paul's day who own all the authority and power. They have all the prerogatives. They owe nothing to the people on the right. They are not beholden to them at all. So Paul is saying that, in all three relationships, each party now has duties and responsibilities to the other. That was not the case in society: all the power and responsibility flowed in one direction, from the left to the right.

As we saw from Plutarch and the sepulcher inscription earlier, not every marriage operated this way. All Christians would not need to be reminded of all forty-one imperatives in Ephesians at all times. However, Paul knew there were households that needed these instructions. Some people would be more up-to-speed than others but regardless, the paradigm for cultural understandings of authority and submission is challenged.

To be clear, Paul is saying that the people with the power—husbands, parents, and masters—have duties and responsibilities to the people without power: wives, children, and slaves.

This is a paradigm shift for ancient thinking. Living in the twenty-first century in the United States, we may say this teaching is obvious, but part of the reason we say that is that we are the children of civilization that was based on Judeo-Christian teaching instead of a society based upon communism, Hinduism, or Islam. People nurtured in these cultures wouldn't find Paul's teaching self-evident.

I read an article recently that said in rural India many Hindu people get offended by women using their own name instead of their husband's name. Women have been beaten because they used their own name to fill a prescription. It comes as no surprise that the early nineteenth-century Christian missionary to India, William Carey, contributed his influence to help stop the Hindu practice of Sati. This was a long-established practice where Hindu widows were burned alive, sometimes forcibly and sometimes not, on their dead husband's funeral pyre.

So there are many cultures to whom Paul's writing would be a new way of thinking. Understanding submission to one another out of reverence for Christ means seeing these paired relationships as one where each person has duties and responsibilities to the other. For the husband-wife relationship, this means the wife submits to her husband and respects him, while the husband loves his wife, giving himself up for her like Christ does for the church.

Sproles: Yes! Recognizing that marriage is a model of Christ and the church brings dignity and clarity to our duties in marriage.

I know many of us wish we could turn in our Bibles to the "Book of Marriage" and read in detail about what really makes a husband a husband or what really makes a wife a wife. (Or what makes a man a man and a woman a woman, for that matter!) But Scripture is fairly silent about the details. It doesn't tell us who does the cooking or who mows the lawn, but it *does* tell us that a wife must live with a spirit of submission and respect for her husband. And it *does* tell us that a husband must live with a spirit of submission and love toward his wife.

Paul Tripp explains it this way:

> The Bible clearly distinguishes men from women. It has essential things to say about God's design for the roles of men and women. But when it comes to the fine-grained detail of masculinity and femininity, the Bible is largely silent. This silence is not some tragic omission. No, it is by divine intention. God's Word really does give us everything we need "for life and godliness." In this way the Bible is comprehensive, but it is not exhaustive. It is always dangerous to ask it to speak in places where it is silent.[111]

Let me give you an example. We tend to think of gentleness or an aptitude for cultivating relationships as feminine, so that when a man demonstrates these strengths, we deem him odd or an outlier. Conversely, we tend to think of objectivity or thinking about "just the facts" as a masculine trait, so that when a woman demonstrates these qualities, we deem her odd or overbearing. Both of these responses ignore the "fine-grained detail" of the sexes.

Regardless of how we are "bent," Scripture tells us there are roles we assume in marriage and the church. How we fulfill those roles as a man and a woman, well, that is a dance unique to each marriage and church.

A man who is sensitive and gentle must still demonstrate the courageous and bold love of Christ toward his wife. Jesus did not take a pass on submitting to God as he took hits from the Jews, Pilate, and the powers of darkness. He laid down his life for us. So you too, husbands, must live this way with your wives.

A woman who is bold and direct must still submit to her husband and respect him. The church does not get a pass on submitting to Christ and respecting his direction. The church must grow and build itself up in love, as each part does its work (Ephesians 4:16). So we too, wives, must live this way with our husbands.

111. Paul David Tripp, "What Makes a Man," March 16, 2015, www.paultripp.com/articles/posts/what-makes-a-man (accessed October 19, 2022).

Q. We see the same teaching on household codes in Colossians. Is there anything we should notice here?

Sproles: Colossians has a similar format to Ephesians. Paul lays a theological foundation in the first three chapters before giving specific instructions.

John Piper notes, "When Paul gets to Colossians 3:12, he has laid a massive foundation in the person and work of Christ on the cross. . . . He exhorts us with words that are explosive with emotion-awakening reality built on Christ and his saving work."[112]

It's on the basis of a God-centered identity, on the work of Christ that brings a "new self" for each of us, that Paul can once again tell us how to behave in the church and in our homes.

> Therefore, as God's chosen people, holy and dearly loved, clothe yourselves with compassion, kindness, humility, gentleness and patience. Bear with each other and forgive one another if any of you has a grievance against someone. Forgive as the Lord forgave you. (Colossians 3:12–13)

Piper pairs these instructions, describing them as inner conditions that lead to outward demeanors:

- Compassionate hearts → kindness (literally "bowels of mercy and kindness")
- Humility → meekness
- Patience → forbearance and forgiveness

Christ followers should have the inner demeanor of compassion, humility, and patience, which leads to the outward demeanor of kindness, meekness, enduring, and forgiving each other. These are crucial for life in the church *and* in marriage. We all love to receive these things, but giving them is much more difficult, isn't it? Well, it's in this context that Paul continues with household instructions:

112. John Piper, "Marriage: Forgiving and Forbearing," *Desiring God*, February 18, 2007, www.desiringgod.org/messages/marriage-forgiving-and-forbearing (accessed October 19, 2022).

> Wives, submit yourselves to your husbands, as is fitting in the Lord. Husbands, love your wives and do not be harsh with them. Children, obey your parents in everything, for this pleases the Lord. Fathers, do not embitter your children, or they will become discouraged. (Colossians 3:18–21)

Submission and love, blanketed with gentleness, are the standard for marriage and the home.

Oster: Again, we see that there's an order and structure to relationships. The husband is not given carte blanche to be whatever kind of husband and father he wants to be; and the wife is not required to be a doormat. Again and again, we see that both husbands and wives have duties and responsibilities to the other. And our society right now is not one that promotes duties and responsibilities to others. Self-control and self-sacrifice are spiritual perspectives that we bring to these concepts of submission and love.

Q. Now we'll turn our attention to 1 Peter. After reading the passage, let's see what is happening in the context of the letter.

> Wives, in the same way submit yourselves to your own husbands so that, if any of them do not believe the word, they may be won over without words by the behavior of their wives, when they see the purity and reverence of your lives. Your beauty should not come from outward adornment, such as elaborate hairstyles and the wearing of gold jewelry or fine clothes. Rather, it should be that of your inner self, the unfading beauty of a gentle and quiet spirit, which is of great worth in God's sight. For this is the way the holy women of the past who put their hope in God used to adorn themselves. They submitted themselves to their own husbands, like Sarah, who obeyed Abraham and called him her lord. You are her daughters if you do what is right and do not give way to fear. Husbands, in the same way be considerate as you live with your wives, and treat them with respect as the weaker partner and as heirs with you of the gracious gift of life, so that nothing will hinder your prayers. (1 Peter 3:1–7)

Sproles: Dr. Oster helped me with this passage when I was writing *On Gender* the first time around. He pointed out that the word "likewise" or the phrase "in the same way" occurs three times in 1 Peter (1 Peter 3:1, 7; 5:5), and this word connects "be subject" with the imitation of Jesus. Peter is telling wives and husbands to act like Christ, just as Paul has in other passages.

How?

They must be holy, speak the truth, not repay evil for evil, and not retaliate or even make threats when mistreated. Instead, they should be "respectful and pure" (verse 2 for wives and verse 7 for husbands) in their behavior.

- Wives likewise submit to your husbands (1 Peter 3:1).
- Husbands likewise treat your wives right (1 Peter 3:7).
- Young men likewise submit to your elders (1 Peter 5:5).

Peter's commands for women come right in the middle of a section on living godly lives in a pagan world. He is helping them deal with their husbands' sins the way Christ dealt with their sin. Peter isn't excusing their behavior. He doesn't deny that these guys are unbelieving brutes (1 Peter 3:1, 6). However, he gives an unexpected course of action: to act so much like Christ that the wives don't even need to use words or beauty to win over their unbelieving husbands.

Words and beauty tend to be powerful tools for women. Peter points out that the most winsome thing about women should be their gentle and quiet spirits. He then explains what he means by mentioning Sarah, the wife of Abraham. Like Jesus, she didn't let fear dictate her behavior but entrusted herself to "him who judges justly" (1 Peter 2:23).

It's easy to think, *If only Peter didn't use those pesky words* obey *and* master. The word Peter uses for "obey" means "acting under the authority of the one speaking" and "really listening to the one giving the charge." It suggests attentive listening and responsiveness.

- It's what the wind and sea did when Jesus spoke (Matthew 8:27).
- It's what many people did when they became obedient to the faith (Acts 6:7).

- It's what Rhoda did when she answered a knock at the door (Acts 12:13).
- It's what children do for parents (Ephesians 6:1).
- It's what we do with Paul's instructions (2 Thessalonians 3:14).

Oster: "Master," the Greek word *kurios*, is a term of respect. There are other examples of this in the Gospels where it means something akin to "sir," but not in a fawning sense. (See Matthew 21:30; Luke 13:8; John 4:11, 15, 19; 5:7; 12:21.) This term *kurios* can be used to refer to a deity (1 Corinthians 8:5–6); clearly in 1 Peter 3, the term is meant as one of honor and respect.

Sproles: That makes sense. If *kurios* is a term of respect, this parallels what Paul was saying in Ephesians: ". . . and the wife must respect her husband" (Ephesians 5:33).

When I looked for *kurios* in Scripture, I found that it was used hundreds of times, sometimes for the Lord, sometimes for human masters. I think this is a clue that points us again to the order of headship. Paul has already noted that Christ is the head of man; man is the head of woman (1 Corinthians 11:3); and woman is the master of the home (1 Timothy 5:14).

So wives acknowledge husbands as "head" in their actions and in their speech. We speak to them and about them with respect. We don't get a pass on obedience to Christ if our husbands act cowardly like Abraham (Genesis 12:11–13), make bad parenting choices like Isaac, Jacob, or King David (Genesis 25:28, 37:3; 2 Samuel 14:1–23), or are unbelieving, selfish boors like Nabal (1 Samuel 25:10–11). We don't ignore them (violating obedience) or write them off as idiots (violating respect). Trusting God, we live in purity and reverence.

Wives, this requires us to change the way we think, taking every thought captive in obedience to Christ (Romans 12:1–2; 2 Corinthians 10:3–5). We must turn off the running commentary in our heads that says to ignore our husbands when they are acting foolish. This is just what Sarah did with Abraham.

What kind of submitting did Sarah do? She respected Abraham in her actions (obeying him) and her speech (calling him "lord"). This principle is repeated throughout Scripture: we are forbidden to say one thing and do another (i.e., hypocrisy).

Think about Sarah. We know she respected Abraham in her speech, but what about her obedience? As we mentioned in Chapter 4, besides going with her husband in faith to a land God would show them, another big example comes to mind. Fearing for his life, Abraham pretended that Sarah was his sister so the Egyptians wouldn't kill him and take her on account of her beauty.

Sarah went along, and sure enough, things got worse before they got better. She got whisked away to Pharaoh's palace as one of his wives. I'm pretty sure this is the point where I'd give way to fear, but this is not the end of the story. Since Abraham wasn't acting like a proper head, God sent plagues on Pharaoh's household, ensuring Sarah's safe return home (Genesis 12:10–20).

What does Peter want us to learn from Sarah? I think one thing is this: Sarah treated Abraham as her head, even when he didn't deserve it, and she trusted God to judge justly, refusing to "fear anything that is frightening." Sarah trusted God, even when her husband didn't.

If you're a woman reading this and find it an impossibly high standard, don't despair. Peter gives husbands some difficult and lofty commands too. And if they don't obey, the warning is clear: their prayers will be hindered.

Oster: We should also remember that submission is voluntary. It is not grabbing somebody by the neck and forcing them to the ground. It is done in the same way that Christ submitted to the will of God. We're not robots being held against our wills by God. It's a *voluntary* submission motivated by respect, out of "reverence for Christ," as Paul puts it. As we ponder all the marvelous, sacrificial things that God's grace and mercy has done for us, we have a commensurate response.

Q. What about the instructions for husbands?

Sproles: Husbands, too, must answer to God for their conduct within marriage. In particular, the words "understanding" and "honor," as well as the phrase "as the weaker vessel," will help us understand the requirements for men in marriage.

Understanding is a word that simply means "to know." Peter is telling husbands to know their wives. There are different ways to know something, and in Scripture we see two types of understanding again and again: information and experience.

- Paul wants the Ephesians to understand how wide, long, high, and deep Christ's love is—a love that surpasses knowledge (Ephesians 3:19).
- Knowledge of God's truth leads to godliness and hope of eternal life (Titus 1:1–2).
- We should make every effort to add understanding to our faith, goodness, self-control, perseverance, godliness, mutual affection, and love (2 Peter 1:5–7).

Laura Ingalls Wilder, author of the *Little House* series, wrote a regular column for a Missouri farm paper under the byline of her husband's name. Her description of how they tended their apple orchard, using information that blossomed with experience, really captures the richness of Peter's use of "understanding."

> I cleared enough land that winter on which to set out the trees from the nursery, broke it the next spring, and put in the trees after I had worked it as smooth as I could. . . . I dug the holes for the trees large and deep, making the dirt fine in the bottom and mixing some wood ashes with it.
>
> I handled the trees very carefully so as not to injure the roots and spread the roots out as nearly as possible in a natural manner when setting the trees. Fine dirt was put over the roots at first and pressed down firmly, then the dirt was shoveled in to fill the hole. Some more wood ashes were mixed with the dirt when it was being shoveled in . . . all trash was raked away, leaving it clean and smooth. . . .
>
> I think that one thing that has made my orchard a success is that I took individual care of each tree. What that particular tree needed, it

> got. Wife and I were so well acquainted with the trees that if I wished to mention one to her, I would say "that tree with the large branch to the south," or "the tree that leans to the north," etc. The tree that leaned was gently taught to stand straight so that the sun would not burn the bark.[113]

Wilder admits that while she and her husband knew how to farm, there were many things they learned only with practice. They personally tended every individual tree in the orchard, bringing a new depth and breadth to their farming knowledge.

Likewise, Christian husbands *know* how to live with their wives when they read Scripture.

They know that the gospel has the power to transform all of their relationships. They know God's order for creation: Christ as the head of man, man as the head of woman, and woman as his strong help. They know they should love their wives and lay down their lives for them. They know they should be gentle with their children.

But, like the Wilders and their orchard, husbands gain so much more knowledge when they put these instructions into *practice*. Obedience brings real understanding.

Knowing her personality, her strengths and weaknesses, her spiritual gifts, even her favorite foods and hobbies, are all ways for a husband to live with his wife "in an understanding way" and love her well. When information intersects with practice, a new kind of knowing emerges—just like reading a book about farming and *actually farming* are two different kinds of knowing. There's knowing and then there's *knowing*.

Husbands, says Peter, *know* your wives.

Q. What does it mean to show honor to your wife?

---

113. Stephen W. Hines, ed, *Laura Ingalls Wilder Farm Journalist: Writings from the Ozarks* (Columbia: University of Missouri Press, 2007), 20–21.

Sproles: Peter explains that when husbands live with their wives in an understanding way, at least part of that will entail honoring wives as co-heirs of Christ. The word "honor" here means a value, or money paid, and by analogy, esteem of the highest degree.

In the church, those who seem weaker are actually *indispensable* and those we think are less honorable, we treat with *special honor* (1 Corinthians 12:22–24). As in the church, so it is in marriage: husbands are to treat their wives with honor, even if he thinks she doesn't deserve it. Even if he doesn't feel affection toward her. Husbands must honor their wives and treat them with gentleness and care.

Check your tone of voice, husbands. Use self-control with your physical presence. Be patient and careful as you would when you handle the crystal. If you have an inner monologue of scorn toward your wife, take those thoughts captive in obedience to Christ (Romans 12:1–2; 2 Corinthians 10:3–5). If you don't do these things, God says your prayers will be hindered (1 Peter 3:7). If this doesn't give you a shiver down your spine, men, then perhaps you should consider how often and about what you are praying.

Q. This "showing honor as with a weaker vessel" sounds demeaning to our twenty-first-century ears. What does Peter mean?

Sproles: The text is literally, "Husbands likewise dwelling with [them] according to knowledge as with a weaker vessel with the female rendering honor as also joint heirs." Peter is using a simile to help explain what he means.

There are lots of similes in Scripture. Jesus used them when he said that he was sending the disciples out as sheep in the midst of wolves, so be wise as serpents and innocent as doves (Matthew 10:16); when he explained that the kingdom of heaven is like a treasure hidden in a field and a merchant looking for fine pearls (Matthew 13:44–46); and when he noted that Pharisees and scribes were like whitewashed tombs (Matthew 23:27). This simile, like all good literary devices, highlights the differences between men and women.

Wendy Alsup helps us out here with some commonsense thinking:

> The feminist response is to downplay the vulnerability of women. Be strong. Be powerful. Don't let men define your identity. The problem is that women's statistically smaller size than men and their bearing of children inherently put them in a vulnerable position. Short of all women taking steroids worldwide, we are not likely to average out to the size and strength of the average male. Ever. And the human race will die out if women don't allow themselves into the vulnerable position of childbirth and rearing. The Bible recognizes this vulnerability, and Peter specifically addresses it and the inherent role of husbands in this vulnerability in 1 Peter 3.[114]

The way you would handle a crystal vase is different from the way you would handle a wooden bowl; you know what they're made of and what it takes to damage each of them. If I carry both of those things in my car, I'll wrap the crystal vase in bubble wrap and gently place it on the seat. If I carry the wooden bowl, I'll toss it in the backseat with no harm done.

Wives who submit to and respect their husbands are voluntarily placing themselves in a position of vulnerability. Husbands must reciprocate with mutual submission, love, and honor, living with them in an understanding way.

Q. Western culture has a hard time understanding these passages, in part because we live in the aftermath of the sexual revolution of the '60s and '70s. Did the Roman Empire experience its own kind of sexual revolution? If so, did it contribute to the downfall of their society?

Oster: When you talk about Rome, there is the Roman Republic followed by the Roman Empire, and the republic did unravel. There are authors who wrote during the end of the Roman Republic who talk about a decline in sexual morality. And they ended up having a Roman civil war in the first century BC. It was a horrific time in those decades, where the fabric of

114. Wendy Alsup. "Hard Words for Women from 1 Peter," *Practical Theology for Women*, January 25, 2010, www.theologyforwomen.org/2010/01/hard-words-to-women-from-i-peter.html (accessed October 19, 2022).

society was coming apart: a crumbling of what had been a centuries-long experience of the Roman Republic.

Around 30 BC, Augustus becomes the first emperor of the Roman Empire. He immediately begins to institute conservative reforms, morally and religiously. He puts up all kinds of temples and institutes all kinds of religious festivals, and Augustus enjoys a long reign.

Q. When taken seriously, these passages on marriage sound like a utopia, and yet we live in a world where we fail each other in marriage and families every day, sometimes horribly. What would you say to someone who is struggling to practice what we've found here?

Oster: We can feel like this is an impossible standard since marriages consist of men and women who are fallen. We can get jaded and think, *Well my wife is obviously not keeping up her end of the deal, so why should I?* Or vice versa.

Sproles: There is a biblical pattern of order between a husband and wife, standards of forbearance and forgiveness, of submission and love, and they aren't contingent on the other person's performance.

Oster: Would you expect your child to honor and obey you even if you weren't being a particularly good parent on a given day? Of course you would. These instructions aren't worded as being contingent on another's behavior. Perhaps that notion comes from our democratic culture, where government is answerable to the people. It is possible to expect too much from a spouse.

We should also remember that Scripture is addressing what should be normative for marriage. The exceptions prove the rule.

Sproles: But certainly there are sins that spouses commit against each other, which push these virtues across a line where they move into the realm of helping the other sin. Things like child abuse, sexual infidelity or abuse, drunkenness, and rage should be taken seriously and navigated with the help of reliable, Spirit-filled church leadership.

So we should use wisdom when we apply these instructions, but we are not going to write them off as cultural or unattainable just because they may be hard.

Oster: This is an area where spending time in intercessory prayer is critical. Before Paul tells his readers anything to do in Ephesians 4–6, he spends three chapters going over what God has done for them. Our tendency in America, even in our preaching and counseling, is to go quickly to how we must change our behavior. We need to ask God to illuminate the eyes of our hearts: "Wake up, sleeper, rise from the dead, and Christ will shine on you" (Ephesians 5:14).

This imperative in Ephesians 5:14 was addressed to believers to stand apart "from the dead ones" who occupy the moral and spiritual cemeteries that surround all of us. Paul finds some of these Ephesian believers once again living in graves, in need of a resurrection like they experienced when they first came to faith (Ephesians 2:5). Without it, none of the challenges to the Christian walk, including a dissatisfying and dysfunctional life with a companion, will be feasibly conquered.

Paul's strategy in Ephesians suggests that we must meditate on what God has done for us and then try to love one another well.

In the next chapter, I'll address the importance of understanding gender in marriage and how it affects our spiritual health. What we believe about these doctrines speaks to our view of the Bible's authority. It speaks to our view of the image of God in men and women. It determines whether we will follow Jesus in strength and health or in weakness and illness.

11

MARRIAGE AND GENDER: HOW HEALTHY ARE YOU?

RENÉE WEBB SPROLES

I speak and write a lot on marriage and gender. Usually, if given enough time, the conversation will end up at the question of importance. It goes something like this . . .

"How much does this really matter? I mean, the issue of what we believe about husbands and wives isn't gospel-level important. The most important thing is Jesus."

"And besides, it's complicated. Words like 'head' and 'submission' sound mean and patriarchal."

"Men have made some big *mistakes in the past. Shouldn't we err on the side of caution and just let everyone choose for themselves what to believe?"*

So how important is this issue?

The short answer is that it's very important. Actually, what we believe about gender and marriage is way more important than most people think.

For the long answer, read on.

In a recent article for *Desiring God*, Joe Rigney explained the idea of "theological triage." This is where you determine how important or serious a teaching is so that you can live a life worthy of Jesus, pleasing him in every way (Colossians 1:9–10).

The questions for "triaging" an issue go like this:

- *Are you alive?* First-tier doctrines answer this question.
- *Are you healthy?* Second-tier doctrines answer this question.
- *What's your diet?* Third-tier doctrines answer this question.[115]

Differences over what it means to be a man or a woman and about marriage are not first-tier. And yet, getting this right matters. Failing to understand what Scripture teaches about men and women makes us unhealthy. The question is, how unhealthy? The answer: very.

Here's Rigney again:

> Differences over manhood and womanhood. . . are directly related to the doctrine of creation, the doctrine of man, and the doctrine of sin. Thus, errors on this doctrine have a greater seriousness.
>
> Additionally, such anthropological error tends to grow over time, especially in the midst of a culture that is fundamentally confused about what it means to be human and hostile to God's design in creation. Like gangrene, contemporary egalitarianism grows and spreads and leads to greater and more deadly error. The frequent move from egalitarianism to the affirmation and celebration of homosexuality is not so much a slippery slope, but simply what cancer does when left untreated.[116]

Understanding what it means to be a man or a woman is important. Understanding concepts like headship, strong help, and submission is important. Understanding how to live as husbands and wives is important.

What we believe about these doctrines speaks to our view of the Bible's authority. It speaks to our view of the image of God in men and women. It determines whether we will follow Jesus in strength and health or in

115. Joe Rigney, "Triage in the Trenches: When do second-tier issues divide?" *Desiring God*, July 10, 2022, www.desiringgod.org/articles/triage-in-the-trenches?fbclid=IwAR3K-j2x58jGPZFV6d2MhS68F27JgaF-6g64I98XSLzzYV36dew2VqvDBgME (accessed October 19, 2022).
116. Rigney, "Triage in the Trenches."

weakness and illness. And when we find errors in our thinking and practice, repentance is as important as addressing cancer with proper treatments when diagnosed.

Scripture shows us that men and women reflect the image of God in complementary ways in marriage. We are not totally distinct from one another, yet we are not interchangeable. Genesis lays a foundation for this by showing the headship of Adam and the strong help of Eve. Later, New Testament writers flesh out these concepts with particular instructions and admonitions to husbands and wives.

So let's start with Genesis and move to other passages of Scripture as we seek to understand this very important second-tier issue: what Scripture says about husbands and wives.

GENESIS 1: MEN AND WOMEN ARE MADE TO COOPERATE

In our modern Western culture where men and women are considered equivalent, not just equal, Genesis 1 sounds good and right and true. God gives his commission to rule and reign over creation to both the man and the woman.

> Then God said, "Let us make mankind in our image, in our likeness, so that they may rule over the fish in the sea and the birds in the sky, over the livestock and all the wild animals, and over all the creatures that move along the ground."
>
> So God created mankind in his own image, in the image of God he created them; male and female he created them.
>
> God blessed them and said to them, "Be fruitful and increase in number; fill the earth and subdue it. Rule over the fish in the sea and the birds in the sky and over every living creature that moves on the ground." (Genesis 1:26–28)

God made sure we'd need each other to fully represent him to the world. Both genders are required to "fill the earth" and create new life. Both genders are commissioned to subdue the earth and rule over all God's creatures.

How do we do this?

We fill the earth through families. We create culture; we work; we build just governments and righteous nations. Every time we do these things, in big ways and small, we reflect the image of our good God.

While the commission to fill, subdue, and rule in Genesis 1 highlights the similarities of males and females, further reading of Genesis exposes differences between the sexes.

GENESIS 2: ADAM HAS DUTIES AND RESPONSIBILITIES

We get more details to the creation narrative in the second chapter of Genesis. God reveals that, while both sexes are made to rule and reign, male and female are not *interchangeable* in how they reflect the image of God.

> The Lord God took the man and put him in the Garden of Eden to work it and take care of it. And the Lord God commanded the man, "You are free to eat from any tree in the garden; but you must not eat from the tree of the knowledge of good and evil, for when you eat from it you will certainly die."
>
> The Lord God said, "It is not good for the man to be alone. I will make a helper suitable for him." Now the Lord God had formed out of the ground all the wild animals and all the birds in the sky. He brought them to the man to see what he would name them; and whatever the man called each living creature, that was its name. So the man gave names to all the livestock, the birds in the sky and all the wild animals. But for Adam no suitable helper was found. (Genesis 2:15–20)

We find an order emerging in Genesis, which is explained later in Scripture. God creates Adam first (primogeniture), moves him into the garden, gives him the command (a priestly duty), and gives him the authority to name the animals as well as his wife. Adam is also responsible for tending the garden and caring for the animals. Authority, strength, and gentleness are all wrapped up in this vision of what it means to be a man.

The Genesis account of man strikes a beautiful balance between work and care. Think about it. Preparation of the soil requires strength. Handling of the roots requires gentleness. Working the orchard season after season requires perseverance. Caring individually for each tree requires attention. Far from creating a gender stereotype of a manly man, the first man reflects the image of God in strength (work) *and* gentleness (care). Yet God says that it was not good for man to be alone (Genesis 2:18). He needed help.

GENESIS 2: WOMAN IS MAN'S COMPLEMENTARY HELP

Now that we have a clearer picture of how man's work of tending a garden reflects the image of God, we'll turn to the words that God uses to describe woman: suitable helper.

> But for Adam no suitable helper was found. So the Lord God caused the man to fall into a deep sleep; and while he was sleeping, he took one of the man's ribs and then closed up the place with flesh. Then the Lord God made a woman from the rib he had taken out of the man, and he brought her to the man.
>
> The man said,
>
> "This is now bone of my bones
> and flesh of my flesh;
> she shall be called 'woman,'
> for she was taken out of man."
>
> That is why a man leaves his father and mother and is united to his wife, and they become one flesh. Adam and his wife were both naked, and they felt no shame. (Genesis 2:20b–25)

The phrase *ezer kenegdo* means something like "a strong helper corresponding to or opposite of him." Eve is Adam's *kenegdo* (suitable or complementary) *ezer* (strength and help) to fill and subdue the earth.[117]

Ezer is a noun that appears twenty-one times in the Old Testament. Here is the tally of its usage:

- Two times in reference to the first woman (Genesis 2:18, 20)
- Three times in reference to nations to whom Israel appealed for military support (Isaiah 30:5; Ezekiel 12:14; Daniel 11:34)
- Sixteen times in reference to God as our help (Exodus 18:4; Deuteronomy 33:7, 26, 29; Psalm 20:2; 33:20; 70:5; 89:19; 115:9–11; 121:1–2; 124:8; 146:5; Hosea 13:9)

Most of the time in Scripture, *ezer,* the same word used of the first woman (Genesis 2:18), is used to describe *God* as a helper. This has startling implications for the intended relationship between men and women.[118]

In the Bible, God, as *ezer,* helps Israel in many ways. He defends them from their enemies again and again. He shields and protects them from foreign

---

117. The Hebrew word here is *kenegdo*. The verb form of *neged* means something like "to be face to face," so as a noun the term means "something that is face-to-face with something else." In Genesis 21:16, we find a form of *neged* when Hagar is described as going some distance away and sitting down "opposite" her son (Genesis 21:16). The prefix *k* means "like" and the suffix *o* means "him" or "his." Putting all of this together, the phrase means something akin to "like his opposite" or "over against him." As for *ezer* (helper), this sounds like such a generic term. It suggests images of a maid, waitress, secretary, or even servant. But if we let the Bible explain itself, we get a very different vision of what it means to be a woman. Far from the gender stereotype of a "girly girl," Genesis shows us how woman is a complementary strength and help for man.

118. Let's look at some of these *ezer* descriptions of God to better understand what kind of help is being described. Moses names one of his sons Eliezer because "My Father's God was my helper; he saved me from the sword of Pharaoh" (Exodus 18:4). "We wait in hope for the Lord; he is our help and our shield" (Psalm 33:20). David asks for help: "But as for me, I am poor and needy; come quickly to me, O God. You are my help and my deliverer; Lord, do not delay" (Psalm 70:5). God as our help is a refrain of a song: "All you Israelites, trust in the Lord—He is their help and shield" (Psalm 115:9–11). God as *ezer* is the well-known first line of a psalm: "I lift up my eyes to the mountains—Where does my help come from? My help comes from the Lord, the Maker of heaven and earth" (Psalm 121:1–2). God indicts Israel because they turned against him, their help: "You are destroyed, Israel, because you are against me, against your helper" (Hosea 13:9).

armies and plagues. He sends his angel armies to fight for them. He empowers them to fight. He rescues them from danger, comforts them when they are weary, and helps the orphan, widow, and oppressed.

Eve was made as a strong helper *opposite* Adam. Genesis shows us that the sexes have complementary strengths.

Can women be shields? Swords? Deliverers? Of course! Every woman who takes up the shield of faith, speaking God's promises to her husband, praying for him, and looking to Christ, helps extinguish Satan's fiery arrows of self-doubt, world-weariness, and fear of failure. Every mother who buckles the belt of truth and wields the sword of the Spirit (the Word) can powerfully disciple her children, speak truth to her husband, and empower them to grow strong and bold in the Lord. *Ezer* women wield the sword of the Spirit, which is the Word of God. We know the Word, pray the Word, and speak the Word in love to our husbands, children, and friends.

While Satan determines to devour the people in our lives, strong women buckle those belts of truth, stay alert, and keep on praying. Open your Bibles and get inspired to live out the image of God, *ezer* women! With the shield of faith in place, we can obey God in holy fear like Noah, follow God into unknown cities like Abraham, face ridicule, shelter the alien, and believe God for all things for our children, including miracles, to name a few.

SUMMARY OF GENESIS

We see it in Genesis, but the rest of Scripture will affirm this truth again and again: there are meaningful differences between the sexes, and there is an order for how we relate to one another. When we acknowledge our differences and fulfill our responsibilities to the opposite sex and the world, we reflect the image of God as he intended. Theologians John Piper and Wayne Grudem put it this way:

> When someone asks if women are weaker than men, or smarter than men, or more easily frightened than men, or something like that, perhaps the best way to answer is this: Women are weaker in some ways, and men are weaker in some ways . . . .

> It is dangerous to put negative values on the so-called weaknesses that each of us has. God intends for all the "weaknesses" that characteristically belong to man to call forth and highlight woman's strengths. And God intends for all the "weaknesses" that characteristically belong to woman to call forth and highlight man's strengths . . . .
>
> Boasting in either sex as superior to the other is folly. Men and women, as God created us, are different in hundreds of ways.
>
> Being created equally in the image of God means at least this: that when the so-called weakness and strength columns for manhood and for womanhood are added up, the value at the bottom is going to be the same for each. And when you take those two columns and put them on top of each other, God intends them to be the perfect complement to each other.[119]

Moving on from Genesis, let's look at Proverbs 31 for more insight into a healthy husband-wife relationship.

PROVERBS 31: HOW TO BE A WIFE (AND A HUSBAND!)

Proverbs was likely originally written as a manual for the instruction of young men. (The readers are always addressed as "sons.") In chapter 31, young men not only get a picture of the kind of wife they should seek, but they also get insights into the kind of men and husbands they should be.

In a 2017 interview with Matt Smethurst, Tim Keller observed that we can learn several things about being an ideal husband from Proverbs 31:

- Husbands should trust and have confidence in their wives rather than trying to control them (v. 11).
- Husbands should consider their wives to be true partners in enterprises rather than disempowered assistants (vv. 13–18).

119. John Piper and Wayne Grudem, *50 Crucial Questions About Manhood and Womanhood: An Overview of Central Concerns about Manhood and Womanhood* (Wheaton: Crossway, 2016), 47.

- Husbands should praise their wives and build them up publicly and privately (vv. 28–29).
- Men shouldn't be afraid of strong women, since the word "noble" used of this wife (v. 10) means to be bold and valiant, a term ordinarily used of warriors (think "Lucy the Valiant" in C.S. Lewis's *The Lion, the Witch, and the Wardrobe*[120]).
- Finally, men shouldn't be nearly as influenced by physical and sexual beauty as they are. It is "deceptive . . . fleeting" (v. 30). Men in ancient times and still today have been far too affected by female appearance—and they tend to assess, accept, and reject women on the basis of their looks rather than on their character and especially their "fear of the LORD" (v. 30).[121]

And what is the ideal wife like?

- She is dependable and has noble character. (Remember, the word *noble* means she is bold and valiant, a term used of warriors.)
- She brings her husband good, not harm, all his life.
- She works hard, getting up early to provide for her family and servants.
- She is a capable businesswoman and is diligent, working into the night.
- She is generous to the poor.
- She plans ahead.
- Strength and honor are her clothes.
- She is wise and can teach others.
- Most importantly, she fears the LORD.

Most women I know cringe at these verses. They tell me that it's too intimidating, too high of a standard. Keller notes, "Some women have complained that such an ideal spouse as depicted here doesn't exist. Yes, but neither does

120. C.S. Lewis, *The Lion, the Witch, and the Wardrobe* (New York: HarperCollins, 1994).
121. Matt Smethurst, "Tim Keller Wants to Help You Become Wise: Gleaning Daily Wisdom from Proverbs," *The Gospel Coalition*, November 6, 2017, www.thegospelcoalition.org/article/keller-wants-to-help-you-become-wise/ (accessed October 19, 2022).

a truly loving person exist—think 1 Corinthians 13—but that doesn't mean we shouldn't aspire to be one."[122]

My grandfather, my dad, and my husband have all had full confidence in me, which I now realize is a rare experience for most women. They praised me and encouraged me to be strong and brave, trying hard things without fear of rejection if I failed. Sometimes we don't understand passages like Proverbs 31 because we don't actually try to do what they say.

When men treat their granddaughters, daughters, sisters, and wives well and understand who God says they are, both sexes are blessed. When women rise to their calling as strong, complementary help to men, both sexes are blessed. With the beautiful standards of Genesis 1–2 and Proverbs 31 in mind, we'll now turn to some New Testament passages to flesh out how husbands and wives should relate to one another to enjoy a healthy marriage.

MARRIAGE IN THE NEW TESTAMENT

Although there are other passages we could explore, these will give us a good understanding of what should be happening in our marriages:

- Marriage means yielding your bodies to one another (1 Corinthians 7).
- Wives are the masters of their homes (1 Timothy 5).
- Husbands are the heads of their wives (Ephesians 4–6).
- Marriage requires Christlike submission and understanding (1 Peter 3).

1 CORINTHIANS 7: YIELDING TO ONE ANOTHER

In 1 Corinthians, Paul gives us insight into the sexual dynamic in a marriage relationship.

> Now for the matter you wrote about: "It is good for a man not to have sexual relations with a woman." But since sexual immorality is occurring, each man should have sexual relations with his own

122. Smethurst, "Tim Keller Wants to Help You Become Wise."

> wife, and each woman with her own husband. The husband should fulfill his marital duty to his wife, and likewise the wife to her husband. The wife does not have authority over her own body but yields it to her husband. In the same way, the husband does not have authority over his own body but yields it to his wife. Do not deprive each other except perhaps by mutual consent and for a time, so that you may devote yourselves to prayer. Then come together again so that Satan will not tempt you because of your lack of self-control. (1 Corinthians 7:1–5)

Husbands and wives have obligations to one another, and Paul is saying that sex is one of them. Hierarchy and authority have no standing in marital sex. Both genders are to "yield" to one another, and neither husband nor wife has "authority" over their own body.

What is most striking, especially in the social world of Paul, is the command for husbands to yield to their wives. There is no precedent for such a view of men in the world of the New Testament. Paul's instructions to men are liberating to women and affirm Jesus' constant teaching about the kingdom virtue of submission.

But why is sex so important in marriage that Paul would write about it and encourage husbands and wives not deprive each other of it? Looking back at 1 Corinthians 6, we find some clues. Urging them to stop their sexual sin, Paul's reasoning goes back to Genesis 2:24 to the phrase "one flesh":

> Do you not know that your bodies are members of Christ himself? Shall I then take the members of Christ and unite them with a prostitute? Never! Do you not know that he who unites himself with a prostitute is one with her in body? For it is said, "The two will become one flesh." But whoever is united with the Lord is one with him in spirit. (1 Corinthians 6:15–17)

C.S. Lewis explains that "a man and wife are to be regarded as a single organism—for that is what the words 'one flesh' would be in modern English. . . . [This is] not expressing a sentiment but stating a fact—just as one is stating a fact when one says that a lock and its key are one mechanism, or that a violin and a bow are one musical instrument."[123]

Sex is much richer, more beautiful, and more important than American culture preaches in our movies, books, and TV shows. It's not just a physical urge like hunger that we satisfy when we feel like it. Lewis continues: "The monstrosity of sexual intercourse outside marriage is that those who indulge in it are trying to isolate one kind of union (the sexual) from all the other kinds of union, which were intended to go along with it and make up the total union."[124] When we have sex with someone outside of marriage, it's creating one kind of union (physical) while ignoring other kinds of union (like the emotional, social, and spiritual unions).

Returning to 1 Corinthians 7, Tim Keller notes that sex is so important because it's "the physical reenactment of the inseparable oneness. . . created by the marriage covenant. Sex renews and revitalizes the marriage covenant."[125] When sex is viewed as a sacred act, it makes sense why Paul would be so specific in his instructions for the "hows" and "whens" of sex in marriage. Keller continues:

> In the Bible oneness is not simply a matter of emotion but is always the creation of a covenant. . . . The Bible is full of covenant renewal ceremonies. When God enters into a personal relationship with someone, he is not so unrealistic as to think that mere emotion can serve as the basis for it. He knows that human emotions come and go and that there needs to be something binding to provide consistency and endurance. . . . But that is not enough. He regularly gets his people together to reread the terms of the covenant, remember the history of his acts of grace in their lives, and recommit themselves through renewal of the covenant. The ultimate covenant renewal ceremony is the Lord's Supper. . . . In the same way, marriage is a

123. C.S. Lewis, *Mere Christianity* (New York: Harper Collins ebooks, 2009), 104.
124. Lewis, *Mere Christianity*, 104.
125. Tim Keller, "The Gospel and Sex." *Q Ideas*, www.208.106.253.109/essays/the-gospel-and-sex.aspx?page=2 (accessed October 18, 2022).

> covenant. . . . The covenant will grow stale unless we continually revisit and reenact it.[126]

The Bible is very practical about our human nature. God knows that we are fickle creatures. We tend to believe that what we feel at any given moment is our full reality, a compass for our decisions. God uses this to his advantage (and ours), for within the covenant of marriage, sex creates feelings that remind us that we are committed to this person for life. Not only this, but the act itself is a physical reminder that we are in this together. We're a team. We're one.

Sex is almost always a barometer of the health of our marriages. Paul knows this and so he writes specifically about it. Our bodies belong to one another in marriage, so we must yield to one another in this "one flesh" union. Paul revisits this concept in Ephesians 5, imploring husbands to treat their wives as well as they'd treat their own bodies.

Why? Because in marriage the image bearers of God are imaging another relationship as well: that of Christ and the church. We'll get to that soon, but first let's look at what Paul says to Timothy about wives.

1 TIMOTHY 5: MASTERS OF THE HOME

> So I counsel younger widows to marry, to have children, to manage their homes and to give the enemy no opportunity for slander. (1 Timothy 5:14)

The phrase translated "manage their homes" is translated "keep house" in the New American Standard Bible and "guide the house" in the King James Version. It is actually the Greek word *oikodespotein*, which comes from two Greek words: *oikos* and *despotes*. *Oikos* means "house," and you might be able to guess what *despotes* means based on a similar-sounding word in English: "despot." *Despotes* means "lord" or "master" (although the word "despot" has come to suggest a tyrannical form of lordship). To clarify, let's see how *despotes* is translated elsewhere in Scripture:

126. Tim Keller, "The Gospel and Sex."

- Simeon, upon meeting the infant Jesus, declared, "Sovereign Lord [*despota*], as you have promised, you may now dismiss your servant in peace" (Luke 2:29).
- When Peter and John were released from prison, the believers praised God in prayer, "Sovereign Lord [*despota*], you made the heavens and the earth . . ." (Acts 4:24b).
- In the letter we are now considering, 1 Timothy, Paul says, "All who are under the yoke of slavery should consider their masters [*despotas*] worthy of full respect . . . those who have believing masters should not show them disrespect" (1 Timothy 6:1–2a).
- See also 2 Timothy 2:20–21, 1 Peter 2:18, 2 Peter 2:1, Jude 4, and Revelation 6:10, which also use "lord" and "master."

Paul names the wife as the *master* of the home. Not the servant. Not even the manager. He calls her the "master." Looking at the Bible as a cohesive, coherent whole, I see Paul's description going hand-in-hand with Proverbs 31. Some of the healthiest marriages I know function with the wife being master of the home while the husband is the loving head of his wife. He listens to her intuition and wisdom, and she respects his viewpoint.

In Proverbs, I see a woman who is the master of her home. I see a strong helper (*ezer kenegdo*) who is competent to run a household and a business while caring for her family and others. It turns the common phrase, "Behind every successful man, there's a woman" on its head, because this successful woman has a husband who "has full confidence in her," who gains respect "at the city gate" because of her, and who "praises her" (Proverbs 31:11, 23, 28).

From 1 Corinthians 7, we see that husbands and wives yield to one another in the covenant renewal ceremony of sex. From 1 Timothy 5, we see that wives, not husbands, are called to be the masters of their homes. Let's turn to Ephesians for more insight into the marriage relationship and specific commands to husbands and wives.

EPHESIANS 4–6: COMMANDS FOR CHRISTIAN LIVING

Paul jumps right into chapter 4 of Ephesians and "insists . . . in the Lord" that both men and women do the following:

- Live completely humbly and gently with one another.
- Be patient (because of their love for each other).
- Be unified in the Holy Spirit through peace.
- Serve one another (so that we can be unified and even help each other mature).
- Put off our old selves and get a new attitude.
- Tell the truth.
- Do not sin when you get angry.
- Stop stealing and work hard so you can share.
- Watch what you say.
- Do not grieve the Holy Spirit.
- Get rid of bitterness, rage and anger, brawling and slander, along with every form of malice.
- Be kind and compassionate to one another.
- Forgive like God forgave you.
- Walk in the way of love.
- Do not let even a hint of sexual sin be among men and women.
- The same goes for impurity and greed.
- Stop being obscene, telling dirty jokes, and talking like a fool.
- Live as children of light.
- Find out what pleases Jesus.
- Live wisely.
- Make the most of every opportunity.
- Again, understand what Jesus' will is.
- Don't get drunk.
- Be filled with the Holy Spirit.
- Speak to one another in psalms, hymns, and spiritual songs.
- Gives thanks to God in everything.

These common duties of ordinary life are for *all* Christians.

So whatever else we say about male headship and female strong help, we must remember that *everyone* is called to live in humility and selflessness. For men this is especially important since male headship has often been misrepresented and even abused. Men, we women have often sinned against you by belittling your God-given headship and disrespecting you, but you have often exacerbated the curse placed on us women through Eve by selfishly insisting that headship means rigid rule, when Scripture commands all of us—men and women—to adopt the position of servant, not ruler.

Next, in Ephesians 5, Paul moves on to how families relate to one another, and he begins with an unpopular concept in our culture today: submission. He says, "Submit to one another out of reverence for Christ" (Ephesians 5:21).

Paul begins his instructions to families with a call to submission. There are a couple different views on who is doing the submitting. One view is that the "submit to one another" in verse 21 is being directed to the wives, because verse 22 actually borrows its verb from the "submit to one another" in verse 21. So verses 21–22 literally say, "Submitting to one another out of reverence for Christ. Wives to your own husbands, as to the Lord." In this view, it is the wives who are to submit, because verse 22 explains *who* is to submit to one another.

Another view is that all Christians are being told to submit to each other—which would include husbands and wives submitting to each other—out of reverence for Christ. And then verses 22–33 flesh out *how* they submit to each other (wives by submitting to their husbands as to Christ, husbands by loving their wives as Christ loves the church). Accordingly, everything that follows verse 21 is qualified by this instruction to "submit to one another out of reverence for Christ." Husbands and wives are to take on a posture of submission to each other because of their reverence for Jesus, although how each of them carries this out looks different. Regardless of which view you hold, it's important to remember the many important responsibilities we all have toward each other (refer to the bullet-point list above).

After verse 21, Paul then moves on to talk about how wives are to relate to their husbands, and the dominant verb is to submit. The Greek word *hupotasso*, which is translated as "submit," is used about forty times throughout Scripture. In military usage, it means to arrange military divisions under a leader. In non-military usage, it means to arrange under, to cooperate, to subject oneself, or to carry a burden. Here are some examples of *hupotasso* in Scripture:

- Jesus submitted to his parents (Luke 2:51).
- We are all to submit to the governing authorities (Romans 13:1).
- We submit to those who serve the Lord's people (1 Corinthians 16:15–16).
- The church submits to Christ (Ephesians 5:24).
- Jesus' power enables him to make all things submit to him (Philippians 3:20–21).
- God submitted creation to humans (Hebrews 2:5–8).
- James tells us to submit to God (James 4:7).

It's worth noting that the only positive example for *involuntary submission* in Scripture is when it is done by God, who places all of creation in subjection (submission) to Christ and who will cause every knee to bow to him one day (see 1 Peter 3:22 and Isaiah 45:23). The submission in view in Ephesians 5:22 isn't something enforced or coerced by the husband. It's an appeal to do so voluntarily to reflect the relationship between Jesus and his church. Here are the verses describing how wives are to relate to their husbands:

> Wives, submit yourselves to your own husbands as you do to the Lord. For the husband is the head of the wife as Christ is the head of the church, his body, of which he is the Savior. Now as the church submits to Christ, so also wives should submit to their husbands in everything. . . . However, each one of you also must love his wife as he loves himself, and the wife must respect her husband. (Ephesians 5:22–24, 33)

Paul tells wives that part of their duties and responsibilities in marriage is to submit to their husbands and respect them. One of the primary ways we can submit to our husbands is to allow them to be responsible for us. (And one of the primary ways husbands can love their wives is to be responsible for them.)

If you need some concrete examples of submission and respect, here are a few: I submit to my husband when I care about him and consider his needs first, when I think about what would bless him (not just in big ways, but also in small, simple ways like making his morning coffee), when I pray for God's will in his life, when I give up something I want to buy or do for him, when I defer to his opinion, when I hold my tongue if I'm right or irritated, and when I speak words of affirmation to him and about him to others. He, by the way, does all of these things for me, too, and considers me a strong help, which makes submission a joy, not a burden.

A wife can have joy and confidence in *hypotasso* (submitting to) and *phobetai* (respecting) a Christlike head who lays down his life for her. A man who enables her to reach her full potential in God's kingdom, who bears the weight of responsibility for her well-being, who gives himself up for her, who seeks her wise counsel and leverages her strong help, is very much a woman's Christlike head.

Therefore, wives should not fear their husbands, but respect and honor them.

Why? It's a Matter of Headship.

Wives are supposed to submit to and respect their husbands voluntarily, but *why*? Paul gives a simple reason: because the husband is the head of the wife just as Christ is the head of the church.

Although this idea of "head" is described much more fully in Chapter 5 ("What's All This Talk About Heads?"), it's helpful to mention here that *head* is a word that has fallen out of favor in our day. I didn't like it at all when I read it at first, which is why I decided to ignore it for years. Sometimes it seems easier to substitute a "synonym" such as "leader" for "head," although the two aren't exactly synonyms. In my home growing up and when I married at age twenty-one, my dad and my husband were acting much more like my *head* than my *leader,* although I didn't know to use the word *head* to describe what I was experiencing: gentleness, devotion, self-sacrifice, support, and, of course, love. Leadership and authority are subsumed in the idea of headship. But when reading what God says about gender and marriage in the Bible, these words are not the primary descriptors of the male/female relationship.

Again, the principle of leadership is encompassed within headship, but it's a poor synonym for it. I cannot find anywhere in Scripture where a husband is called the leader of his wife. I can, however, find several places where the husband is called the head of the wife. Not only that, but leadership and authority have been abused for millennia, so if we are to use these loaded terms, we must define them as Jesus and Paul define them. Service, deference, care, gentleness, sacrifice, and selflessness are how all disciples of Jesus are to exercise leadership and authority when given the opportunity.

Kephale is the Greek word used for "head" in this passage and in others. It is found about seventy-five times in the New Testament. Almost every time we find it in Scripture, it means a literal head that sits atop a neck.[127] Many egalitarians, who tend to see no meaningful gender distinctions in Scripture, argue that *kephale* means "source," so that husbands are the source of their wives, just as Adam's rib was the source of Eve. In this interpretation, any additional responsibility or authority is minimized. Yet this interpretation seems to ignore the plain meaning of the word. Complementarians, who acknowledge gender distinctions in Scripture with specific roles for the sexes, tend to argue that *kephale* means "authority;" therefore wives are under their husbands' authority and leadership. Yet, this also seems to miss the plain meaning of the word.[128]

---

127. For example, Jesus says not to swear by your head (Matthew 5:36). He also says to anoint your head with oil when you fast (Matthew 6:17). The hairs of our head are numbered (Matthew 10:30). John the Baptist's head was brought on a platter (Matthew 14:11). A woman anointed Jesus' head with costly perfume (Matthew 26:7). A crown of thorns was placed on Jesus' head (Matthew 27:29). A cloth was wrapped around Jesus' head in his tomb (John 20:7). Paul shaved his head because of a vow (Acts 18:8). Being kind to our enemies heaps burning coals on their heads (Romans 12:20). Women pray and prophesy with covered heads, men with uncovered heads (1 Corinthians 11:4–5).

128. Refuting evangelical feminists, Wayne Grudem pushes hard on his assertion that *kephale* means "authority over." While I don't disagree that *kephale* contains within it the notion of authority, Jesus redefines authority in ways that are counterintuitive to fallen human beings who crave and misuse power. Men are doing themselves (and their wives!) a disservice to only imagine and embody the idea of "authority" when they act as "head." See Wayne Grudem, *Evangelical Feminism: A New Path to Liberalism?* (Wheaton: Crossway Books, 2006), 194–95.

I will also mention that if we read the few places in Scripture where *kephale* is *not* talking about a literal head, we get some helpful insight into this order of creation called headship. It's an order that was hinted at in Genesis 1–3 and is explained quite thoroughly with the progression of God's revelation in Scripture. Christ is called the head (*kephale*) of the church as well as the head (*kephale*) cornerstone. (Again, for more on the biblical uses of "head," as well as "cornerstone," see Chapter 5: "What's All This Talk about Heads?").

Paul goes on to describe what it means for the husband to be the wife's "head." It has everything to do with Christlike, sacrificial love:

> Husbands, love your wives, just as Christ loved the church and gave himself up for her to make her holy, cleansing her by the washing with water through the word, and to present her to himself as a radiant church, without stain or wrinkle or any other blemish, but holy and blameless. In this same way, husbands ought to love their wives as their own bodies. He who loves his wife loves himself. After all, no one ever hated their own body, but they feed and care for their body, just as Christ does the church—for we are members of his body. "For this reason a man will leave his father and mother and be united to his wife, and the two will become one flesh." This is a profound mystery—but I am talking about Christ and the church. However, each one of you also must love his wife as he loves himself, and the wife must respect her husband. (Ephesians 5:25–33)

Paul calls husbands to care for their wives and love them as Christ loves the church. He then tells them to love their wives as they love their own bodies. Amidst a culture often characterized by misogyny, suspicion, and domination of women, Paul's instructions for husbands sound slightly ridiculous. What man would serve his wife, loving her and giving himself up for her so that she could be sanctified? Who thinks of Christian marriage as modeling Christ and the church for the world?

Let's unpack these words Paul writes to husbands.

Love. *Agape* is one of four words for love in Greek and is mentioned over 300 times in the New Testament. Distinct from the affection of friendship (*philos*), the passion of sexual love (*eros*), and the warmth of familial love (*storge*), the ultimate expression of love is unconditional, self-sacrificing love, which the early Christians described by using the Greek word *agape*. *Agape* is the kind of love that prompts God's rescue mission for humanity through Christ. Associated with the exercise of the will, *agape* involves both feelings *and* action.

- In Matthew 5:44, Jesus commands us to *agapao* (love) our enemies and pray for them.
- In John 3:16, God *agapao* (loved) the world and gave us Jesus so that we might have eternal life.
- In John 14:15, 21, 23, Jesus says that if we *agapao* (love) him, we will keep his commands.
- In Romans 5:5, the *agape* (love) of God has been poured out into our hearts through the Holy Spirit.
- In 1 Corinthians 13, *agape* (love) is thoroughly described as, among other things, patient, kind, not envious, boastful, or puffed up, not easily angered or grudge-keeping. *Agape* (love) rejoices in the truth, always protects, always trusts, always hopes, and always perseveres.

Agape love is a description of the high call to love for Christian husbands. It is modeled on Christ's love for the church and would have been a radical departure from the type of marital affection expected in antiquity. I daresay it's a radical departure from what most marriages look like today.

Trust/Vulnerability. Paul says Jesus "gave himself up" (Ephesians 5:2, 25), and husbands are to "love your wives, just as Christ loved the church and gave himself up for her" (Ephesians 5:25). This word, *paradidomi*, is mentioned more than 100 times in the New Testament. It means to give into the hands of another with a sense of close personal involvement, to deliver something to keep, to entrust, and even to arrest.

- Jesus said a man going on a journey *paradidomi* (entrusted) his wealth to his servants (Matthew 25:14).
- Jesus *paradidomi* (gave up) his spirit when he died on the cross (John 19:30).

- Paul and Barnabas *paradidomi* (were committed to) the grace of God for the work they completed (Acts 14:26).
- Paul and Barnabas *paradidomi* (risked their lives) for Jesus (Acts 15:26).
- Paul said those who are alive are being *paradidomi* (given over) to death so that Jesus' life may be revealed in their bodies (2 Corinthians 4:11).

There is a sense of vulnerability and trust, especially in light of Christ giving himself up for the church, that husbands are called to exhibit in their relationships with their wives. This giving up, this entrusting of husbands to their wives, is a great gift for women. Indeed, it's an honor for us when husbands do this.

What can this "giving up" look like? The examples are endless.

My husband entrusts himself to me when he shares his dreams for our future; when he confides in me his feelings of failure, insecurity, or disappointment, especially regarding work; when he gets up in the night to take care of a crying baby; or when he asks my advice or perspective. In these ways and so many others, I know that he is not only loving me *like* his own body (Ephesians 5:28); sometimes he is loving me *more than* his own body.

Sanctification. "To make her holy" (Ephesians 5:26). The word Paul uses here is *hagiazo*, which means to make holy, purify, or consecrate. Tim Keller, in his book, *The Meaning of Marriage: Facing the Complexities of Commitment with the Wisdom of God*, talks about sanctification in marriage.

> Within this Christian vision of marriage, here's what it means to fall in love. It is to look at another person and get a glimpse of what God is creating, and to say, "I see who God is making you, and it excites me! I want to be part of that. I want to partner with you and God in the journey you are taking to his throne. And when we get there, I will look at your magnificence and say, 'I always knew you could be like this. I got glimpses of it on earth, but now look at you!'"[129]

129. Tim Keller, *The Meaning of Marriage: Facing the Complexities of Commitment with the Wisdom of God*. (New York: Penguin Books, 2011), 132.

Adam failed in this commission of holiness. Instead of washing Eve with water through the word of truth, he stood by, watched her sin, joined her sin, and then blamed her when God asked what happened. Ever since then, husbands have struggled to sacrificially love and entrust themselves to their wives so that they may become holy through the word of truth. But now, in Christ, as instructed by his apostle Paul, men get the chance to make it right. You get the chance to show the whole world how men and women can complement, complete, and inspire each other in holiness.

A Final Note to Husbands

Husbands, if you starve your wife, you starve yourself. If you hurt your wife, you hurt yourself. If you neglect your wife, you neglect yourself. Paul says husbands should love their wives as they love their own bodies, feeding and caring for them. Jesus is your model.

You don't see Jesus lead with authority in worldly ways. He doesn't *make* us submit to him through intimidation. He doesn't *insist* on getting his way or keeping his thumb on his disciples as their leader. He doesn't *make demands* by yelling or bullying.

What does insisting on your way look like? It can look like changing jobs frequently; being financially negligent; overworking; going out after work with friends instead of coming home; embracing a hobby that is expensive and time-consuming; failing to help around the house or with the kids; and choosing how to spend the family's money. I know a woman whose husband came home one night with a new, fully loaded sports car, yet he flatly refused to let her buy so much as a new outfit without his permission.

Jesus shows men another way. He modeled holiness and then challenged and empowered his disciples to follow his example (Matthew 10). He made time to talk to marginalized people whom others would ignore (Matthew 19, Mark 5, Luke 10, John 4). Jesus prayed (a lot!), cared for the hungry and the sick, and laid down his life.

In contrast to the husband who insists on his own way and bullies, Jesus left heaven to come rescue us. He steadfastly went about his Father's business. He got up early in the morning and stayed up late at night to pray. He taught lessons of grace and truth, and he patiently explained himself again and again to disciples who just didn't understand who he really was. He endured public humiliation and scorn for our benefit, even enduring torture and death so we could have life.

Summary of Ephesians 4–6

Husbands who submit to their wives with sacrificial love, trust, and care exemplify what a head truly is. They give the world a picture "in the flesh" of Christ's love, trust, and care for the church, his bride. Wives who submit to their husbands and respect them exemplify what strong help truly is. They give the world a picture "in the flesh" of the church's submission and respect for Christ, her husband. And when a Christian marriage fails in submission, love, and respect, the "one flesh" of their marriage causes both partners to be weak and sick.

Peter gives yet another angle on this submission that wives must do as well as this loving and giving up that husbands must do. Let's turn to 1 Peter 3.

1 PETER 3: WIVES OF COURAGE, HUSBANDS OF UNDERSTANDING

> Likewise, wives, be subject to your own husbands, so that even if some do not obey the word, they may be won without a word by the conduct of their wives, when they see your respectful and pure conduct. Do not let your adorning be external—the braiding of hair and the putting on of gold jewelry, or the clothing you wear—but let your adorning be the hidden person of the heart with the imperishable beauty of a gentle and quiet spirit, which in God's sight is very precious. For this is how the holy women who hoped in God used to adorn themselves, by submitting to their own husbands, as Sarah obeyed Abraham, calling him lord. And you are her children, if you do good and do not fear anything that is frightening. (1 Peter 3:1–6, ESV)

This passage begins with the word "likewise," so we should look back at the first use of submission to get more understanding. Likewise connects the "why" of slaves submitting to masters in 1 Peter 2:18: in the fear of God. Each subsequent group "likewise" submits because of the fear of God.

Here are the uses of the Greek word for "likewise" or "in the same way" (*homoios*), which occurs three times in 1 Peter (1 Peter 3:1, 7; 5:5):

- Slaves **submit yourselves** to your masters in the fear of God (1 Peter 2:18).
- Wives *likewise* **submit yourselves** to your husbands (1 Peter 3:1).
- Husbands *likewise* treat your wives right (1 Peter 3:7).
- Young men *likewise* **submit yourselves** to your elders (1 Peter 5:5).

Peter, just like Paul, is telling wives *and* husbands (beginning in 3:7) to imitate Christ.

Why? Because we fear God.

How? They must be holy, speak the truth, not repay evil for evil, and not retaliate or make threats when mistreated. Instead, they should be "respectful and pure" (v. 2 for wives, and v. 7 for husbands) in their behavior. They should *entrust themselves* to God (sound familiar?) to make things right. He's calling out both sides to change the way they're acting.

Wives: Submit to Win

Peter's commands for women come right in the middle of a section on living godly lives in a pagan world. He helps them deal with their husbands' sins the way Christ dealt with their sins. You don't see Peter excusing their behavior—he doesn't deny that these guys could be unbelieving brutes (1 Peter 3:1, 6).

Yet Peter gives an unexpected course of action: act so much like Christ that you don't even need to use words or beauty to win over your unbelieving husband. Beauty and words can be powerful tools for women, but Peter points out that the most winsome thing about women should be their gentle and quiet spirits. And this is not new information. It has always been this way, he says, for Sarah, the wife of Abraham, did this exact thing. Like Jesus, she didn't let fear dictate her behavior but entrusted herself to "him who judges justly" (1 Peter 2:23).

Before we dive into this passage, let me give a disclaimer: I am not talking about emotional, physical, or sexual abuse or illegal behavior in this section; women should not stay in a home that is dangerous.

What kind of submitting did Sarah do? She respected Abraham in her actions (obeying him) and in her speech (calling him "lord"). This principle is repeated throughout Scripture. We aren't to say one thing and do another. The Bible's word for this duplicity is "hypocrisy." Jesus talks about hypocrisy in the Sermon on the Mount multiple times: when giving to the needy, when praying, when fasting, and when correcting others (Matthew 6:2, 5, 16; 7:5). You cannot be a hypocrite, Peter says. You speak and do what Christ expects of you.

If only Peter didn't use those difficult words, "obey" and "master," these instructions would seem so much more appealing. But let's stick with the words Peter uses and see what the Bible has to say for itself.

Obey. The word Peter uses is *hypakouo*, which means "really listening to the one giving the charge." Letting the Bible explain itself, let's explore where else *hypakouo* is used:

- It's what the wind and sea did when Jesus spoke (Matthew 8:27).
- It's what the spirits did when Jesus spoke (Mark 1:27).
- It's what Rhoda did when she answered a knock at the door (Acts 12:13).
- It's what children do for parents (Ephesians 6:1).
- It's what we do with Paul's instructions (2 Thessalonians 3:14).

Again, *hypakouo* suggests "attentively listening" and being "responsive."

Master. The word Peter uses here is *kurios*, meaning "master" or "lord." It's used hundreds of times in Scripture to refer to both the Lord and human masters. Dr. Oster's explanation for *kurios* from Chapter 10 teaches us that it's a term of respect, meaning something akin to "sir" in the Gospels but not in a fawning sense. Paul has already written that Christ is the head of man, man is the head of woman, and woman is the master of the home. Now Peter seems to be using "master" or "lord" as a shorthand for the order of headship.

What does Peter want us to learn from Sarah? I think it's this: Sarah trusted God, even when her husband didn't. Sarah treated Abraham as her head, even when he didn't deserve it, and she trusted God to judge justly, refusing to "fear anything that is frightening." Throughout Genesis, we see that God delivers her from danger and keeps his promise to her, allowing her to become mother to the promised son, Isaac (Genesis 21:1–5). As Wendy Alsup puts it,

> There is something very powerful about a calm reaction by a wife to a very serious problem in her husband. There is a response that does not rely on words but nevertheless influences others powerfully towards repentance and righteousness. Most of us don't really believe this—we don't grasp that God has methods that are much more powerful for change than the ones we normally use.[130]

Wives acknowledge husbands as head in their actions and in their speech. They speak to and about them with respect. They don't get a pass on obedience to Christ if their husbands act cowardly like Abraham (Genesis 12:11–13), make bad parenting choices like Isaac, Jacob, or King David (Genesis 25:28; 37:3; 2 Samuel 14:1–23), or are unbelieving, selfish boors like Nabal (1 Samuel 25:10–11). They don't ignore them (violating *hypakouo*) or write them off as idiots (violating *kurios*). Trusting God, they live in purity and reverence. Wives, this requires us to change the way we think, taking every thought captive in obedience to Christ (Romans 12:1–2; 2 Corinthians 10:3–5). Turn off the running commentary in your brain that says to ignore your husband when he's acting stupid.

And for those women (and men) reading this who have suffered losses so great that they will not see justice from our God in this life, in the very next chapter, Peter reminds them that everyone "will have to give account to him who is ready to judge the living and the dead" (1 Peter 4:5). I encourage you to "leave room for God's wrath, for it is written: 'It is mine to avenge; I will repay,' says the Lord" (Romans 12:19b). God keeps his promises.

---

130. Wendy Alsup, "Hard Words to Women from 1 Peter," *Practical Theology for Women*, January 25, 2010, www.theologyforwomen.org/2010/01/hard-words-to-women-from-i-peter.html (accessed October 19, 2022).

If you're a woman reading this and find it an impossibly high standard, don't despair. Peter gives husbands some difficult and lofty commands too, and if they don't obey, the warning is clear: their prayers will be hindered, and they, too, will have to answer to God for their conduct in marriage.

Husbands: Understand and Honor

> Husbands, in the same way be considerate as you live with your wives, and treat them with respect as the weaker partner and as heirs with you of the gracious gift of life, so that nothing will hinder your prayers. (1 Peter 3:7)

First of all, remember that "likewise" word which reminds wives *and* husbands to imitate Christ because we fear God. How? They must be holy, speak the truth, not repay evil for evil, and not retaliate or even make threats when mistreated. Instead, they should be "respectful and pure" (v. 2 for wives, and v. 7 for husbands) in their behavior. Instead, they should *entrust themselves* to God (sound familiar?) to make things right. Both husbands and wives should change the way they're acting.

Let's look at the words "understanding" and "honor," as well as the phrase "as the weaker vessel."

Understand. The word *gnosis*, which is translated as "understanding" here, is a word that simply means to know. Peter is telling husbands to know their wives. There are different ways to know something, and in Scripture we see two types of *gnosis* appear again and again: information and experience. Here are just three examples:

- *Information*: Paul considers knowing Christ of utmost value in his life; everything else is like garbage (Philippians 3:8).
- *Experience*: Paul wants the Ephesians to grasp how wide, and long, and high, and deep is the love of Christ and "to know this love that surpasses knowledge" (Ephesians 3:19a).
- *Information and Experience*: Paul prays that the Colossians will be filled with the knowledge of God's will and that they'll always be growing in the knowledge of God (Colossians 1:9–10).

Information + Experience = Understanding

In the last chapter, we saw how "Little House" series author Laura Ingalls Wilder wrote about how she and her husband tended their apple orchard, using information that, when put into practice, gave them great understanding and skill to care for the land.

Wilder and her husband had plenty of *information* about how to farm, although she admits that there were many things that could only be learned with *experience.* The Wilders personally tended every tree in their orchard. They prepared each hole "large and deep, making the dirt fine in the bottom." They handled the tree with gentleness "so as not to injure the roots." Most notably to me is that they "took individual care of each tree" so that when they mentioned a tree, one of hundreds, they could simply say, "that tree with the large branch to the south." Their *information,* put into practice with *experience,* brought a new depth and breadth to their *understanding of* farming.[131]

Likewise, Christian husbands "know" how to live with their wives when they read Scripture. They know that the gospel of Jesus Christ has the power to transform *all* of their relationships. They know God's order for creation: Christ as the head of man and man as the head of woman. Husbands know the instructions for conduct in marriage, like submission, love, and holiness.

But husbands should also know *their particular wives,* so that they can love them well. Knowing his wife's personality type, her strengths and weaknesses, her spiritual gifts, even her favorite foods and hobbies, are all ways for a husband to live with his wife "in an understanding way."

A husband *knowing* that he should be the Christlike, submissive, self-sacrificing, entrusting, sanctifying head of his wife and *being* that kind of husband are two different kinds of knowing. A wife *knowing* that she should be the respectful and submissive strong helper made in God's image and *being* that kind of respectful, submissive, strong helper are two different kinds of knowing. This is just like how reading a book about swimming and actually

131. Hines, ed., *Laura Ingalls Wilder Farm Journalist,* 20–21..

swimming are two different kinds of knowing. There's knowing and then there's *knowing*. Husbands, says Peter, know your wives.

Honor. Husbands should live with their wives in an understanding way, "showing *time* (honor) as with a weaker vessel." At first, this sounds contradictory to God's design of woman as strong help. Is woman a weaker vessel or is she a strong helper? As discussed in Chapter 10, the text is literally translated, "Husbands likewise dwelling with [them] according to knowledge as with a weaker vessel with the female rendering honor as also joint heirs . . ." Peter is asking husbands to live with their wives in a particular way, and he follows this instruction with the simile "as with a weaker vessel with the female" to help explain what he means.

The way you would handle a crystal vase is different than the way you would handle a wooden bowl. Women are like "crystal vases" among the "wooden bowls" of men in many ways. Despite what is promoted in our media today, the biological reality is that most wives are smaller and physically weaker than their husbands. Husbands must be physically respectful and gentle with them. Women's bodies are made to carry children in pregnancy and feed them in the first years of life. This makes them more physically vulnerable than men, who have a fleeting involvement in the process of creating new life. Wives who submit to and respect their husbands are voluntarily placing themselves in a position of vulnerability. Husbands must reciprocate with mutual submission, agape love, and honor, living with them in an understanding way.

Valuing. When husbands live with their wives in an understanding way, Peter says that at least part of that will entail honoring wives as co-heirs of Christ. The Greek word for honor (*time*) means a value, or money paid, and by analogy, esteem (of the highest degree), especially to someone with an office or rank. In Scripture, we see the forms of *time* meaning literal money, as well as honor of others. It's especially helpful to notice how this word "honor" is used again and again to call us to esteem others *regardless of rank*.

- The thirty pieces of silver that Judas received for betraying Jesus and the money that Ananias and Saphira received for selling their property were both called *timen* (Matthew 27:6, 9; Acts 5:2–3).

- The islanders of Malta honored (*timais*) Paul and his companions in many ways (Acts 28:10).
- Paul even uses both meanings in the same letter when he writes, "You were bought with a price [*times*]; do not become slaves of human beings" (1 Corinthians 7:23) and "Just as a body, though one, has many parts, but all its many parts form one body, so it is with Christ. . . those parts of the body that seem to be weaker are indispensable, and the parts that we think are less honorable we treat with special honor [*timen*]" (1 Corinthians 12:12, 22–23a).

As in the church, so it is in marriage: husbands are to treat their wives with honor because of their joint standing in Christ's salvation. Even if you think she doesn't deserve it, even if you don't feel affection toward her, even though you enjoy the responsibility of headship, Peter says husbands must honor their wives and treat them with gentleness and care.

Husbands, check your tone of voice. Use self-control with your physical presence. Be patient and careful like you would when you handle the crystal. And if you have a running commentary of scorn about your wife going through your head, change the way you think and take every thought captive in obedience to Christ (Romans 12:1–2; 2 Corinthians 10:3–5). As I've mentioned, if you don't do these things, God says your prayers will be hindered.

If this doesn't give you a shiver down your spine, men, perhaps you should consider how often and about what you are praying.

SO ARE YOU HEALTHY?

Here's a summary of what we've seen so far in these Scriptures: The image of God in husbands, described as a head, must look like Jesus as our head. The instructions to submit, sacrificially love, and, in a spirit of trust, make themselves vulnerable to their wives, honoring them as co-heirs of Christ, are good news for women (and men)!

The image of God in wives, described as a strong helper or ally, must also look like Jesus. The instructions to be the masters of their homes, submit because of a divine order called headship, and respect their husbands are good news for men (and women)!

I began this chapter by claiming that understanding and obeying what Scripture teaches about men and women is a second-tier issue critical to our spiritual health.

So how's your health?

To be truly healthy, we must believe and obey the gendered instructions for marriage found throughout Scripture. There is an order to the marriage relationship, and it's modeled on Christ and the church. When men and women fail to acknowledge this, we become sick and weakened in our ability to live abundantly in Christ.

I'm passionate about this because I've lived it all my life. Headship didn't curse me. It's the best thing that ever happened to me. It didn't stifle me. It helped me grow and become strong. It didn't limit me. It gave me the potential to do things I never could have done alone. Not only this, but it set the course of my marriage. Headship, strong help, and mutual submission make *both my husband and me* stronger.

This information is not just good news for a world full of hurting marriages. It's the best news around! Unfortunately, though, for too many people, these instructions are just that: words divorced from experience. The beauty of headship and gender intended in Genesis 1–3 is redeemed in Jesus Christ, if we'll only obey.

In John 14, our Lord gives us a clear barometer of our love and devotion to him: obedience. With the help of our advocate, the Holy Spirit, we can, indeed, keep his commands (John 14:15–16). And as Jesus told his disciples, "Now that you know these things, you will be blessed if you do them" (John 13:17).

In the next chapter, discipleship minister Michelle Eagle and I give advice on how leaders can implement soft complementarianism with eyes open to people's needs and ears open to people's perspectives.

12

ADVICE FROM COMPLEMENTARIAN WOMEN TO LOCAL CHURCHES

MICHELLE EAGLE, RENÉE WEBB SPROLES

"Change is at the heart of leadership because a leader's job is to take people from where they are to where they need to be. You can't do that without ushering in change."
—Carey Nieuwhof[132]

Renew.org upholds gender complementarity as God's good design for men and women. Indeed, it is beautifully described from the creation of male and female in the beginning pages of Genesis to Paul's letters, which explain marriage and the church.

In this chapter, we address the how-to's of practicing broad complementarianism in our churches, as found in Scripture. To move to an egalitarian position or remain entrenched in rigid traditionalism are both errors that dishonor God and hurt men and women. We must, with the help of the Holy Spirit, seek to align ourselves with what we find in Scripture for our good and God's glory. Often, this alignment involves change, and change can be difficult at best and divisive at worst, even when it is for our good.

Think about Moses and Aaron. They were liberating the people of Israel from slavery in Egypt, a change one would think should rank among the least

132. Carey Nieuwhof, "7 Signs Your Church Will Never Change," Church Job Finder, October 5, 2020, www.churchjobfinder.com/articles/7-signs-your-church-will-never-change (accessed September 30, 2022).

controversial across the greatest number of people. Yet once they began traversing the wilderness, the grumbling began. "If only we had died by the Lord's hand in Egypt! There we sat around pots of meat and ate all the food we wanted, but you have brought us out into this desert to starve this entire assembly to death," they complained to Moses (Exodus 16:3). Change—even liberating change—can be hard.

Likely, you have a church filled with strong-minded, educated, successful, faithful, Spirit-driven women. You want your church to empower such women to their fullest ability while remaining true to the norms of Scripture. Perhaps you are now asking the question, What does a healthy complementarian church look like in my context? Michelle Eagle, discipleship and women's minister at Harpeth Christian Church, and I give our perspectives on the practical working out of complementarian theology in the local church.

Q. What can male elders and senior ministers/pastors do to facilitate the full inclusion of women in the many roles that are available to them?

Sproles: Many leaders in churches who practice a rigid, traditionalist type of complementarianism are hesitant to bring up the issue of more fully involving women. They aren't up for the pushback from a noisy minority and think, *Maybe they won't notice that women have no visible part in our assemblies. Perhaps they won't notice that all the visible positions of influence are men. And, after all, our children's minister is a woman.*

I can guarantee you this is wrong-minded. We definitely notice the absence of women in visible positions, and our young men and women notice and mind even more than previous generations.

On the other hand, many leaders in churches that have practiced egalitarianism (or who hold egalitarian views) will be hesitant to restrict the role of elder and senior minister/pastor to men, regardless of whether Scripture teaches this. They think, *How in the world can I stop including women in these roles if we already have them there? Won't it seem regressive or oppressive? Does this teaching even still apply to the church today? A lot of women are leaders in the workplace: they are board members, CEOs, lawyers, judges, doctors, professors. Isn't it kind of embarrassing to restrict women, even in just a few ways, at church?*

I think many of us conflate the secular world and gospel community. When the Church of England was considering ordaining women as priests, C.S. Lewis made a thoughtful point about the difference between the two. In the secular world, men and women can and must be treated as unisex, as interchangeable citizens and workers, as a safeguard. However, that is a fiction we are allowed to shed when we return to the world of reality, God's world. There, we may resume our real identities as men and women.

> The innovators are really implying that sex is something superficial, irrelevant to the spiritual life. To say that men and women are equally eligible for a certain profession is to say that for the purposes of that profession their sex is irrelevant. We are, within that context, treating both as neuters.
>
> As the State grows more like a hive or an ant-hill it needs an increasing number of workers who can be treated as neuters. This may be inevitable for our secular life. But in our Christian life we must return to reality. There we are not homogeneous units, but different and complementary organs of a mystical body. . . And the kind of equality which implies that the equals are interchangeable (like counters or identical machines) is, among humans, a legal fiction. It may be a useful legal fiction. But in church we turn our back on fictions. One of the ends for which sex was created was to symbolize to us the hidden things of God. One of the functions of human marriage is to express the nature of the union between Christ and the Church. We have no authority to take the living and sensitive figures which God has painted on the canvas of our nature and shift them about as if they were mere geometrical figures.
>
> This is what common sense will call "mystical." Exactly. The Church claims to be the bearer of a revelation. If that claim is false then we want not to make priestesses but to abolish priests. If it is true, then

> we should expect to find in the Church an element which unbelievers will call irrational and which believers will call supra-rational.[133]

Sam Allberry, in an interview with Rosaria Butterfield and Jackie Hill Perry, noted a similar distinction between the secular world and the church.

> If you take the framework of submission and leadership out of the Gospel, out of the example of Christ, it is ugly. Because, I think fallen minds cannot be trusted with that subject. It is because we see this in the life of Christ himself, we are able to see it in a wholesome, healthy way. We can use these things to bless the other person. The husband is loving his wife the way that Christ loved the church, and I think it's uniquely beautiful within a Gospel-shaped context. I don't think it can be beautiful apart from that.[134]

Eagle: If your church follows the biblical standard of complementarianism, meaning men and women are equally loved and valued in the eyes of God but have separate and distinct roles in the church body and in the family, but you never talk about your position or why, you will face a different kind of problem. You will eventually be "found out" by women who assume men simply want to keep the positions of leadership within your church. Instead of giving women and men the chance to listen and investigate the biblical doctrines you strive to uphold, you will give them the legitimacy to assume that what the world believes about the conservative Christian church is true: it's a good ole boys club or worse, anti-woman.

Q. How did you two get here in the first place, with so many churches embracing egalitarian doctrine while others remain entrenched in rigid traditionalism?

---

133. C.S. Lewis, "Priestesses in the Church," in *God in the Dock: Essays on Theology and Ethics by C.S. Lewis*, ed. Walter Hooper (Grand Rapids: Eerdmans, 1970). An online version of this essay can be found at www.files.allsaintsaustin.org/files/Lewis-Priestesses_In_The_Church.pdf (accessed October 19, 2022).

134. Sam Allberry, Jackie Hill Perry, and Rosaria Butterfield, "How to Depict the Beauty of Complementarity," YouTube, www.youtube.com/watch?v=15IS87Ad3HE (accessed October 19, 2022).

Eagle: I believe many women have had an identity crisis in recent decades. I know that I did. For as long as I can remember, I was told by the world and my parents that I could do and be anything. I went to college and began practicing medicine as a physician assistant. I competently treated patients and led an office staff. I was active in church and was asked to be an elder. During this time, my husband was not a spiritual head for me. Because I had witnessed similar dynamics growing up, I took on the role of leader within my home with ease and confidence. My professional, personal, and childhood experience all reinforced the idea that a woman and a man are equal in every respect and, as such, are equally qualified in all areas of life. Why would this not also apply to my roles in the church? My identity was in what I could do, not in who God said I was.

I turned to Galatians 3:28, which is actually talking about equality in Christ, and applied it to all roles in marriage and the church just as I did in the workplace.[135] Men and women weren't just equal in my mind, we were interchangeable based on our talents and gifts.

My perspective was that if the church limited the roles I could fill, then obviously they doubted my abilities and must be against me. This worldview had been shaped from childhood and reinforced by what the world told me was true.

I believed that Christians needed to be countercultural in so many areas, but I couldn't apply it to gender roles. The idea that I could do anything better than a man was deeply embedded in my soul. It was also evident in my world: many of the men around me were not living examples of sacrificial spiritual leaders; many women in my life had been deeply wounded by the men who were supposed to love and care for them. Raising a young woman to be independent and self-sufficient (as a stopgap against the deficiencies of men) was a no-brainer, especially since I believed that there was no role I could not fill and probably do a better job than a man.

135. The context of Galatians 3:28 makes it abundantly clear that men and women are equal in Christ: they are equally justified by faith (v. 24), equally free from the bondage of legalism (v. 25), equally children of God (v. 26), equally clothed with Christ (v. 27), equally possessed by Christ (v. 29), and equally heirs of the promises to Abraham (v. 29). But Galatians 3:27–29 does not address gender roles or the doctrine of headship.

Sproles: By my thirties and early forties, I also believed I was egalitarian. For all my life, I lived in two different worlds. The culture at my church, my Christian elementary school, and my Christian university, was what I would now describe as rigid complementarianism or traditionalism. I never saw a single woman pray, read Scripture, or even speak in gatherings where men were present. Only male teachers and boys could participate up front in chapel at school, and a female teacher couldn't pray aloud in the classroom if boys were present.

My family life, however, was very different. A high-functioning team, my mom and dad started their own business out of our garage while raising three kids. My grandparents lived behind us on their farm, and they too relied on each other's strengths and complemented one another in ways that helped them thrive.

At twenty-one, I married a man who loves me to this day with a self-sacrificial fierceness and loyalty that is hard to describe. He too has ministered to me with words of affirmation, prayers of blessing, and attentiveness to my needs and the needs of our two children. Our mutual submission, respect, and love make us a high-functioning team.

The dissonance between my church life and home life grew as I entered my late twenties. *Why does my church believe women can't pray when 1 Corinthians 11 clearly indicates that they were, and Paul did not forbid them to continue? Why are men the only ones baptizing people? Why are female teachers relegated to the children's ministry?* I was loved and empowered at home but felt insulted at church. Without looking more closely at what Scripture had to say about this, I simply declared that if that was complementarianism, I wasn't that. The only other option in my mind was to become egalitarian.

Q. What changed for each of you?

Eagle: Well, I matured spiritually, and as my husband matured as well, I became increasingly aware that the way my beliefs played out in my marriage and church were not in line with God's best. This created confusion and uncertainty. I wondered, *Does God really think I'm less than my* *husband? Does he think that I can't teach or lead the church as well as my male counterparts?*

I was putting this challenging question in a different category than some of the other countercultural questions I was wrestling with, like forgiveness, turning the other cheek, having the light of Jesus' hope in a dark world, or loving my enemy.

The issue of gender got to the root of who I was, and I believed that equality in gender meant men and women were interchangeable. It took a long time to tease apart the fact that while women are made in God's image and equally loved by him, the genders are designed for different roles. I had confused my roles with my identity. I saw some of the roles of women as being less than that of a man instead of just being different: power equated to value.

As my husband grew in his spiritual formation, we changed churches. God was renovating my marriage and emphatically telling me to let my husband be my head. This was extremely uncomfortable, and I am so grateful that I was discipled by a woman who was divorced and understood firsthand what it looked like to lose a marriage. She coached me in real time, showing me how to handle situations in a God-honoring way instead of a worldly way. She taught me to hold my sharp tongue and to approach conversations with respect, instead of taking an adversarial stance.

Sproles: When I came on staff at North Boulevard, I began to have some conversations on gender with our senior minister, David Young. Taking my frustrations seriously, he encouraged me to dig into Scripture and see what I found there. He engaged me in several conversations about what I was learning. At about the same time, I was reading *The Reason for God* by Tim Keller and came across this passage that changed how I was approaching the topic of gender.

> Now, what happens if you eliminate anything from the Bible that offends your sensibility and crosses your will? If you pick and choose what you want to believe and reject the rest, how will you ever have a God who can contradict you? . . . Only if your God can say things that outrage you and make you struggle (as in real friendship or

> marriage!) will you know that you have gotten hold of a real God and not a figment of your imagination. So an authoritative Bible is not the enemy of a personal relationship with God. It is the precondition for it.[136]

I needed to look again at the texts that talked about gender in marriage and church and let them offend me. (And they did, at first!) However, what I eventually discovered was that I wasn't egalitarian, after all. I was using the word *egalitarian* in response to the heavy-handed complementarianism in my church and schools. Scripture portrayed a beautiful, broad complementarianism that was empowering and valuable for men and women.

Q. Tell us about your experiences working as paid staff at your church. How does a complementarian theology play out in that environment?

Eagle: I joined the staff at Harpeth Christian Church as an administrative assistant to the home group minister. It was a ten-hour-a-week position making $10 per hour. This pastor was a respectful minister, but he didn't know my past job experience very well. As I worked for him, God taught me how to be humble and how to submit to male leadership. I was frustrated, and God met me in my frustration. He put people in my path who reminded me to bloom where I was planted instead of constantly moving on and being dissatisfied.

That minister moved on and our lead pastor, Bobby Harrington, filled in for the position of home group minister. This required me to increase my hours as well as my responsibility. I became part of the team. We had conversations about how best to move this ministry forward, and I was asked to implement those directives. Eventually another home group minister was hired, and on one occasion, this minister was very disrespectful to me. Bobby found out about it, and it was not tolerated. He called me to get details from my side and, as he did, he apologized for not protecting me and said that no man on staff will treat another person, especially a woman, that way. He viewed his role as lead pastor and leader of the staff as protector. He

136. Tim Keller, *The Reason for God: Belief in an Age of Skepticism* (New York: Riverhead Books, Penguin Group, 2008), 118.

wasn't looking at it from a human resources perspective, but from the biblical call to headship.

As I worked with other ministers on staff and had more interactions with men in the church, it became evident that they respected and loved how God had designed women differently from men. We are to complement one another, not compete, and I felt that tangibly while on staff. My opinions and experiences were heard and valued. We didn't always agree, and the decisions didn't always go my way, but I knew that I had not just been dismissed.

Sproles: After David Young and I began to have more and more conversations about gender and the church, he became more intentional in engaging the women on staff at our weekly meetings and other team settings. When you come from a long tradition of rigid complementarianism, this is no small thing. Women were invited to pray or read Scripture alongside men in meetings, and we were always viewed as valuable members of the staff. Our voices and opinions were heard and respected. This was an excellent step in embracing the freedoms of complementarity we find in Scripture.

Q. How can a culture of complementarity be cultivated in churches today?

Eagle: The best way to cultivate this is through discipleship. Women need to disciple women in what it really looks like to follow Jesus in a world that wants to define our worth very differently than God does. If you are a lead pastor or a discipleship minister, you must have a strong program that actively disciples women, not just puts on conferences or does women's Bible studies. Those are great and need to happen but, just like men, women need to be in each other's lives, guiding and shaping each other to conform to God's truths instead of passively allowing the world to mold how we see our identity. We need women in our lives who are not afraid to tell us when we misstep and give us examples of our mistakes. We need to hear that male leadership will not always be perfect; and yet, we must respect them.

Women coming from different backgrounds will react differently to male leadership, so I suggest that you match young, strong, women with women who will understand the struggle. If I had been discipled by a woman who had a strong, godly father and a husband who led their family as God directed him, I would not have related at all. Most of those women will not struggle with male leadership. Let God lead the matching of women to disciple makers who will understand and be able to guide them from personal experience.

Sproles: Yes. I had such a different experience from you, Michelle, in terms of discipleship and headship in the church (rigid) and home (healthy). Churches of Christ are traditionally so different from the egalitarian church experience of your early marriage. Many of our women are so used to male-dominated church settings that they don't question it. It's just the way it is. They don't see themselves as the strong help God made them to be, and therefore are hesitant to speak up and offer their perspectives. Some are even afraid to pray aloud around other women, much less other men, even their husbands! Because of these experiences that women in our churches have had, we need intentional woman-to-woman discipleship that will spur them to embrace their role as "strong help."

In addition, many men feel unequipped or inadequate in their role as the sacrificial, loving head of their wives. In the parenting class that my husband and I have co-taught for almost twenty years, we've reached a tipping point: a majority of our young moms and dads now come from divorced or dysfunctional homes. They know they want to be different from the example of their parents, yet they are afraid they'll repeat the same failures in their role as head and strong help. Asserting sacrificial authority scares and confuses the men, because they haven't experienced the headship they want to live out for their family's good and out of obedience to God. They, too, need discipleship in this area.

Eagle: So you must develop a team of male and female disciple makers. That means you will have to put time and resources into developing women leaders, just as you do for the men on your team. Do not assume that if you send the men on your staff to a discipleship conference, they will gather and bring back the information to the women disciple makers. Training is necessary for the women on your team, whether they are paid staff or volunteers. Do not leave discipleship up to chance in the female population of your church. If you do, you will reap what you sow.

If your church is like most in the U.S., ours included, women are the ones who will bring their families to church. They will do the web searches, talk to their friends, and suggest which church to try when the family is church shopping. Many are the spiritual heads of their families. While that is not ideal, we are grateful for whatever circumstances bring a family through our church doors. We are teaching them truth on Sunday mornings and in our home groups, and hopefully the husbands and fathers are discovering their role as leaders of their families. Do not expect the women to just step down gracefully. They must be discipled to understand and be equipped to allow their husbands to step into godly male leadership. In most women's minds, they have been leading spiritually, and it has been going fine. So why should she trust this role reversal?

Disciple men specifically in their role as servant leaders. Teach them how to honor their wives and daughters in practical ways that uphold Scripture's teachings on love. Men must have other men in their lives who are living this out and are willing to call it out in them. Examples must be shared over coffee as well as from the stage. And the best place to showcase the appropriate, God-honoring roles of men and women is in the home. The world is discipling our men to be passive and telling them that in remaining passive, they are best serving their families. This is a lie that men must call out in other men through discipling relationships.

Q. What can lead ministers/pastors and elders do to create an environment where women are honored, maximizing their talents and spiritual gifts?

Here's a list of steps to take if you are serious about creating an environment that empowers women to maximize their talents and spiritual gifts in the context of the church:

1. Respect women
2. Protect women
3. Actively seek women out for ministry
4. Showcase women
5. Support women

6. Encourage teamwork
7. Bring diversity on stage

#1 - RESPECT WOMEN

Eagle: Show respect to the women in your church, on your staff, and those serving as key volunteers. Women need to feel loved. We need to know that we are valued. There are ways to subtly do this that most women will not miss. It may seem trivial to a man, but a woman will pick up on nuances that will help her understand the lead pastor values women.

In sermons, mention your wife helping in the sermon prep or getting her opinion about important topics. Speak often about how amazing your wife is in ways that are unexpected. I remember Bobby talking about how his wife was such a wonderful example to their kids because they knew that when they woke up early, they'd always catch her at the kitchen table starting her day off in the Word. He said how much he respected her commitment to start every day that way and how grateful he was that his kids had that example. From that small story in a sermon, I knew that Bobby respected and valued his wife and her spiritual contribution to their family.

Give sermon illustrations that involve strong, independent women leading in biblically appropriate areas and not just children's ministry. Make it a goal to show what God deems appropriate, instead of what he doesn't. We have a husband-wife team that leads our community service outreach. Most of the correspondence and stage time are shared between the husband and wife. She is competent and passionate about this ministry, and it is obvious they are partners in leading it.

Sproles: I wholeheartedly agree. One of the consequences of rigid complementarianism is that many men, consciously or unconsciously, don't value the input of intelligent, competent, strong women in their marriage or in the church. I honestly think that usually this is not malicious; it's just what happens after years of misapplying Scripture and living it out wrongly. Repentance involves respect for women in actions and in speech. Through announcements, sermons, articles in a newsletter, and live or video interviews with women, let the church know the valuable contributions women have made. Leaders should speak to and about their spouses and other women with respect, modeling healthy complementarianism.

As I mentioned, my husband and I co-teach a marriage and family class on Sunday mornings. We have been interviewed during the Sunday morning service, showing the congregation that our church values healthy marriages and seeks out male and female perspectives on such important matters.

#2 - PROTECT WOMEN

Eagle: Lead ministers/pastors and elders must get involved in marriages that are messy. I have heard from many women that they did not feel protected or supported when they went to church leadership when their marriages were falling apart, especially when their husband had an addiction or was unfaithful. Thankfully, this is completely foreign to me in my experience in our complementarian church. I have seen our leadership surround couples and hold men accountable for their actions. I have seen church discipline centered on Matthew 18 save marriages and allow women the confidence to submit to male leadership that was not their spouse when necessary.

While this can be abused by some women, err on the side of protecting the woman and being the tough love that many men need. Do not allow women to feel alone or unsafe to come to leadership when they are in difficult situations in their marriages. I have had several women come to me with marital problems, and I have never hesitated to go to our leadership for help. I know that these men will drop everything to intervene and protect a wife and children when the situation necessitates it, and that they will stay involved. We have systems in place to do this. We have a very active Celebrate Recovery program, as well as counselors and money dedicated to helping families navigate difficult times. No woman should feel alone or abandoned by her church leadership.

#3 - ACTIVELY SEEK OUT WOMEN

Eagle: Look for ways to include women in decision-making processes. I'm not an advocate for committees and bogging down the system with lots of meetings, but you should know the skills and resources you have in your church. Here's an example: Women will be less likely than a man to tell you they are a mortgage broker. Typically, you aren't as likely when you first meet a woman to ask about their occupation. But if your church is looking to refinance, see if there are any women brokers. Or, when it is time to put that addition on the church, include women on the team who have the experience you are looking for. A woman may be a stay-at-home mom now, but she could have been a structural engineer before she had kids and decided to stay home.

When you are evaluating new ministries to include in your church, look for women who are passionate about them. I guarantee that there are confident female leaders in your church who are leading somewhere. You might as well use them to move the agenda of your church forward. These women will put their energies into advocacy groups, homeschool tutorial boards, parent-teacher organizations at school, community service organizations, and other places that are not your church unless you actively recruit them for ministries that align with the vision of your church.

If your eldership is wrestling with a topic, look for a woman's voice to weigh in. Do not be afraid to seek out a female perspective. If you are a church leader, you should not use the excuse of male leadership to ignore the wealth of knowledge and experience the women in your church have.

Sproles: It is critical to remember that every woman, because she's a part of the body of Christ, has a role to play in the church's work and the spread of the gospel.

The broad participation of women in the body of Christ is so important. Women might serve on or lead the finance committee, sermon team, adult teaching ministry, or inner-city ministry. You get the idea. We need to allow women to participate in a myriad of ways in the church and stop relegating them to children's ministry. This isn't diminishing the work of children's ministry; it is vitally important! However, we should remember that all of Jesus' followers, men and women, are commanded to make disciples, baptizing and teaching them. We must encourage one another, instruct one another, and help one another grow into maturity, and this means women should be active participants in the life of the church.

#4 - SHOWCASE WOMEN LEADERS

Eagle: When your church stands for complementarianism, you will not have a problem showcasing male leadership. It will be obvious as soon as anyone looks at the website and views an entire male board of elders and male teaching ministers/pastors. What won't be obvious is the positive influence women have in your church, especially in non-traditional women's roles.

Do not back away from highlighting the women who are making a difference in your church and in the community. Use examples of women in the Bible, as well as in the local, national, and international community in your sermons as illustrations. You will not lose respect from men by doing this, but you will gain so much from the women in your sphere of influence. In preparing their sermons, many ministers/pastors often think about how their words will land with the young people in the audience. But they may not think about how they can do this to reach at least 50 percent of their audience by highlighting women—and not just in their roles as moms.

#5 - BE THE EXAMPLE

Eagle: Involve men in supportive roles. When a woman sees a man who is involved in children's ministry or serving in an area normally dominated by women, it gives her hope for male leadership. It shows a humility that says, "I'm so at ease in my role as a male leader, I can serve at the potluck (or I can teach the kindergarteners or hold babies in the nursery) just as comfortably as I can serve as an elder." It sounds counterintuitive, but seeing a man serving in a role generally reserved for women encourages male servant leadership. It shows men what it looks like to support and empower their wives and daughters. No job is greater than another, and nothing is off the table when it comes to serving one another. It doesn't lower our respect or give the appearance that a woman is running over her husband; rather, it honors the wife. As lead pastor or other men in leadership roles, serve at the potluck alongside your wives. Take a turn in children's ministry, and then talk about it from the stage.

#6 - SERVE AS A TEAM

Eagle: As I mentioned, I am a full-time staff member as one of our discipleship and women's ministers, and my husband is an elder in our church. Separating the staff and elder's wife role can be challenging, but we had very healthy conversations with Bobby, our lead pastor, prior to my husband becoming an elder. There are things that, as a staff member, I take to our executive minister or Bobby to take to the elders, instead of going directly to my husband. As an elder, my husband has to keep certain issues confidential. But besides those rare scenarios, we do much ministry together. We meet with couples; we bounce disciple making plans off one another and lean into each other's strengths.

We also share this process with other people. My husband wants me to succeed in my ministry efforts, and I want to support his. I do not hesitate to ask him when I need tech support for an online women's event, but I also let the women know he is doing that. I want them to appreciate the way he supports my ministry efforts from behind the scenes. If I have a discipleship training, he is usually there as a participant but also as a support for my role. He wants to show the men in the audience that he loves me well by helping me in my ministerial responsibilities. When I teach, I share stories that showcase the men in my life who love me well. I intentionally share that the elders are excited about a women's event or that Bobby is concerned about a specific issue of particular importance to women.

When an elder's wife's responsibility comes up, or my husband is teaching a class, I try to be supportive in whatever way possible. We are transparent with those around us about our struggles and our victories. When we meet with couples, we admit that we don't get it right all the time, and we make a point of sharing the positive ways our spouse loves us well. Because leadership needs to be an example of the church at its best, find ways to involve your wife in the church that showcase how you work as a team. Show off each other's strengths. This will provide both men and women with examples that are countercultural but biblical.

Sproles: My husband and I taught a parenting class with two other married couples for almost twenty years. This not only blessed us personally but it was also the training ground for serving together in ministry. A few years ago, our elders asked us to begin a Sunday morning class for families, so now we teach people in all stages of life, not just those raising children. This ministry is encouraged by the leadership. I know of other husbands and wives who have served in the children's ministry together or who are devoted to missions, serving on the committee, hosting missionaries, and traveling together to see how the ministry is going firsthand. Leveraging the strengths of men and women in teamwork blesses not only the men and women working together but also the body of Christ as a whole.

#7 - ON-STAGE DIVERSITY

Eagle: Give women stage time and video time. If there is a Scripture reading, prayer, devotional, or announcements, share the stage with women. Go out of your way to look for women to serve in this way, and include a variety of ages. As their kids get older, many women lose their sense of purpose; let young women, more seasoned women, and everyone in between participate in the Sunday morning service to show diversity on your stage. This may seem subtle to you, but it will not go unnoticed by women.

Recently at church, we showed a video that I did based on a blog I'd written for Renew.org about the book of Jeremiah. I got wonderful feedback from men and women. Another recent video we showed was a Priscilla Shirer clip. Lead pastors need to insist that there is a woman's voice regularly featured from the stage, whether live or on video. This needs to be an intentional process, and it's one that a complementarian church will have to work at—but it will be worth the effort.

Sproles: I spoke to one minister who helped transition a rigidly complementarian church to a healthier version of complementarianism. The elders did a study, which they eventually presented to the church in summary form. They also offered a more comprehensive packet of materials to their members for those who wanted the detailed theological arguments. Finally, the senior minister preached two or three sermons on the topic. Their principle goal was to get women more involved as the rule rather than the exception, citing the long-term best interests of the entire congregation. They didn't want any surprises that would disrupt the unity of the church, so they committed to limiting the changes to what was publicly discussed, returning to the topic if they broadened their scope for female participation.

All these steps were helpful, but we all know that change can still be very hard, even with prayerful consideration and much study. So the leadership of the church took pains to implement visible changes slowly. One practical step in this process was to move the Scripture reading and prayers via microphones to the back of the auditorium on Sunday mornings. In this way, men and women could read Scripture and pray and were heard, not seen. Eventually, both men and women moved to the front of the auditorium, and the transition was well-received. Using video testimonies of women or conducting interviews with women during the assemblies was another gentle way to help the congregation align practice with their theology. Small groups were also encouraged to use both men and women in teaching and prayer.

I appreciate this church's courage to do the hard thing and obey God's teaching on men and women where they had previously been in error. Many times (and maybe more times than not!), obedience precedes understanding. So it is the responsibility and privilege of godly leadership to help us get there.

Eagle: Complementarity is God's best for the church. In our society (both within the church and in our families), it is an uphill battle worth fighting.

Our men need to be taught servant leadership, and our women need to understand and submit to the roles that God has empowered us to fill. The leadership of our churches needs to encourage headship and strong help in families, constantly seeking examples of how this plays out in ways that bless men and women. As male leaders of churches, you have the position given by God to make a difference and initiate change. Do not back down from it just because we (the strong women in your church body) start to put up a fight. When we see that you are fighting for us and not against us, and that you are protecting and serving, then we will understand that God is honored by complementarianism and that we are at our best when we work with it instead of against it.

Sproles: I also encourage leaders in rigidly complementarian churches to not back down just because your church is overreaching in its application of 1 Timothy 2 or 1 Corinthians 14. Please repent of the church's past mistakes and teach us the beautiful complementarity we find in Scripture. Then, help us live that way. When we see you are for us and not against us, we will trust your leadership and know your love for God's Word and concern for each of us in the body of Christ.

Good leaders facilitate change and point people to God while doing it. Moses and Aaron told Israel:

> "In the evening you will know that it was the LORD who brought you out of Egypt, and in the morning you will see the glory of the LORD, because he has heard your grumbling against him. Who are we, that you should grumble against us?" . . . While Aaron was speaking to the whole Israelite community, they looked toward the desert, and there was the glory of the LORD, appearing in the cloud. (Exodus 16:6–10)

Scripture upholds a beautiful standard of complementarity for men and women. God is glorified when we get this right. The church, as the bride of Christ, must wrestle with these truths and live them out in ways that include both women and men as revealed in Scripture. In a culture that insists equality means sameness and in religious traditions that silence the voices of women, we can do better. Leaders can make the changes necessary for the benefit of women (and men!) and for the glory of God.

In the next chapter, we'll see an example of one church that implemented these types of changes for the benefit of both men and women.

13

GENDER ROLES: ONE CHURCH'S REAL-WORLD FIGHT

JARED ELLIS

It's one thing to talk about complementarianism and egalitarianism in terms of a theological debate. But what does it look like to see these theological positions engage each other in the local church? More specifically—what does it look like for a church that has been more or less egalitarian transition to a more complementarian framework? That's the story told here by Jared Ellis, preaching minister at Fellowship Regional in Iola, Kansas.

Blinding lights swing and sway across a massive Vegas venue. Deafening stadium anthems play at eardrum-bursting decibels. The bass is not heard as much as it is felt, rattling your lungs. Suddenly the lights and music are cut. Tangible darkness overtakes you. In those brief seconds, the thousands of people in attendance roar with eager anticipation.

Suddenly a single spotlight illuminates a dapperly dressed figure centrally located in the center of a chain-link octagon. His sequined suit coat reflects a myriad of tiny lights that dance in the darkness like a murmur of perfectly orchestrated lightning bugs. Faithful fight fans know the silhouette by his expertly quaffed hair and showman swagger. In this moment, the Veteran Voice of the Octagon—UFC announcer Bruce Buffer—speaks into the microphone, his voice booming through the speakers. It is only two words, but these two words send the crowd into a frenzy. Those who know the familiar introduction join in with him, shouting it out in unison, "It's time!"

These two words are like a starting pistol. They carry in their wake a host of unexpected events and semi-controlled chaos. "It's time" signals the start of several wars. From this point forward, anything can happen. This is only the beginning. These words are the preface to carnage, mayhem, and stitches.

Many of the same thoughts, emotions, and reactions are conjured when the words "gender roles" are uttered.

BUILDING BETTER MEN

For many reasons, the words "gender roles" are rife with angst and controversy, and they often trigger a barrage of combative emotions. Even now, you may have the urge to back into your own corner on the issue or begin to bounce on your toes and dance about while cracking your neck and knuckles in preparation for a fight. If so, then you may be disappointed in where we go from here.

This article is not a scholarly report. It does not read like a business white paper, a persuasive speech, or a "Complementarian's Guide to Success." This is simply our church's story.

On January 19, 2020, for Sanctity of Life Sunday, I shared this statistic as I closed in on the final point of my sermon: "Over 90 percent of the women seeking abortions reported that they were heterosexual."[137] I used this bizarre statement to establish the fact that abortion is a *man problem.* More specifically, it is a *weak* man's problem. It was a heavy morning for us all.

As the sermon concluded, I asked for every man to step out of his seat, surround the rest of the congregation, and hold hands. We confessed our own sins and the sins of our nation. We apologized to our wives and kids for being lazy and self-centered. We renewed our commitment to be what God wanted us to be—leaders, protectors, and teachers. We invited the Holy Spirit in to heal our hearts and bodies of bitterness and abuse. There was weeping from men and women alike. Confessions of abortions, remorse for

---

137. Jenna Jerman, Rachel K. Jones, and Tsuyoshi Onda, "Characteristics of U.S. Abortion Patients in 2014 and Changes Since 2008," Guttmacher Institute, www.guttmacher.org/report/characteristics-us-abortion-patients-2014 (accessed October 14, 2022).

failed relationships, prayers for prodigal sons and daughters, and conviction to step up and lead all made appearances that week.

Yet the most memorable moment of that service happened after the closing prayer.

I stood at one of the exits and shook hands with folks as they left, and through quivering lips and cheeks smeared with eyeliner and mascara, nearly every woman said the same two words: "Thank you." In the words of U2 front man, Bono, "Some days are better than others." This was one of those days.

Within a couple of months, the landscape of the church completely changed. Like most places in spring 2020, we became an online church due to the pandemic. During this time, we—the elders and staff—observed and prayed for our church, community, state, and nation, trying to make sense of it all. Two things became very apparent to us:

1. There were many weak men in decision-making positions, both locally and nationally.
2. We needed to build better men.

We had no way of addressing the first, but we could do something about building better men.

For this season, we decided that every sermon would be geared toward men. On Sundays, we ran a livestream, but it was stripped down to nothing more than a devotional thought with a discussion guide uploaded to our webpage. Our goal was to put men in a teaching position within their homes. We strongly suggested that our men lead their families through the Scriptures and the discussion guide. Some never did it. There were those who did, but only sporadically.

However, others did it religiously. We were building better men. We heard from many wives how this was such a blessing and how pleased they were at their husbands' newfound spiritual fervor. Even the men began to check each other: "Did you do your questions this week?" one would ask. "No, I didn't," the other would respond. Then the gouging would start: "Fella, get it done!"

After months of preaching specifically to men, what's happened in our church has been remarkable and unexpected. But let me take you back to the beginning.

REVISITING GOD'S WORD

Our church did not start off as a Christian Church (within the "Restoration Movement," the movement of which I'm a part). It was originally a "nondenominational" church. However, the founding pastor was partially supported by his denomination. After five or six years, the pastor at the time decided that, for the ministry to remain fresh, he would begin transitioning out and handing over the leadership of the church to younger guys. He homed in on me and my lifelong friend, another Christian Church guy named Luke Bycroft.

So, this was not the stereotypical denominational pastor or church. Nonetheless, we anticipated many theological wrinkles that would need to be ironed out. Surprisingly, those happened quickly. Within two years, Luke and I were both on staff and the man who had planted, nurtured, and tended this church began helping us establish our new roles for when he would be gone.

Pragmatically, when the church began, the pastor surrounded himself with a team of people made up of five husband-wife couples. They were a wonderful support to him and the ministry, but Luke and I struggled with the fact that the men on the leadership team, though completely qualified, were not elders as we understood the term. Additionally, their wives served beside them in the same role. This was completely foreign to us.

Suddenly we found ourselves in quite a predicament.

This was our thought process: First, what they were doing was working. Second, our church history and education had informed our understanding of the various gender roles within the church, but this wasn't the only model out there. Third, like many ministers across the world, we had experienced the hypocrisy, politics, and power moves within our preferred model of church structure and leadership. We were tempted to say, "If it ain't broke . . . ."

Ministry moments like these should always force us back to God's Word.

Even as I type that, it sounds blatantly obvious. Unfortunately, often we take the path of least resistance, or the path that keeps us employed, or the path that looks progressive, or the path that *feels* right or helps us make friends. We expressed all of this to the lead pastor and told him that, more than anything, we just wanted God to bless this ministry and that at the end of the day, whenever we have the ability to bring our friend, spouse, business, or church into obedient alignment with the Bible, we should do it.

At the next leadership team meeting, he opened the meeting by saying, "As I begin to transition out, there will be some things that will change, as we've talked about before." Turning to me, he said, "Jared, go ahead and let the team know what we've been talking about." I don't know if you've ever been punched in the kidney before, but there are certain sensations that go with the punch. I was feeling them all. To be clear, it wasn't as if he threw me to the wolves. There was no ill intent. He was doing exactly what he said he was going to do: transition out and transition us in.

So I simply expressed the same thoughts to the team that I had expressed to him. As I spoke, I felt completely inside out, humble, and probably a little scared: "I really just want God to bless this ministry, and I believe that he will if we are obedient. After wrestling with the Scriptures, we think for us, it's going to be important for the women to step out and the men to step up." One lady spoke up. "I agree. That is what the Bible says," she said. Another woman began nodding her head in agreement. Then one of them asked, "Do we need to leave now, or after the meeting?" I was floored.

From that point forward, the leadership team transitioned to a team of men we call elders.

God blessed us as leaders with a spirit of peace and unity, but there was something about this decision that began to change the culture of our church as well. We announced to the church that the structure of the church had changed a bit, and we introduced the men to the congregation as elders. We explained that when a big decision, disagreement, or complaint arises, the staff defers to these men as the elders of the church.

SHIFTS IN THE CHURCH CULTURE

I could go on for paragraphs about each of the men, but instead, let me tell you the impact they as a team have had on the culture of our church. Because they took seriously the challenge to "step up," they have held that standard for the rest of the men. They have preached, led parenting and marriage classes, led small groups, and frequently taught children's church. Above all that, they are loving husbands to their wives, and their expectation is that other men will follow them as they follow Christ.

Another cultural shift happened a few years later. As we began to grow and try to cover all the bases, the elders sat down with the staff and helped us define our job descriptions. I remember mine clearly: "Jared, you preach. If you want to do some marriage counseling for couples in need, feel free. But the focus for you needs to be preaching. Show up on Sunday and preach your heart out. You lead us from there. When you are done, you do whatever keeps you healthy until it's time for you to preach again, then preach your heart out." Their decision to prioritize scriptural preaching and emphasize the need to keep ourselves healthy had a natural trickle down.

We want to continue this focus, especially as we get more focused on disciple making. We now have clear staff values, a clear purpose, and a healthy church, and our congregation has come to desire and expect the same things. A phrase I've heard repeated by one of our elders is, "We would rather be a mile deep than fifteen miles wide and a dime thick." As a church, we desire health and depth. This pursuit means we have had to make some hard decisions. Another phrase we often say is, "We do hard things." We don't do hard things because they are popular, or because we are tough guys. We do them because we want God to bless our church and our efforts. He has.

Among evangelical churches across the U.S., men occupy roughly 35 to 45 percent of the sanctuary seats on Sunday mornings. This isn't surprising news. For the last couple decades, most congregations have become increasingly more female. Why are so many men neglecting weekend church services? Many have attempted to unravel this mystery, throwing the blame in nearly every direction: the pastor's kid-gloves, weak preaching, and modern worship music, just to name a few.

Yet, in Iola, Kansas, over the last few years, our church has seen an increase in the number of men in attendance. It happened subtly. We had never tried to make our services more appealing to men. We did not launch a men's ministry.

But we did spend a lot of time, energy, and money on marriages—from classes and counseling to couples' studies and an annual, sometimes biannual sermon series on the Song of Solomon. We stuck to our guns on the roles of men and women within marriage, while banging loud the drum that men were to uphold their responsibilities as husbands by loving their wives as Christ loved the church. We have emphasized that men are called not only to lay down their lives for their wives but also to rise and live for them by elevating their wives' status as co-heirs with Christ with gentle consideration so that their prayers are not hindered (1 Peter 3:7).

There is one other thing that we suspect has happened, although it's just our best guess. Even when the majority of our congregation was women, we were preaching the same high-standard messages concerning men and their weighty responsibilities as husbands and fathers. We suspect this gave many of our women hope and faith that their non-attending and non-engaging husbands could actually become better. It seems as if these women came to pray and believe that their husbands would catch fire for Christ. It was as if, instead of going home and hounding that man to begrudgingly follow her to church, she started putting him in the presence of God through her prayers. She no longer had to contend with her husband, but she contracted the job out to the Great Shepherd, who is always looking for the "one."

During that season, our church became 56 percent men, largely thanks to our women (it's likely even higher now). Their faithful prayers, submissive hearts, and desperate tugs at the hem of the Christ were seen and heard.

When we began a season of preaching specifically to men, here is what we saw: More women and young girls were baptized during this time than at any other time in the history of our church. We saw more husbands climb into the baptistry and baptize their wives than ever before. A wonderful women's ministry also appeared, and simultaneously, two new men's groups and a college class started.

WHAT I KNOW

One side will cry that gender roles are the remnants of the male patriarchy. Another side will appeal to science, citing that skeletal, muscular, and hormonal differences have predetermined these roles. All I know is that obedience to God's Word should be the first step. Understanding it may come later, but the harvest is the important part.

I apologize if any part of this sounds like bragging. God has done this all on his own. He never needed us to accomplish it. We are merely grateful to witness it.

We are no Vegas venue. You'll probably never see a sequined suit at our church. We have some lights and music, and although my voice will never be as smooth as Bruce Buffer, I can tell you what we do have. We have women who have fought for their husbands on bended knee in desperate prayer, and we have husbands who cherish their wives. They love them and they live for them.

In the next two chapters we move from an in-depth look at the complementarity of men and women to address the LGBTQ+ movement. We will examine its cultural influence before offering advice on how Christians should respond to transgenderism, in particular.

14

UNDERSTANDING THE PRESSURES OF THE LGBTQ+ MOVEMENT IN FIVE DECADE-CENTERED SHIFTS

PAUL HUYGHEBART

The New Testament theologian Richard Oster said in Chapter 6, "Culture and the problems arising from churches living in culture are responsible for everything and every letter in the New Testament." If we want to faithfully and effectively communicate and live out God's timeless truths regarding gender, we need to understand contemporary *cultural moods toward gender. And if we want to understand where our current culture stands on gender, we need to understand the influence of the LGBTQ+ Movement. In this chapter, Atlanta-area senior minister Paul Huyghebaert articulates the LGBTQ+ Movement in five historic, decade-centered shifts. These shifts help explain some of the strongest cultural pressures to soften and even rewrite biblical teachings on gender.*

"The times they are a-changin'," sang the prophet Bob Dylan in a song by the same name.

The year was 1963, and the winds of change were definitely blowing. The American Civil Rights Movement was at work to advance the cause of African Americans through the influence of prominent leaders such as Martin Luther King, Jr., and John Lewis. The ideas that would later characterize the postmodern period were taking root in American society. The sexual revolution was in full swing. The Vietnam War was surfacing tensions within the younger generation, and those tensions were nearly at a breaking point.

When you read the words of Dylan's song, it's clear he had a sense of what was coming.

Fast-forward twenty years, and the seeds of yet another change movement were beginning to germinate—one that today is referred to as the LGBTQ+ movement—and once again, the times they were a-changin'. A leader in the Renew Network, Guy Hammond, has done an excellent job documenting the history of the progression of LGBTQ+ ideology from the late 1950s until now. Guy Hammond is a homosexually attracted Christian. Before giving his life to Christ, he lived as a gay man until he was in his mid twenties. Today he is a Canadian pastor and the executive director of Strength in Weakness Ministries, an organization that provides support to Christian men and women who live outside the heterosexual mainstream. In an article such as this, we won't have time to drill as deeply into the history as he does, so I will recommend his book, *Gay & Christian?,* for further reading.

A SHIFT IN ATTITUDE AND BEHAVIOR

What I want to examine are the cultural shifts over the last five decades in the accepted, or you might even say *expected*, attitudes in relation to those who are a part of the LGBTQ+ community. I also want to show you demonstratively why we who hold to traditional biblical values must not ignore what is happening around us. Last year, Gallup released the results of a study that indicates just how quickly attitudes are changing—and it's not just attitudes that are changing anymore. As a part of the study, Gallup was able to determine by generation the percentage of Americans who self-identify as LGBTQ+, beginning with Traditionalists (born before 1946) and working through Generation Z (born between 1997 and 2003).[138] Here is what they found:

- Generation Z: 20.8 percent
- Millennials: 10.5 percent
- Generation X: 4.2 percent

138. Jones, Jeffrey M., "LGBT Identification in U.S. Ticks Up to 7.1%," Gallup, February 17, 2022, www.news.gallup.com/poll/389792/lgbt-identification-ticks-up.aspx (accessed October 19, 2022).

- Baby Boomers: 2.6 percent
- Traditionalists: 0.8 percent

If you have not previously seen this data, you may find yourself—as I did—feeling a bit shocked. The numbers indicate a rapid rise in LGBTQ+ identification. In another study from Barna, the numbers are even higher for the Millennial and Gen Z categories, at 30 percent and nearly 40 percent, respectively.[139] These numbers give us an understanding of what is happening, but they don't tell us much about why. We could simply resort to Bob Dylan's line and say, "Times are changing," but I'm guessing that approach wouldn't be particularly satisfying.

No matter where you find yourself in the debate about LGBTQ+ issues, each of us should want to understand how such a cataclysmic shift—not only in thinking but also in behavior—has occurred. In five words, here's my best take at explaining the dominant cultural attitude in each of the five decades from the 1980s and before until now: *condemnation, toleration, affirmation, celebration, participation.*

Before we go any further, I want to make a few quick acknowledgements. First, I know this is a heated issue, and I will undoubtedly receive pushback on what I'm about to share. Second, yes, I'm wading in anyway. And finally, I want you to know that I'm writing because I care, not because I don't.

THE ASSESSMENT

1. CONDEMNATION (1980s AND BEFORE)

Prior to 1980, any sexual behavior outside of normative heterosexual activity—except in small and mostly hidden pockets of society—was largely condemned. This attitude was only reinforced by the onset of the AIDS epidemic in 1981. In the earliest days of this epidemic (late 1970s through mid 1980s), the vast majority of the cases of HIV and AIDS were found within

139. Paul Bond, "Nearly 40 Percent of U.S. Gen Z's, 30 Percent of Young Christians Identify as LGBTQ, Poll Says," *Newsweek*, October 20, 2021, www.newsweek.com/nearly-40-percent-us-gen-zs-30-percent-christians-identify-lgbtq-poll-shows-1641085 (accessed October 19, 2022).

the homosexual population—specifically homosexual males. Many within the dominant culture took the attitude that the epidemic existed directly as a result of deviant and abhorrent behavior. Some even went so far as to suggest that gay men were simply getting what they deserved.

This attitude prevailed for most of the 1980s, although as the decade marched on, AIDS-related deaths of prominent figures such as Rock Hudson and Freddie Mercury undoubtedly had an effect on public sentiment. It was also in the 1980s that ideas connected to pro-gay ideology and pro-gay theology began to find limited traction. Guy Hammond writes in detail about Yale Professor John Boswell, author of *Christianity, Social Tolerance, and Homosexuality*.[140] Boswell's book marks one of the earliest, and certainly most cogent, efforts to move the dial on public attitudes toward homosexual behavior.

2. TOLERATION (1990s)

The 1990s saw a definite shift in attitude toward the LGBTQ+ community. Whereas before the predominant cultural posture had been one of condemnation (you shouldn't live like that), this decade saw the posture shift toward toleration (if you want to live like that, it's your business. . . just don't make it mine). This was the liberal idea of "live and let live."

Probably the best example of this new way of engaging the LGBTQ+ community was the "Don't Ask, Don't Tell" policy the military embraced in late 1993. As a result of this policy, same-sex attracted military applicants—many of whom had previously been excluded from armed service—were no longer asked about their sexual orientation as a part of the application process. As long as you kept your same-sex attraction to yourself, there would be no issues.

140. John Boswell, *Christianity, Social Tolerance, and Homosexuality: Gay People in Western Europe from the Beginning of the Christian Era to the Fourteenth Century* (Chicago: University of Chicago Press, 2015).

3. AFFIRMATION (2000s)

The move into a new millennium saw yet another grand shift in the way culture at large engaged with the LGBTQ+ community. To many, on both a mental and emotional level, this shift felt like a giant leap. It was one thing as people in the 1990s made the choice to accept that behaviors they objected to morally existed behind closed doors. It was an entirely different thing to see those behaviors accepted in open society.

The movement toward cultural affirmation came to a head in 2005 with the release of the movie *Brokeback Mountain*—the story of two male ranch hands who carried on an illicit love affair over the course of roughly twenty years. Keep in mind, they were both married to women as well. It was in this decade that the NBC TV sitcom *Will and Grace* became popular. According to IndieWire.com, eleven shows debuted gay characters from 2000–2009.[141] This was more than either the previous decade or the decade following, as of the publishing of this article in 2014.

With pop culture leading the way, the attitude that eventually dominated was one of affirmation. For most people, this was expressed somewhere on a spectrum between "this is okay" to "this is good."

4. CELEBRATION (2010s)

The next decadal shift is easily explainable. After all, if something is good, it should be celebrated, right? To disagree that something should be celebrated is to disagree that it is good.

Between 2010 and 2019, the pressure to link arms with the Gay Pride movement hit full swing. We saw a wave of corporations who signed on with endorsements in celebration of the LGBTQ+ agenda. A 2018 Vox article titled "How LGBTQ+ Month Became a Branded Holiday" addresses this

141. "Reader's Poll: The 25 Most Important LGBT Television Series," *Indie Wire*, June 15, 2014, www.indiewire.com/2014/06/readers-poll-the-25-most-important-lgbt-television-series-214082/ (accessed October 19, 2022).

phenomenon in some detail.[142] Rainbow flags were suddenly everywhere. Even churches were seen joining in Gay Pride parades.

This decade saw the true institutionalization of things like LGBTQ+ History Month, even though it had been established in 1994. LGBTQ+ people had found their own cultural heritage, and it was worth celebrating. . . and the rest of society was expected to join in.

5. PARTICIPATION (2020s)

We are only three years into this new decade and already so much has changed. If the shift from the 1990s to the 2000s could be characterized as a "giant leap," this shift we're experiencing now might be better equated with a transcontinental flight. I want to relate to you just a little of what I'm observing and hearing anecdotally as we find ourselves in the early years of this new decade.

First, I will point you back to the statistics. Nearly 21 percent of those in the Generation Z demographic self-identify as LGBTQ+. Not long ago, I heard a story about a middle school classroom where all the girls but one identified as LGBTQ+. A pastor recently shared with me a conversation that took place in his youth group concerning the near-constant pressure some of his teens were facing to participate in homoerotic behaviors: "A high school boy recently told me that it's hard to find a girlfriend because all the girls are dating other girls."

The most fitting word for this new decade is "participation," and this trend will likely only increase for the next several years. This is the new dominant attitude embraced by much of culture toward LGBTQ+ people and behaviors. Life is short. Experiment a little. You might discover something about yourself.

---

142. Alex Abad-Santos, "How LGBTQ Month Became a Branded Holiday," *Vox*, June 25, 2018, www.vox.com/2018/6/25/17476850/pride-month-lgbtq-corporate-explained (accessed October 19, 2022).

WHAT NOW?

Bob Dylan was right, but not because he's a prophet—not in the biblical sense anyway.

Situations, people, and opinions about what's right and what's wrong are always changing, and the last fifty years have been no exception. That's not to say that the last fifty years haven't brought some unique changes. It's also not to argue that the changes we are experiencing aren't happening more quickly than in other times of recorded history. If we had taken a seat across a table from each other five decades ago, and I had told you about the changes that were coming in relation to the dominant cultural attitude toward the LGBTQ+ community, you would likely have blown me off as a catastrophist.

And remember, we're not talking only about the dominant religious attitude. It's the dominant cultural attitude we have been speaking to. Things have changed. . . dramatically.

As people who follow Jesus, we must strive to understand the times in which we live (recall the men of Issachar from 1 Chronicles 12:32 who "understood the times and knew what Israel should do"). As long as we have our heads buried in the sand, as long as we live in denial about what is happening around us, we will find ourselves at the mercy of the movement of culture, be it in a positive or a negative direction. When we take the time to educate ourselves, however, we will inevitably emerge more prepared to handle what lies ahead. Parents, it is imperative that you understand what your kids are facing. Only then will you be able to disciple them in the way of God and guide them through the turbulence of these shifting cultural sands.

Here then is my hypothesis concerning the shift in attitudes toward, and perception of, the LGBTQ+ movement and LGBTQ+ people over the last five decades. Before the 1990s, if someone were to identify as gay, much of society would have responded negatively. I have characterized this reaction by using the word condemnation. In truth, there is another word I could have used: alienation. The typical reaction toward gay people was to keep them at arm's length. Remember, again, this is not simply the religious culture of the 1980s we are talking about. It was the culture at large.

The typical reaction toward gay people was to keep them at arm's length.

I am grateful that we have reached the point where we can acknowledge that hateful condemnation and alienation of those who are wrestling with same-sex attraction is just plain wrong. That's not what grace or love looks like. It shouldn't have been the dominant response pre-1980, and it should not be the way we treat people today. With that said, it is important to note that this truth—and in particular the twisted application of it—is at the root of much of the shift in both attitude and behavior from the 1990s forward. What do I mean by this? I'm glad you asked.

Can I ask a question in return? Have you ever been called a "hater"?

If you are over forty, the answer may be no. If you are a Millennial or younger, you may be thinking about the last time someone threw this accusation in your direction. Haters are judgmental. Haters are unkind. Above all, haters aren't loving. As Christian author Natasha Crain explains, we live in a time in which "judging is the ultimate sin."[143]

Judging is the ultimate sin. . . let that sink in for a moment.

I don't believe the current data on those identifying as LGBTQ+ are completely accurate identifiers of how many within the younger generations are actually living with same-sex attraction.

Allow me to explain.

If judging is the ultimate sin, how do we indicate that we aren't judgmental? What's more, what does the dominant culture around us need to see from us if we are to demonstrate a non-judgmental attitude? In the 1990s, we did so by moving away from condemnation toward toleration. In the 2000s, the standard shifted to affirmation. By 2010, celebration was necessary. And now? That's right. Now, in order to be seen as a non-judgmental

---

143. Natasha Crain. *Faithfully Different: Regaining Biblical Clarity in a Secular Culture* (Eugene, OR: Harvest House Publishers, 2022).

person, especially if you are a part of the younger generation, participation is fast becoming the standard.

This is at least part of the reason why so many of our young people are currently self-identifying as LGBTQ+. Who doesn't want to be seen as a loving person, especially as the culture around us is radically redefining love to mean unconditional affirmation?

"Hold on!" I hear some saying. How could anyone equate respectful non-participation with the act of judging?

First, remember that perception is everything in our postmodern world. What you intend by your words or actions is not what ultimately matters to people. What matters is how others receive your words and actions.

Second, let me share a quick story from my time in high school that will illuminate what I believe is happening today. During my senior year, I was at a party where a bottle of alcohol was being passed around. We were sitting in a circle, and the bottle had started its way around the group almost directly across from me. As I watched different people take a drink, then pass it to the next person, I knew I was going to have to make a choice. By the time the bottle reached me, I had resolved that I was not going to participate. I simply passed it to the next person. The boy sitting next to me noticed that I had chosen the stance of non-participation. Instead of simply letting it go, he chose to challenge me.

"Aren't you going to have a drink?"

"No," I replied.

I have never forgotten his next words. "What? Do you think you are better than the rest of us?" My non-participation was immediately received as judgment. It wasn't received as merely a personal choice to abstain. Somehow by passing the bottle to the next person without having taken a drink myself, I had unknowingly and unintentionally condemned all those who were drinking.

My non-participation was immediately received as judgment.

This is the dilemma I believe many in the younger generations are facing today. It's no longer good enough to accept that some people will make the choice to embrace a lifestyle you don't agree with, and in response take a live-and-let-live posture. It's no longer good enough to condone the actions of the LGBTQ+ community. It's no longer good enough even to celebrate the choices and the bravery of those who "come out." If you do all of these, but fail to participate, you may still be seen as judgmental and unloving. And judging is the ultimate sin.

OUR RESPONSIBILITY

Church, we absolutely have a responsibility to love the LGBTQ+ community and individuals within that community. We need to make sure, however, that we are embracing the biblical definition of love. True love means wanting people's ultimate well-being, not just their temporary happiness. True love means wanting what God wants for others. And what does God want more than anything for all of earth's 7+ billion people? He wants them to be renewed, to see his image restored in them. This will only happen as we each embrace his way for us, which will increasingly lead us to say no to our own desires insofar as they are contrary to God's good design for us. One thing I find amazing about the God we serve is that he never calls us to be different and better without guiding us on that path.

He's given us his Holy Spirit-inspired Word as a lamp for our feet and a light to direct our path (Psalm 119:105). He places his Holy Spirit inside of those who have given their lives over to him—and as the apostle Paul says, it's through the power of the Spirit that we are able to put to death the deeds of the body (Romans 8:13). This all points to a God who reaches out relationally in response to his fallen creation. He has not abandoned us, even when we have abandoned him. He offers hope. He offers help. As a community seeking to follow Jesus, relationship will be one of our most powerful tools as well. As Guy Hammond told me recently:

> Often the church's emphasis has been on behavior, not on the heart and/or on the relationship with God. Personally, as I have fought to say "no" to my own homosexual desires these last thirty-five years, it

> has been ultimately my relationship with God and his love for me that has propelled me to say "no" to something that feels so natural to me.

It is my prayer that this chapter will be received in the spirit in which it is intended. I am truly concerned for the next generation. As someone with a background in the field of mental health, I am concerned for the damage this latest cultural shift will cause. Sexual experimentation is not without consequences—emotional, physical, or otherwise.

It is not wrong to want to protect the next generation from those consequences. And we must do this without demonizing those who are same-sex attracted. How do we do this? Let's never forget these words from John 1 and the example we see in them: Jesus came from the Father "full of grace and truth" (John 1:14). He didn't come from the Father trying to figure out how to strike a balance between some grace and some truth. He chose to embrace both of these virtues to the full. If we are to faithfully navigate these changing times, we will do the same.

15

THOUGHTS OF A THEOLOGIAN AND A THERAPIST ON THE TRANSGENDER DEBATE

JOHN WHITTAKER, ELLEN RADCLIFF

The previous chapters have asked what the Bible says about God's purposes for creating men and women and how those purposes can be lived out in the church and home. This chapter takes a step back and examines the concept of gender itself.

Part of LGBTQ+ orthodoxy is the belief that gender is a fluid, socially constructed concept, and, as such, gender can be separated from a person's birth sex. Hence, the LGBTQ+ claim that whatever a transgender person identifies as is that person's fullest identity. How should Christians respond to transgenderism and transgender activism? How should Christians relate to transgender people?

To help us navigate this cultural moment, we talked with both a theologian and a therapist. John Whittaker is a New Testament theologian and creator of the Bible in Life online teaching ministry and The Listener's Commentary on the New Testament. *Ellen Radcliff is a provisionally licensed clinical mental health counselor (LCMHCA) and a provisionally licensed marriage and family therapist (LMFTA), who also serves as part of the executive staff of Strength in Weakness.*

Q. Ellen, can you tell us your story?

Radcliff: I grew up in a Christian home with God at the center of my household and with unconditionally loving parents. Even still, my heart was fraught with insecurity growing up—mostly about my femininity. I grew up in a home where my dad was the traditional male stereotype: rough, tough, gruff. And my mom is the opposite. She's the traditional female stereotype: gentle, quiet, and nurturing. I was—and am—a lot more like my dad in personality and in character, which is something I'm very proud of now. But I wasn't always.

As a young girl with a tender heart and lots of insecurities—and assumptions based on those insecurities—I concluded that I was broken as a woman. I felt that something was wrong with me because I didn't live up to this bar of femininity that I had set for myself. That bar was my mom's example of femininity, which I could not naturally emulate. I didn't realize at the time that there are multiple ways to be feminine or masculine.

I walked around with this incredible shame that I unknowingly masked as anger and hardness and superiority, especially directed toward my mom because deep down I resented her example of femininity and the feeling of inadequacy it bred in my heart. Eventually, I went looking for validation that I was woman enough.

So when I got into high school after harboring this insecurity and shame my whole life, I very innocently befriended a girl I admired. She was a bit more like me. She was opinionated, strong-willed, and outspoken, but she seemed okay with those parts of her—whereas I had grown up ashamed of those parts of me. As our friendship developed, so did my infatuation with her. She eventually became my idol. It got to the point where my entire identity and sense of self-worth were wrapped up in her and in our friendship. The relationship became emotionally enmeshed very quickly. For me, it bordered on obsessiveness.

Honestly, when this level of emotional attachment and idolatry in a friendship is reached, especially among women, it's easy for a physical relationship to follow. And that's exactly what happened. This experience sort of springboarded me into a life of homosexuality. I lived as a lesbian for a time before I eventually surrendered my heart to God.

Long story short, I became a Christian, and I'm now happily married. My husband and son and I live in Eastern North Carolina. As a therapist and mental health counselor, I help individuals and families who are wrestling through sexual and/or gender identity, whether in their own lives or the lives of a loved one.

Q. It sounds like having gender stereotypes that are too rigid can cause confusion?

Radcliff: Yes, and the Bible itself challenges rigid gender stereotypes.

There are many men and women in the Bible whom God lifts up as righteous examples who may not have lived up to our culturally constructed gender stereotypes: Deborah led the men into war. The story of Jael is incredibly violent. Ruth provided for her mother-in-law the way a son would, sweating and toiling in the fields. The Proverbs 31 woman provided for her family and bought properties. David the warrior king wrote poetry that exuded tremendous emotion and vulnerability. Jesus showed strong emotion. He even likened himself to a hen gathering her chicks.

If we aren't careful, too rigid stereotypes can feel oppressive to kids like me throughout their childhood. What I've found is that kids aren't typically able to communicate this until their teenage years. When they say, "Mom and dad, I'm transgender," what we don't see in that teenage proclamation is the decade or more of confusion, isolation, and shame—even perceived failure to meet the cultural and societal stereotype of their gender.

I believe we need to be confronting these gender stereotypes in our own hearts and homes so that the people living outside of the norm in this way don't feel that they're inherently sinful just because they lack the stereotypical masculine or feminine traits the world has implemented.

Although I grew up very insecure in my femininity, I never experienced a strong desire to live as a man. I did really like wearing baggy clothes and playing basketball, and I hated dresses and being soft-spoken, but, given the time that I grew up in, these thoughts didn't lead me to the conclusion that I should live as a man. If I had grown up as a teenager today, I wonder if I would have applied the term "transgender" to my experience of simply rebelling against the socially constructed gender stereotypes that I felt were oppressive to me.

Q. Even though we ought to challenge rigid gender stereotypes, should Christians follow the trend of opposing the gender binary altogether?

Radcliff: It seems clear to me that there is an explicitly stated male-female binary in the Bible. Genesis 1:27 talks about the creation and humans, and it says that, "God created mankind in his own image, in the image of God he created them; male and female he created them." There's the binary. And whenever humanity is referred to in the rest of the Bible, it's in binary categories. Husbands and wives, brothers and sisters. And when the Bible mentions crossing gender boundaries, it speaks only in the negative (1 Corinthians 6:9; Deuteronomy 22:5).

Whittaker: Yes, Scripture is explicit that there is a gender binary. Genesis 1:26–27, which Ellen mentioned, is the foundational text for this. It makes it clear that when God created human beings, he made two genders: male and female. And throughout the rest of the Scriptures, humans are only ever described as male and female. Not only that, but Genesis 1 continues by telling humans to "be fruitful and increase in number" (Genesis 1:28), which indicates that being male and female entails their bodies and their ability to reproduce together. In fact, Genesis 2 describes male and female humans as so complementary that, when they come together sexually, they become "one flesh."

Q. Let's talk about some important terms. For example, what is "transgender" and "gender fluidity"? What other terms do we need to know?

Whittaker: To engage this conversation thoughtfully, it's important to understand some of the vocabulary.

"Transgender" is an umbrella term for all the different ways people experience their gender identity as not corresponding to their biological sex. In this conversation, the word "sex" refers to a person's birth sex or biological sex.

Until recently, the term "gender" was tied to a person's biology and referred to how people expressed their sexuality as biologically male or female. The term is increasingly used for the *feeling* of being either male or female, a combination of both, or some other identity entirely. As a psychological experience, gender has begun to refer to how a person perceives and feels themselves to be (e.g., either male or female), regardless of biological sex. A biological male may perceive himself to be female and a biological female may perceive herself to be male. This perception is their "gender identity."

"Gender dysphoria" is a fairly new term adopted by the American Psychiatric Association to describe the distress a person experiences over the incongruence between their gender identity and their biological sex.

"Transexual" describes a person who has undergone medical intervention in an effort to make their body match their gender identity. This may range from hormone therapy to surgery.

There are two other terms that sometimes appear in this conversation and might be helpful to know. "Non-binary" refers to a person who rejects being put into the categories of male or female. "Intersex" refers to an extremely rare physiological condition in which a person is born with atypical features in their sexual anatomy.

Knowing these terms will help us have meaningful conversations about this subject. There are other terms that may come along, and the best thing we can do is graciously ask what a term means if a person uses one we are unfamiliar with.

Q. Transgenderism has become an incredibly polarizing issue. Why does it seem that the LGBTQ+ community and Bible-believing Christians live on separate planets when it comes to the transgender discussion?

Radcliff: Well, I think we live by different standards. When it comes to Christianity, God's capital-T Truth, as laid out in the Bible, is our compass for knowing how he calls us to live as Christians. The Bible makes it clear that our emotions are not good moral compasses (Jeremiah 17:9). No matter how we feel, we are to live for God. If we love him, we will obey him (John 14:23).

Following God instead of our hearts is a difficult concept for our society to understand. In our modern, morally relativistic society, nothing trumps love of self. This concept of striving to love God more than self is becoming a foreign concept, especially among the youth of today. Instead, we hear these phrases often: "I have to be true to me." "I have to be unapologetically me."

There is a sense in which I agree with these affirmations; I just do not see how they make sense outside of God. Who else knows my true self more than my Creator, who carefully knit me together and knows every hair on my head? Being true to me *is* living for God. Only out of an overflowing love for God, resulting in obedience to the standards that he calls me to live by, can I become fully who I was made to be by my Creator.

Q. As followers of Jesus who believe the Bible, how should we think about transgender ideology?

Whittaker: The first thing we need to come to terms with is that truth is determined by reality, not by how I feel or what I prefer. A common phrase today is to "live your truth." But ironically, that's not an attitude based in truth because that's not how truth works. There is no such thing as "my truth" and "your truth." There is only *the* truth . . . which is when something you believe or say matches up with reality.

And reality is unyielding regardless of my feelings or the way I want things to be. Once I was driving a group of students in the school van. We were cruising down I-5 between Olympia, Washington, and Portland, Oregon. The fuel gauge said I had a third of a tank left. But suddenly, the van started sputtering and lurching, and it died right there on the freeway. I had deeply and sincerely believed I had plenty of gas to get to the next exit. The fuel gauge even told me I had enough gas. But it wasn't true. Reality didn't yield to my sincerely held belief, no matter how badly I wanted it to do so.

Not only is reality unyielding but feelings are notoriously fickle and unreliable. They vacillate. They are unpredictable. They are deceitful. Feelings make poor masters and better servants.

Our preferences and feelings don't change reality or make things true. They are an unreliable guide to truth. And thus, we must ruthlessly embrace facts over feelings, no matter how deep or how loud or how strong or how persuasive the feelings are. If we're going to live in the real world, we must ensure that our ideas, beliefs, and feelings match up with the way things actually are.

Q. How does truth factor into this conversation about transgenderism?

Whittaker: Because our culture now takes pride in transgenderism, many people, including many Christians, are sympathetic to trans ideology or even tempted to be supportive of it. But as disciples of Jesus, our source of truth must be the Bible, and our values must be shaped by its teaching and worldview—not by culture.

And the Bible goes against transgenderism.

Yet—and this is very important—it doesn't directly counter transgenderism by proposition or explicit command (e.g., "Thou shalt not practice transgenderism). Rather, the Bible negates it by teaching an entire worldview about reality and what it means to be human. Again, if we are going to be disciples of Jesus, we must submit to Jesus' authority. And one way he carries out his authority is through the Bible. So we *must* submit to and be formed by the Bible's teaching about the nature of reality and what it means to be human.

Q. What does the Bible teach about what it means to be human?

Whittaker: The first thing is very simply that there is a human nature. This may sound like stating the obvious, but it's terribly important. If there is no inherent human nature, and no intrinsic design, meaning, and goal for human beings, then we are free to (or forced to) create our own meaning and goal. We can determine our own identity. You can be whatever you want to be.

Take that notion and place it in the midst of the deeply rooted individualism of present-day Western culture, and you end up with varying degrees of radical individual self-determination. Each person determines their own identity and their own meaning for existence.

But the worldview of the Bible has a totally different vision of what it means to be human.

According to the Bible, we humans are creatures, formed and fashioned by a Creator. He designed us and brought us into existence. And when he did so, he determined that we would be created in his image. "Let Us make man in Our image, according to Our likeness," he said (Genesis 1:26, NASB). Therefore, humans are creatures made to be the very image of God.

The most basic implication of this throughout the Bible is that we don't exist for ourselves, but for God. Radical self-determination is contrary to the biblical view of God as our Creator and our nature as human beings. We belong to God, and he determines who we are, what it means to be human, and why we exist.

The second thing the Bible teaches about human nature that is relevant to the trans conversation is that to be human means to be embodied as male or female.

Genesis emphasizes that when God made humans in his image, this is connected to being male and female, and that being male and female entails human bodies. Genesis 1:27–28a says, "God created man in His own image, in the image of God He created him; male and female He created them. God blessed them; and God said to them, 'Be fruitful and multiply, fill the earth, and subdue it'" (NASB).

Humans are intrinsically sexed beings. I suppose it's possible that God could've have made androgynous, sexless beings. But he didn't. When he made humans, he made them sexed—male or female. This is God's design, not a social construct.

What's more, being created male and female necessarily entails our bodies and is tied in verses 27 and 28 to the ability to reproduce. In other words, this nature as image-bearing creatures who are male or female is an embodied nature. According to the Bible, you can't separate the gender identity of male from a male body that is capable of reproduction. And you can't separate the gender identity of female from a female body that is capable of reproduction. (Interestingly enough, the urge to transition the body in trans ideology seems like tacit acknowledgement of this inherent aspect of our humanness.)

This leads to another important part of the Bible's teaching about what it means to be human, namely, that the body is essential to human nature and identity—not optional, accidental, or peripheral. In the Bible, human beings are embodied beings.

It's not as if the real me is the inner me and I merely wear a body. We're not spirits who happen to have bodies. Our bodies are an essential and permanent part of us.

Humans, body and all, are part of God's good creation. Indeed, the creation of humans is the culminating moment when God says all that he has made is very good (Genesis 1:31).

Furthermore, the incarnation demonstrates the goodness of the body. In Jesus, all the fullness of deity dwelt in a body (Colossians 1:19).

Jesus' resurrection and our promised resurrection demonstrates the permanent goodness of human bodies. We will be embodied forever with a glorified resurrection body that is like Jesus' resurrection body.

Our bodies are good. Our bodies are ultimately a permanent part of us. Our bodies are essential to our human and gender identity. And what we do with our bodies matters. This is why the apostle Paul says that the body is "for the Lord, and the Lord is for the body" (1 Corinthians 6:13).

So according to the Scriptures, male and female entails our whole self, including our body. This is the way things are. Feelings don't change this. Physical alterations can't change this. It is impossible for puberty blockers, hormone therapy, and even surgery to truly change a male into a female or a female into a male. Our embodied nature as male or female humans cannot change. It is a biological impossibility for a man to become a woman or a woman a man because our maleness or femaleness is written in every cell of our body.

Therefore, gender is embodied; our biological sex displayed in our body is indispensable and intrinsic to our gender identity. It is ineradicable. Male and female identities are inherently tied to our bodies and can't be discovered or known without reference to our bodies. Our gender identity and our biological sex are designed by God to be one and the same. Thus, as Preston Sprinkle says, "Scripture does not seem to allow for—and in a few places explicitly prohibits—identifying as a sex or gender that's different from your biological sex."[144]

Q. What are some implications of the Bible's teaching on sexuality and gender for how to approach this topic in the church today?

Whittaker: One implication is that while we do need to avoid rigid (and often culturally created) gender stereotypes as Ellen talked about above, we also need to recognize and communicate that every time gender distinctions are blurred in Scripture, it is described as a negative thing.

One example of this is the prohibition against homosexual practice in Romans 1:26–28. Engaging in homosexual sex is described as exchanging "natural relations" for what is "contrary to nature." The creation of male and female in Genesis 1–2 lies behind this passage. Thus, "contrary to nature" means what is contrary to the way God has designed human sexuality. Therefore, the blurring of sexual difference—male and female—in sexual activity is contrary to God's design.

Another example of this principle, this time from the Old Testament law, is the strong prohibition against cross-dressing in Deuteronomy 22:5: "A woman must not wear men's clothing, nor a man wear women's clothing, for the Lord your God detests anyone who does this." Once again, the blurring of gender difference and expression in something as mundane as clothing is condemned in the strongest language. As Jason DeRouchie points out, this law assumes a "fundamental rule—that there are only two biological sexes—male and female—and that what is gender normative in God's world is that one's biological sex should govern both one's gender identity and expression."[145] As with many passages in both testaments, the backdrop is the Genesis 1–2 framework of our createdness as either male or female.

144. Preston Sprinkle, "Pastoral Paper: A Biblical Conversation about Transgender Identities," The Center for Faith, Sexuality, and Gender, www.centerforfaith.com/resources/pastoral-papers/12-a-biblical-conversation-about-transgender-identities, 8.
145. Jason S. DeRouchie, "Confronting the Transgender Storm: New Covenant Reflections on Deuteronomy 22:5," *Journal of Biblical Manhood and Womanhood* 21 (Spring 2016): 58–68.

This is consistent throughout the Bible. Scripture always joins gender identity and expression to biological sex, so much so that to confuse that by means of clothing or behavior, or in any other way, is staunchly prohibited.

Another implication is that what we do with our body sexually speaking is intrinsically linked to our relationship with God as his imager bearers and thus matters deeply. One of the places this is most explicitly taught is in 1 Corinthians 6:12–20, which we briefly quoted from earlier.

The context in this passage is sexual immorality. To support his point, Paul quotes from the account of the creation of man and woman in Genesis 2 because it is foundational for a biblical understanding of human nature and sexuality. In this context, Paul writes that "the body is not for immorality, but for the Lord, and the Lord is for the body" (1 Corinthians 6:13b, NASB). Then he mentions the essentiality and permanence of our body by referring to Jesus' resurrection and our resurrection. This leads him to make a rather startling statement in verse 15a: "Do you not know that your bodies are members of Christ?" (NASB).

He doesn't say our spirits; rather he says our *bodies* are part of Christ. That's how central our body is to our human identity and to our relationship with Jesus. And this is specifically stated with regard to our sexuality and what we do with our sexuality in our body. In fact, Paul describes our body as sacred when he says, "Do you not know that your body is a temple of the Holy Spirit who is in you, whom you have from God, and that you are not your own?" (6:19, NASB).

Let me make two important observations about this well-known verse. First, notice that you are essentially equated with your body in this sentence (*your body* is a temple and *you* are not your own). That's because, as we noted above, the Bible understands human beings fundamentally as embodied beings, with the inner person and outer person as one embodied whole.

The second observation is the last phrase: "You are not your own." As disciples of Jesus, we don't belong to ourselves. We aren't free to determine our own identity or meaning. We don't get to live "our truth." For followers of Jesus, there's no such thing as "my body, my choice." Our body is not our own. We belong to God, for we "have been bought for a price: therefore glorify God in your body" (6:20, NASB). Glorifying God with our sexuality is directly tied to our body and what we do with it.

Q. Let's talk about personal relationships in a church setting. As a Christian, when you know somebody who has come out as transgender, how do you approach that relationship within the church?

Radcliff: Let me mention first that I think our churches need to be really clear about what the Bible teaches on this issue.

Some of the most heartbreaking stories are of trans people coming to a church for several months, even years, and after developing deep relationships and establishing a feeling of belonging, *then* they end up learning that the church holds to a historically Christian perspective of gender identity and sexual ethics. I think we need to be really clear about our beliefs and lead with conviction. We never want anyone to feel duped by us or by God. Of course, once you've been clear with a person about your convictions, restating it unsolicited over and over may only serve to fuel isolation and shame in the other person and ultimately create a barrier between you and them.

That said, we need to create safety within our churches to allow people to talk about their struggles with gender identity incongruence. Shame multiplies in silence. And when it comes to personal relationships, we're primarily dealing with people, not issues. We want to see these people through the eyes of God. These are people God sees as his beloved creation. Just because they struggle with something we don't struggle with doesn't mean that God doesn't want them in his kingdom.

We need to remember that each person has a story that needs to be unpacked. We can get to know them and their unique experience, which requires listening and loving. I think sometimes we are hesitant to ask questions; maybe we're afraid that engaging in dialogue will appear as though we are affirming their decision. This is not the example Jesus set for us. Seeking to understand someone's experience does not negate our convictions. And every trans person I've met has been more than happy to answer my questions when

I've approached them respectfully and lovingly. So, when you ask questions, ask open-ended questions that help you to understand their experience and draw out their story.

Whittaker: Tone is terribly important. There are always two parts to a subject as deeply personal as this one. There's the truth and then there's what we do with the truth. Do we use it as a club to beat people into submission? Do we use it as a wall to keep "those people" out? When we know the truth, what do we do with it?

As disciples of Jesus, we must both live and speak the truth in love (Ephesians 4:15). The Greek phrase here literally reads "truthing in love." Certainly that involves what we say, but it also involves what we do. In our words as well as our actions, we demonstrate the truth of Christ. It is in that way, Paul goes on to say, that we all will grow to maturity in Christ.

Q. As Christians, what are some ways we can help people in our churches who are struggling with gender dysphoria or transgenderism in some way, but haven't yet come out as transgender?

Whittaker: Speaking the truth in love in this kind of situation has a number of implications. For example:

- It means we're honest and clear about what the Bible says and what it does not say about this issue.
- It means that we create gracious, compassionate environments for people to dialogue about their experience and what the Bible says.
- It means we enter into real relationships with people, not treating them as a problem to be solved or an issue to get rid of but a person to be loved, known, and valued.
- It means we listen rather than assuming we already know what they're like or what they're going through.

Now to be honest, I am co-writing this chapter with some apprehension. Not because I'm worried about what people might think of the biblical view or about being "canceled." My apprehension stems from the fact that this is such a deeply personal subject, and I'd much rather sit down over coffee and have a conversation about it. That way, I could ask questions. I could listen and hear your thoughts. You could ask me questions and hear my tone of voice. I'm convinced that time, space, and compassion for real relationships and meaningful conversations are some of the most important things we can do.

Q. How should we relate to those who are activists of transgender ideology?

Whittaker: I do think that trans ideology and its activists need to be distinguished from those who are genuinely suffering and struggling with gender confusion. When dealing with an activist who is promoting trans ideology in the church, we need to clearly and directly challenge the false ideology. We need to firmly but gently ask them to refrain from promoting it if they are going to be a part of the church. We need to do this with wisdom, grace, and truth.

Q. Ellen, what is one thing that would have helped you as a child struggling with gender questions?

Radcliff: I think the most important thing we can do, especially with our young children, is talk about this and other uncomfortable things. Our kids are learning about sex, sexuality, gender, and other complex constructs from their misguided peers, social media, and television. We do not want our kids to get their foundational understanding about such complicated topics from these sources. As parents, we must create open, honest, and loving dialogue surrounding some of these complex issues so that our kids are hearing it from us *first*. This reduces shame, creates connection and belonging, and gives our kids a much better foundation for understanding such topics.

Also, it would have helped if when I was growing up, my parents had said to me, "Wow, Ellen, you are so passionate like Jesus! Sometimes you remind me of Jesus in the temple flipping over the tables!" Or, "You can be so direct! Like when Jesus called the Pharisees whitewashed tombs! Of course, maybe you can incorporate more of Jesus' love next time . . . but we love seeing you be an image bearer of Christ in your passion, your zeal, and your desire for justice. Way to go!" If this had been the sentiment for me growing up, perhaps I would not have convinced myself that these were good traits for a man to have, but shameful for me to have.

So I think we need to be really mindful and confrontational in our own hearts of what exactly is a biblical representation of masculinity and femininity—and what has been distorted by rigid gender stereotypes.

Q. Among Bible-believing Christians, one area of disagreement that I have observed is regarding pronouns. If I call a biological male a "she" or a biological female a "he," am I building bridges—or am I giving into a false ideology?

Radcliff: I would say that this really is a matter of conscience before God.

I think you have to determine what you feel comfortable with in this. I would never suggest to anyone that they transgress upon their conscience or what they feel the Spirit prompting them to do or not to do. I personally refer to a non-Christian however they wish to identify; I have found this to be a powerful gesture that helps keep a bridge of communication open with a lot of people who might have otherwise written me off simply because of my faith. My conscience allows this because they have not yet agreed to live under God's law, and it is not breaking the earthly law that they live under.

Paul tells us in 1 Corinthians 5 that we are not called to judge those outside of God's kingdom. We are only called to hold those *within* God's kingdom to his standards. So if a non-Christian does not abide by the same biblical ethics that I do, I'm not surprised or offended. If, however, a Christian wishes to identify as a sex different from their natal sex, I believe we have a biblical duty to exhort that brother or sister toward obedience and righteousness.

Whittaker: I really appreciate Ellen's perspective on this. Personally, I have gone back and forth in my thinking on this topic. When it comes to unbelievers, I am comfortable using their preferred pronouns as an act of hospitality, with the hope that I might win some (1 Corinthians 9:19–23).

But for someone who claims to be a follower of Jesus, I struggle a bit more. My default position would be to use pronouns in keeping with their biological sex because that's more in sync with the teaching of the Bible, and I don't want to be complicit in promoting a false ideology.

But I also know that I don't understand the depths of gender dysphoria and how something as simple as a pronoun can trigger their dysphoria in real and painful ways. If I don't take a recovering alcoholic to a bar out of deference to where they've come from, perhaps I should be just as sensitive to my brother or sister who has endured deep gender dysphoria and not use a pronoun that might wound them.

Hence my struggle, and I don't have a fully settled position on this question.

Q. In addition to resources at Strength and Weakness, if someone wants to delve deeper into this topic, what are some resources you recommend?

Whittaker: This is a huge topic with a wide range of perspectives, so let me mention just a few resources that I've found reliable and helpful.

One of the most helpful books that explores the Bible's teaching on this topic, as well as a number of practical issues, is *Embodied: Transgender Identities, the Church, and What the Bible Has to Say*, by Preston Sprinkle. The thing I most appreciate about Preston's work is that he is a biblical scholar who digs deep into the teaching of Scripture but also has real relationships with people across the spectrum. He speaks out of deep biblical understanding and meaningful relationships with people.

In addition to Preston's book, you can find papers and video resources that provide guidance for churches and individuals on specific questions and issues at the Center for Faith, Sexuality, and Gender (Preston is the president of the organization), centerforfaith.com. Especially helpful are the video courses for parents and youth workers.

Another resource that explores what the Bible has to say on the subject is Andrew Walker's book *God and the Transgender Debate: What Does the Bible Actually Say about Gender Identity?* This book aims to help the church get caught up on the revolution that's happening in Western culture regarding sexuality and gender and provide a compassionate guide to the Bible's teaching.

16

TEN QUESTIONS FOR EGALITARIAN CHURCHES

BOBBY HARRINGTON, RENÉE WEBB SPROLES, DANIEL MCCOY

If you are a church leader leaning toward an egalitarian approach to men and women in church leadership, we want to engage you in a deeper conversation on the implications of an egalitarian approach. We acknowledge that there is so much pressure to adopt egalitarianism, and there are many writings by good scholars that advocate methods of interpretation that will help you get there. We understand how easy it is to adopt this viewpoint. But we are asking these questions to help you see if the egalitarian approach is really, truly taught in God's Word.

Male headship is the doctrine that says men have a unique responsibility for leadership in the home and church. There are an increasing number of Christians who reject this belief, seeing it as an unnecessary barrier to reaching a people in our culture that has long recognized the equal giftedness of men and women in the workforce and in the home. It is becoming hard for many to justify anything less than egalitarianism in the local church.

In Western culture, many see churches that insist on male-only elders and senior ministers/pastors as behind the times *at best*, but increasingly more cynically as men cloaking their hunger for male power in a guise of faithfulness to the Bible.

Many call such churches *misogynistic* (hating women). All the while, there are more and more churches of influence to point to in the evangelical community who are abandoning male headship for an egalitarian approach to leadership based on giftedness, not on gender.

Does male headship only *feel* like faithfulness in the minds of conservatives—when it's really just a tradition or an unnecessary barrier between an egalitarian culture and the church?

Perhaps you are already on your way to transitioning away from male headship and embracing egalitarianism in the church (for a definition, see page 24). Or maybe you're actually convinced that male headship is biblical, so you're not going anywhere, but you are struggling with how to explain it or how to help others. Either way, we humbly ask you to think through these questions and explore what Scripture says about these issues at a more comprehensive level.[146]

If you take this journey with us and have an open-minded humility before God, we can just about guarantee it's not going to be comfortable. You'll face strong contrary winds from at least two directions: 1) the cynicism of Western culture toward biblical authority and toward anything the Bible says about gender, *and* 2) the "large-and-in-charge" tradition-bound leadership culture of many churches. The teachings of the Bible challenge both trends.

So wherever you find yourself in this debate, may we ask you to pause and ask for God's help in prayer as you seriously work through these ten questions?

1. How did the earliest Christian leaders get it so wrong?

This question helps us test our exegesis. If the apostles truly did teach the egalitarian posture, as most egalitarians claim, then we should find circumstantial evidence of that posture in the writings of those discipled by the apostles. Put another way, if the egalitarian viewpoint is true, the earliest leaders, called the Church Fathers, should reflect it in their writings.

---

146. We want to thank Professor Rick Oster, Joe Shulam, Bob Russell, Jim Putman, and Gary Johnson for their helpful input on these questions.

The Church Fathers wrote starting in the year AD 90 and on into the second century.

The Church Fathers:

- were discipled by the apostles
- led in the churches established by the apostles
- spoke the same language as the apostles
- lived in the same culture as the apostles

It is helpful to see if they embraced the egalitarianism that many tell us is the true interpretation of what the apostles taught.

So what do the writings of the Church Fathers show us? There is no hint of the egalitarian view in their writings. It does not exist.

Thus, for egalitarians to ground their position in New Testament exegesis, they must argue that their unique understanding was present in the apostle Paul and the first church, and then it evaporated before any leader in the early church adopted it and wrote about it.

How could these early Christians have gotten it so wrong, so fast?

Instead, we find that the earliest Christians championed complementarian arguments and said they were based upon what they learned from the apostles. They believed they were explaining the natural reading and understanding of the original text. To be sure, we can find some misogynistic statements in early church writings, but at the same time, please note the second- and third-century complementarian affirmations:

- They stated their belief in male and female equality.
- They stated their belief in male headship in the home.
- They stated their belief in only male preachers and elders of the gathered church.
- They supported female teachers for ministry outside the gathered church.
- They supported female deacons for baptisms, anointing for prayer, etc.

- They supported a special order of female widows for prayer, care of the sick, and benevolence.
- They supported female missionaries.

Again, consider this first question: If egalitarianism is right, how did those discipled by the apostles get it so wrong?

2. Why did God create from scratch—not based on culture—male leadership roles in the Old Testament, in the ministry of Jesus, and in the New Testament church?

The egalitarian argument is that male headship was not created by God, but rather, it was an accommodation to the Fall or the surrounding culture of patriarchy. Egalitarianism with no gender roles was God's truest intention, to be realized gradually in the new covenant age, we are told.

So why did God not start things with Abraham and Sarah that way? Or why not course-correct at the time of Jesus and the twelve apostles, if egalitarianism was indeed the intention? And it's not as though it works to say that God was simply accommodating to the culture when God led his people to do many other things that were *contrary* to their culture. Jesus also started something in his public ministry that was radically new and different—but he still focused on developing twelve male apostles.

We are often told that equality of male and female roles in the church and home is a social justice issue. But if egalitarianism was the path of rightness and justice, why did God not set things up that way?

Please note the following roles that God created, all the while feeling free to deviate from cultural norms:

- The selection of Abraham, Isaac, and Jacob as *patriarchal heads* of the Jewish people
- The selection of twelve tribes based upon *the twelve male descendants of Jacob*
- The appointment of male-only *priests in the Old Testament* (although pagan religions had women priests)
- All *God-ordained royalty* who led over Israel were men

- All the *major Old Testament prophets and all the known writers of the Old and New Testament* were male
- All *twelve apostles* whom Jesus chose were male
- In the New Testament, we read that only men were authorized by God to be appointed as *elders*. More on this below.

Again, if God wanted egalitarianism, why did God not establish it in the Old Testament, in the ministry of Jesus and the twelve apostles, and with elders?

3. Why make giftedness and not the created order the starting point? Another way of stating this question is to ask, "Where does Scripture teach us to start the conversation on male headship?"

Headship in the Bible is connected to the concept of *primogeniture,* which simply means "born first." When the apostle Paul writes about headship, primogeniture is the go-to concept he brings up. In particular, he rewinds to the first chapters of Genesis where we see Adam being created before Eve. The Spirit inspires Paul to refer back to this created order as the basis for male headship in the church:

> I do not permit a woman to teach or to assume authority over a man; she must be quiet. *For Adam was formed first, then Eve.* And Adam was not the one deceived; it was the woman who was deceived and became a sinner. (1 Timothy 2:12–14)
>
> For man did not come from woman, but woman from man; *neither was man created for woman, but woman for man.* It is for this reason that a woman ought to have authority over her own head. (1 Corinthians 11:8–10a)

These passages present the primogeniture argument. God created the man first to have a headship role in the home and church. We are not generally familiar with this posture as an argument, but it was understood as authoritative by many in the ancient world, whether in homes or in society at large.

A modern-day example of primogeniture is found in the British monarchy. The Duke of Cambridge, Prince William, was the firstborn son of Charles, the Prince of Wales, and Diana, Princess of Wales. As firstborn, William will one day be king. When this happens, he will not have a license to do whatever he wants; rather, he will have great responsibilities toward the subjects of the United Kingdom. He will submit to the needs of his subjects, and his subjects will submit to his authority.

Again, we do not often see this argument in our culture. We are far removed from it naturally making sense to us. Yet the primogeniture/headship argument is the posture of the New Testament regarding men and women when it comes to some church functions, grounded in the first chapters of Genesis.

Sometimes egalitarians locate male-female roles as a result of the Fall (i.e., where God says to Eve in Genesis 3:16, "Your desire will be for your husband, and he will rule over you"), but this is not what the New Testament teaches. The conflict of Genesis 3:16 is best seen in context as describing fallen marriage, not marriage as God intended it.

We point you to the created order as originally established by God before the Fall. Wayne Grudem lists ten arguments that show there was indeed male headship before the Fall. The Fall didn't create gender distinctions and roles; rather, the Fall distorted those roles into ugly power plays. Here, in brief, are Grudem's ten arguments:[147]

1. The order: Adam was created first, then Eve (note the sequence in Genesis 2:7 and 2:18–23; 1 Timothy 2:13).
2. The representation: Adam, not Eve, had a special role in representing the human race (1 Corinthians 15:22, 45–49; Romans 5:12–21).
3. The naming of woman: Adam named Eve; Eve did not name Adam (Genesis 2:23).
4. The naming of the human race: God named the human race "Man," not "Woman" (Genesis 5:2).
5. The primary accountability: God called Adam to account first after the Fall (Genesis 3:9).
6. The purpose: Eve was created as a helper for Adam, not Adam as a helper for Eve (Genesis 2:18; 1 Corinthians 11:9).

147. Wayne Grudem, *Evangelical Feminism and Biblical Truth: An Analysis of More than 100 Disputed Questions* (Wheaton: Crossway, 2012), 109.

7. The conflict: The curse brought a distortion of previous roles, not the introduction of new roles (Genesis 3:16).
8. The restoration: Salvation in Christ in the New Testament reaffirms the creation order (Colossians 3:18–19).
9. The mystery: Marriage from the beginning of creation was a picture of the relationship between Christ and the church (Ephesians 5:32–33).
10. The parallel with the Trinity: The equality, differences, and unity between men and women reflect the equality, differences, and unity in the Trinity (1 Corinthians 11:3).

If we follow Scripture, any conversation around male headship roles should start with the creation account. Unfortunately, this is not what egalitarians tend to do in the discussion.

We have found that they tend to ignore the creation account and instead start with Galatians 3:28: "There is neither Jew nor Gentile, neither slave nor free, nor is there male and female, for you are all one in Christ Jesus."

Why start here as the foundational posture? The context of Galatians 3:28 makes it abundantly clear that men and women are equal in Christ: they are equally justified by faith (v. 24), equally free from the bondage of legalism (v. 25), equally children of God (v. 26), equally clothed with Christ (v. 27), equally possessed by Christ (v. 29), and equally heirs of the promises to Abraham (v. 29). But Galatians 3:27–29 does not address gender roles or the doctrine of headship.

Creation is the consistent starting point for the apostle Paul when it comes to gender functions. What is Paul's reason for his appeal to Adam's creation prior to Eve? It's to explain why women should not be the main teachers in the church (1 Timothy 2:11–15) and why women are to honor male headship when they are praying or prophesying (1 Corinthians 11:3–10).

Here is the question restated: How can we justify ignoring primogeniture as the foundational basis Scripture gives for understanding male headship?

4. Why reject the priest/rabbi/synagogue role as a historical background for key texts in 1 Corinthians 11:3–5, 1 Corinthians 14:29–34, and 1 Timothy 2:11–13?

When it comes to crucial texts on gender in the church, such as 1 Corinthians 11:3–5, 1 Corinthians 14:29–34, and 1 Timothy 2:11–13, it is important to consider the cultural and historical background. A careful reading of the book of Acts shows that the early church started in the temple courts and drew its first members out of synagogues. The early church was formed with the synagogue as its background.

The synagogue is an extension of the Old Testament model where male priests were the authoritative teachers; pagan religions had female priests, but not Israel. The Old Testament taught that only qualified men could be priests (Numbers 4:1–3; 1 Chronicles 23:12–32). With the emergence of the synagogue, this authoritative teaching role passed on to the rabbis in the synagogue who, again, were only qualified males.

Many of us were not taught much about the role of male priests as the teachers in the Old Testament. We mainly thought of them as making animal and other sacrifices. But Malachi 2:7 describes their role this way: "For the lips of a priest ought to preserve knowledge, because he is the messenger of the Lord Almighty and people seek instruction from his mouth." Prophets—male and female—appeared here and there. But the burden of teaching day-to-day in the Old Testament was on the male priesthood in Israel.

This male teaching model continued as the norm in the synagogue in the first century. Hughes Oliphant Old notes that in those meetings, "There was a large core of dedicated men who had given their lives to the study of the Scriptures, and who prepared themselves to preach when the leadership of the synagogue invited them to do so."[148] The synagogue thus became a natural model for male leadership in the early church.

Consistent with the synagogue norm and God's intention in the created order, God inspired Paul to teach that women are not to serve as authoritative teachers in the gathered church (1 Timothy 2:11–15), and women are to honor male headship when they pray or prophesy (1 Corinthians 11:3–5). Likewise, Paul taught women to be silent during the disruptions in church or the judging of prophecies (1 Corinthians 14:29–34).

148. Hughes Oliphant Old, *The Reading and Preaching of the Scriptures in the Worship of the Christian Church*, Vol. 1: The Biblical Period (Grand Rapids: Eerdmans, 1998), 102.

This was not just a local prohibition for women in Corinth; according to both Corinthian texts, this was to be the norm for *all churches* (1 Corinthians 11:16; 14:33).

This also helps explain why Jesus' twelve apostles were men. And it also explains why elders are exclusively male in the New Testament (in 1 Timothy 3:1–7, Titus 1:5–9, and 1 Peter 5:1–3). These practices fit the Old Testament and synagogue norm.

We find that most egalitarians are uninformed about the priest/rabbi historical background for the male teacher-elder role in the church. Scholars use ideas about the cult of Artemis in Ephesians or use other pagan sources as the background, but they point to these backgrounds without a clear biblical basis and ignore the known formative role of synagogues in the early church. For insight on the misapplication of the Artemis cult, how it connects with Ephesus, and its historical background, see Chapter 8: "Does God Allow Women Preachers in 1 Timothy 2?"

This continuity of male headship that spans both testaments and is tied back to creation teaches that God intended male headship to be transcultural—something that should not be derailed by cultural winds of change.

In summary, why not take the priest/rabbi role as a crucial historical background for the discussion on women teaching in the early church?[149]

5. How do Jesus and the church mutually submit to each other?

Egalitarians like to use the phrase "mutual submission" to summarize the instructions for households in Ephesians 5. I get it. I (Renée) did this myself for years. But careful reading of this passage shows something more nuanced than an interchangeable submission between husbands and wives. Paul is calling spouses back to the original *order* of love through the redemption won for them in Christ.

Put another way, Jesus tells the church to follow him, but the church does not tell Jesus to follow her. The roles are not interchangeable. And so,

149. We are grateful for the input on these points by Professor Richard Oster of Harding School of Theology and Joe Shulam of Netivyah Training Institute in Israel, two experts in first-century backgrounds for the early church.

neither are the roles for husbands and wives interchangeable, as articulated in this passage:

> Submit to one another out of reverence for Christ.
>
> Wives, submit yourselves to your own husbands as you do to the Lord. For the husband is the head of the wife as Christ is the head of the church, his body, of which he is the Savior. Now as the church submits to Christ, so also wives should submit to their husbands in everything.
>
> Husbands, love your wives, just as Christ loved the church and gave himself up for her to make her holy, cleansing her by the washing with water through the word, and to present her to himself as a radiant church, without stain or wrinkle or any other blemish, but holy and blameless. In this same way, husbands ought to love their wives as their own bodies. He who loves his wife loves himself. After all, no one ever hated their own body, but they feed and care for their body, just as Christ does the church—for we are members of his body. "For this reason a man will leave his father and mother and be united to his wife, and the two will become one flesh." This is a profound mystery—but I am talking about Christ and the church. However, each one of you also must love his wife as he loves himself, and the wife must respect her husband. (Ephesians 5:21–33)

The power of headship is fleshed out in these verses as the errors of Adam and Eve are corrected. When Adam and Eve fell, they fell into the abuses of their roles: women being either manipulative or doormats; and men being either passive or domineering. In this passage, we see the curse (Genesis 3:16) reversed in the gospel through submission, respect, and love.

How Wives Submit: Model the Church

As convenient as it would be to be able to read egalitarian, mutual, no-set-roles submission into the marriage relationship, the Christ-church metaphor makes this impossible. It's true that Jesus submitted to the cross for the sake of the church, but his submission is not interchangeable with the church's submission to him.

Wives submit to their husbands as the church submits to Jesus. A wife may have joy and confidence in submitting to and respecting a Christlike head who lays down his life for her. A husband who uses his strength for her good, who enables her to reach her full potential in God's kingdom, who bears the weight of responsibility for her well-being, who gives himself up for her, who seeks her wise counsel and leverages her strong help, is very much a woman's Christlike head.

And it's not just Ephesians 5 that teaches wives to submit to their husbands. Other passages in the New Testament leave no ambiguity on this point.

> Wives, submit yourselves to your husbands, as is fitting in the Lord. Husbands, love your wives and do not be harsh with them. (Colossians 3:18–19)
>
> Wives, in the same way, submit yourselves to your own husbands so that, if any of them do not believe the word, they may be won over without words by the behavior of their wives when they see the purity and reverence of your lives. . . . Husbands, in the same way be considerate as you live with your wives, and treat them with respect as the weaker partner and as heirs with you of the gracious gift of life, so that nothing will hinder your prayers. (1 Peter 3:1–2, 7)

Submission and respect are the divine calling of a wife to honor and affirm her husband's headship and help carry out that headship according to her gifts.

How Husbands Submit: Model Christ

There is a sense of vulnerability and trust, especially in light of Christ giving himself up for the church, that husbands are meant to exhibit in their relationships with their wives. This giving up, this entrusting of husbands to their wives, is a great gift for women.

Adam failed in this commission of holiness. Instead of washing Eve with water through the word of truth, he stood by and watched her sin. Ever since then, husbands have struggled to sacrificially love and entrust themselves to their wives, like Christ did for the church, so that they may become holy through the word of truth. But now, in Christ, as instructed by his apostle Paul, we get the chance to make it right. We get the chance to show the whole world how men and women can complement, complete, and inspire each other in holiness.

Husbands, if you starve your wife, you starve yourself. If you hurt your wife, you hurt yourself. If you neglect your wife, you neglect yourself.

Paul says husbands should love their wives like they love their own bodies, feeding and caring for them. In marriage two people really are "one flesh" (Ephesians 5:28–31). And if this weren't enough to inspire obedience, Paul's second point surely should. This "one flesh" mystery testifies about Christ and the church to the world (Ephesians 5:32).

Husbands who submit to their wives with sacrificial love, trust, and care give the world a picture "in the flesh" of Christ's love, trust, and care for the church, his bride. Wives who submit to their husbands and respect them give the world a picture "in the flesh" of the church's submission and respect for Christ, her husband.

When Christian men love their wives like Jesus loves the church, headship is life-giving. It's a beautiful thing when lived out by sacrificial husbands following Christ's example.

Headship and love are the divine calling of a husband to take primary responsibility for Christlike servant leadership, protection, and provision in the home.

Salvation and Submission

In the larger context of 1 Peter 3:1–7, the blessing of being joint heirs "of the gracious gift of life" (v. 7) is directly related to the same kind of equality language in Galatians 3:27–29 that egalitarians rely upon.

This section of Scripture explicitly shows that equality of standing in salvation does not take away gender roles. Peter provides an exhortation for women to submit to their husbands (v. 1) and for their husbands to treat their wives with respect "as the weaker partner" (v. 7). In other words, Peter saw no conflict between the neither-male-nor-female principle regarding our inheritance (Galatians 3:27–29) and the headship-submission principle regarding male-female roles.

Yes, these passages are unpopular culturally. And, yes, these passages have been abused by large-and-in-charge husbands trying to make power plays by mistreating their wives with forced submission. But even though it has been abused, the male headship model has been a good, life-giving model, where Christian men love their wives like Jesus loved the church. And we also note, like the passages on leadership in the church, that the husband's headship is connected to creation *before the Fall* (Ephesians 5:31). It's a beautiful thing when lived out by sacrificial husbands following Christ's example.

Husbands representing Jesus have a unique leadership role with their wives, who have a unique role representing the submission of the church to Jesus. We suggest that explaining Ephesians 5:22–24 as interchangeable submission and headship wrongly represents who Jesus and the church really are and how they work together.

6. Does it bother you that you must redefine the understanding of so many passages and key words?

Again, the egalitarian viewpoint requires the reinterpretation of the male headship role God created in both the Old Testament and the ministry of Jesus. If we include the whole Bible, the full discussion on gender in Scripture requires egalitarians to reinterpret hundreds of passages. This is contrary to what egalitarians typically tell us, which is that there are really only two passages that restrict the kinds of authority women exercise in the church—1 Timothy 2 and 1 Corinthians 14—and that the restrictions found in these two passages aren't actually meant to be taken transculturally.

There are hundreds of passages that can't easily be made to fit egalitarian ideals. There is the centrality of the patriarchs, the male-only priesthood in Israel, the major prophets in Israel, the apostles of Jesus, elders in the New Testament, etc., and *then* we get to 1 Timothy 2 and 1 Corinthians 14. To be a true egalitarian requires one form of reinterpretation or another when it comes to all these passages.

There are also key words that must be reinterpreted from how they have been understood for 2,000 years. Here are four words at the heart of this discussion that must be redefined, according to an egalitarian lens:

- "head"
- "authority"
- "helper"
- "submission"

For more on how these words have needed to be redefined against the historic church's understanding, we recommend reading "On Gender and the Bible: Where Does Egalitarianism Lead?"[150] Respected contemporary scholars such as Tim Keller, D.A. Carson, and Thomas Schreiner show that the interpretive consensus over twenty centuries about these words is the most accurate one, not the egalitarian redefinitions, contrary to what is typically alleged.[151]

Throughout history, almost no one has adopted the hermeneutical views of egalitarians on the Bible. These views are still rejected in the majority of churches around the world today. Yet egalitarians argue that their reinterpretation of these words is the new scholarly consensus. In our studies, we have not found this to be true. Even if this were the new scholarly consensus, this fundamental fact would remain unchanged: a person who studied the Bible thoroughly without the pressure of our Western secular culture would not naturally end up with an egalitarian understanding of the key words. This is what history shows us.

We must ask ourselves: Are we trying to find reinterpretations that fit our culture; or are we letting the original and historic meaning of the text serve as our final authority?

150. Bobby Harrington and Renée Sproles, "On Gender and the Bible: Where Does Egalitarianism Lead?" Renew.org, www.renew.org/on-gender-and-the-bible-where-does-egalitarianism-lead-part-9/ (accessed October 17, 2022).
151. See Thomas Schreiner's summary article supporting the historic consensus on these words in Thomas Schreiner, "Paul and Gender: A Review Article," *Themelios* 43, no. 2, www.thegospelcoalition.org/themelios/article/paul-and-gender-a-review-article/ (accessed October 17, 2022).

7. What can you teach from Scripture on what makes a man distinct from a woman?

This question gets at the heart of our cultural moment and the clash of its consistent egalitarianism with a Judeo-Christian worldview. The Bible teaches that God made us male and female (Genesis 1:26–27) and that the strengths and importance of each are meant to play out throughout life, not just in sexual reproduction.

Yet our culture is fast rejecting the goodness of the distinctiveness of maleness and femaleness.

The result is deep confusion and sometimes even self-hatred directed at one's own body as a gendered creation. We now have millions of men alienated from women because of this confusion: many shrink from any signs of manliness on the one side while others maintain a distorted, brutal, and toxic manliness on the other.

And there is now a crisis for young men, especially in their teens, twenties, and early thirties in America. Why have so many young men lost their way and become directionless? Why are many struggling with shame at being male (seeing it as toxic) and contemplating a new gender identity (just visit a local high school and listen to the conversations)? With a fuzzy understanding of the purpose of maleness and femaleness (see Chapter 1: "What Does Nature Tell Us Sex and Gender Are For?"), many churches remain silent on the issue.

As C.S. Lewis said, "We are producing men without chests."

Although "toxic masculinity" can denote toxic traits such as misogyny and sexual abuse, many secular and Christian egalitarians believe that *masculinity itself* is toxic. The upshot is that to be accepted in our culture, men must become more like women. The culture and many churches are embracing the belief that a person can change genders and that gender itself is a cultural construct that ought to be deconstructed.

The church ought to speak into this confusion with clarity, affirming the goodness and distinctiveness of how God created us as male and female. Yet churches that go egalitarian struggle to biblically answer even basic questions about what it means to be male and female. An increasing number are now explicitly adopting the viewpoint of the secular culture when it comes to gender.

So what does it mean to be a man or a woman? And, importantly, what passages from Scripture will you rely upon to frame your answer?

Years ago, I (Bobby) read a book by a popular egalitarian leader from Willow Creek Community Church in Chicago on a biblical view of marriage. Willow Creek has been one of the most influential churches among evangelical, Bible-believing churches, and it is an explicitly egalitarian church. I was surprised when I discovered that the book was missing all the major passages on husbands and wives from the New Testament. Then I realized that the author didn't use them because he believed they were culturally bound and no longer applicable.

Here's the uncomfortable reality: when church leaders interpret passages on gender through an egalitarian lens, they lose clarity on some of the most pressing questions for everyday Christians and parents in this cultural moment.

We believe this question of what makes a man and a woman different is more important than most people realize. Below, we summarize a longer post we published that explains the complementary relationship between men and women highlighted in Scripture:

1. God created males and females to be different.
2. God created male headship (authority) in the beginning.
3. Male headship (authority) in the home means that husbands mimic the leadership role of Jesus.
4. Wives respond to the headship (authority) of their husbands the way the church responds to Jesus.
5. Male headship in the local church is reflected in the teaching-authority and elder roles.
6. Men and women are to honor and submit to the authority of male headship in the church.
7. Honoring Jesus-style male headship will bring blessings on the family and the church.

We articulate the distinctives of men and women in more detail in Chapter 1 ("What Does Nature Tell Us Sex and Gender Are For?") and in this book's Conclusion. In this crucial time in our history, we must help people to understand their unique calling, especially men feeling directionless and unnecessary because of the messages sent by their culture. BetterMan.com has an excellent course for churches on how men are called to uniquely live out their masculinity along the lines we laid out above.

How we address the distinctiveness of gender is foundational to being able to address much of the chaos created by a culture furiously fighting against anything that suggests God's authority and our createdness.

If egalitarians cannot help the people in our churches with a biblical answer to these questions, then people will adopt the secular culture's viewpoint because that is the only viewpoint they are hearing.

Again, what does *Scripture* teach about the purpose and uniqueness of men and women?

8. How will you use Scripture as a basis for appointing female elders?
One of the most important things a local church does, when it is following the Bible, is appointing elders. The words *elder, overseer*, and *shepherd* are synonymous in the New Testament with one body of godly, proven leaders who oversee the local church (1 Timothy 3:1–7; Titus 1:5–9; 1 Peter 5:1–4; Acts 20:28–31; James 5:14).

So when churches seek to appoint elders, if they are discipling their people well, they will typically go through the passages on elders and help the members of the church to join in appointing those who meet the criteria to be elders, as described in the key passages.

When we read about the qualities, character, and lifestyle of those who are to be appointed as elders, it is not just that in general their roles sound more masculine; we also see how the passages explicitly only describe men. Here are some examples:

- "Now the overseer is to be above reproach, *faithful to his wife*, temperate, self-controlled, respectable, hospitable, able to teach." (1 Timothy 3:2)
- "He must *manage his own family well* and see that his children obey him, and he must do so in a manner worthy of full respect. (If anyone does not know how to manage his own family, how can he take care of God's church?)" (1 Timothy 3:4–5)
- "An elder must be blameless, *faithful to his wife, a man whose children believe* and are not open to the charge of being wild and disobedient." (Titus 1:6)

Women elders are simply not in view in these passages. So will you guide the everyday members of your local church to sidestep the gendered nature of these passages? Egalitarians will typically ignore, reinterpret, and add to them. Once you abandon the norm of Scripture, you will be forced to create human norms for guidance. You will replace what God teaches with your own tradition. Scripture will no longer be the norm for how you appoint elders.

If you are committed to egalitarianism, what Bible passages will you use to guide your church to embrace female elders? What will you tell them to sidestep the absence of women in the sections of Scripture that tell us what to look for in elders?

9. Why do churches not grounded in secular Western egalitarianism tend to read these passages so differently?

It is not fun to think about, and we mentioned it above in passing, but many Christians in Western nations live in times where vast numbers are turning from Judeo-Christian views in general and Christianity in particular. We are losing a lot of the historic cultural support we once had for many of our beliefs about the Bible and the ways of Jesus.

The upshot is that many Western Christians attempt to make their views palatable for those who do not like what the Bible says. Contextualizing the teachings of the Bible in terms that make sense to Western ears is a good thing. However, changing the teachings of the Bible to fit secular Western ideals is not. Changing our teachings to better fit in with culture means we end up marrying "the spirit of the age."

But it will not work, over time.

Trading historic Christianity for progressivism has historically led to decline and then eventual apostasy (more on that below). Most egalitarians believe that they are creating an "on ramp" that will help secular people come into the church. But they are actually creating an "exit ramp" where church members do not uphold a biblical view and instead defer to the beliefs of the dominant culture. Over time, they are subtly and unwittingly encouraging church members to embrace the values of the culture over those taught in the Word of God.

Western cultural ideals, including egalitarian ideals, are powerful. However, the vast majority of churches around the world still believe that male headship is the biblical norm. The Roman Catholic Church, the Orthodox Church, and most Protestant churches in the global South are in general agreement on the historic consensus on male headship. The male headship view is the norm:

- For nearly 2,000 years
- For all kinds of cultures
- For all kinds of countries
- For all kinds of Christian traditions

Yes, there are exceptions, but they do not overturn the norm. Only in the secular, egalitarian culture of the West is a different view becoming prevalent. Culture is winning over more and more churches in the West to the egalitarian viewpoint.

So here is the question stated differently: Honestly, if you took away Western cultural pressure, would Scripture lead you to adopt an egalitarian posture?

10. How will you stop the drift to gay, lesbian, and transgender affirmation and other forms of progressivism in your church?

Most church leaders who become egalitarians do not plan to embrace same-sex unions and transgender lifestyles as acceptable for godly people. Yes, some do plan to embrace these things too, but most strongly protest that they will not follow that path.

The problem is that egalitarian *methods of interpretation* lead to those results.

The same tools used to explain away the passages on gender are typically used by others to explain away the passages on LGBTQ+ issues and other hard doctrines.

This is a trajectory that is better measured not in years, but in decades.

Wayne Grudem has discovered and documented this trend: Throughout history, the interpretive methods that get you to egalitarianism typically will be used by your disciples over time to explain away other hard teachings.[152] That same slide, based upon the same hermeneutical methods, leads to progressivism (liberalism) and ultimately to the slow death of churches.[153]

You might spend some time looking at the historical trajectory over recent decades of the seven major mainline denominations in the U.S.[154] Check out the United Church of Christ, the Episcopal Church, the Disciples of Christ, and other denominations that have embraced liberalism. They made these same egalitarian moves decades ago, bringing women into all levels of leadership, and now they embrace the goodness of homosexuality and transgenderism, multiple paths of salvation, and often a denial of the reality of hell. They are all on the historical trajectory of decline leading to death as denominations.[155]

Why?

---

152. Wayne Grudem, *Evangelical Feminism: A New Path to Liberalism?* (Wheaton: Crossway, 2006).
153. For more on this trajectory, see David Young's *A Grand Illusion: How Progressive Christianity Undermines Biblical Faith* (Renew.org, 2019).
154. Josiah Aden, "'Seven Sisters' of Mainline Protestantism Still Bleed Members," *Juicy Ecumenism*, September 25, 2019, www.juicyecumenism.com/2019/09/25/mainline-protestantism-decline-continues/ (accessed October 17, 2022).
155. Ed Stetzer, "If It Doesn't Stem Its Decline, Mainline Protestantism Has Just 23 Easters Left," *Washington Post*, April 28, 2017, www.washingtonpost.com/news/acts-of-faith/wp/2017/04/28/if-it-doesnt-stem-its-decline-mainline-protestantism-has-just-23-easters-left/ (accessed October 17, 2022).

Because in each case, the logic is the same: based on the perceived harm that our traditional interpretations of these passages have done (e.g., to women, homosexuals, transgender people, the lost), we need to reinterpret these passages in ways that bring justice and equality.[156]

If you choose egalitarian methods of interpretation—especially in the name of seeking justice and equality—how will you not end up at the same destination? Don't look at the short term when the implications take a little longer to work out; take a longer view. What will make you different from mainline and progressive denominations twenty or twenty-five years from now?

AN OBJECTION

We have heard people say, "I do not want to be on the other side of eternity and have Jesus say, 'Why did you restrict women in the use of their gifts for my kingdom?'"

That sounds like a powerful argument against complementarianism, doesn't it? Yet let us offer some pushback because we believe this confuses eldership/senior ministry with the work of ministry.

When we connect all of the important roles women play in the New Testament church with our all-important work of making disciples, the New Testament picture is not one of restricting women at all. Rather, the picture of elders and authoritative teachers is one of *empowering* women and men "for works of service, so that the body of Christ may be built up until we all reach unity in the faith and in the knowledge of the Son of God and become mature, attaining to the whole measure of the fullness of Christ" (Ephesians 4:12–13).

There are so many important ministry works outside of being the main preacher/teacher or an elder that it should be obvious this is not an issue of gift utilization. We never want to adopt the false view that the truly

156. For more on this logic, see Daniel McCoy, "How to Read the Bible like a Progressive," Renew.org, www.renew.org/how-to-read-the-bible-like-a-progressive/ (accessed October 17, 2022).

important and gifted people are the preacher/teachers and elders. At their root, the jobs of these men are to equip the rest of the church to serve God in countless ministries that are vitally important in the eyes of God—including the most crucial job any of us could have: making disciples.

The New Testament describes women prophesying (Acts 21:9), serving as deacons (Romans 16:1–2), mentoring younger women (Titus 2:3–4), making disciples (Matthew 28:18–20), and doing other important and visible acts of ministry. The New Testament teachings as a whole make it clear that women are to be empowered for countless vital ministries.

In the meantime, here is another painful potential question by Jesus on the other side of eternity to think about:

> *Why did you cave to the pressure of cultural ideals that contributed to the breakdown of gender identity and created gender confusion? Why did you undervalue the authority of my Word and not observe the trajectory of the progressive churches who went before you?*

Considering this trajectory, our tenth question may be the most important of all to ponder: If you explain away all the passages on male headship to become egalitarians, how will you prevent those methods of interpretation from being used by those who come after you to move further in the slide toward full progressivism?

CONCLUSION

Before we finish, let us add some important context.

First, we do not think this topic is a salvation issue. To us, it is an issue about honoring God and pursuing God's best for us based upon the created order. And it is about a concern over the long-term implications of new methods of interpretation.

Second, we love our egalitarian brothers and sisters, and we empathize with them. It can be difficult for churches to address these issues today because of the pain involved. Many church leaders are embarrassed by the history of how their churches have restricted and mistreated women. There are also many husbands who have misused Scriptures about male headship as excuses to "lead" in domineering ways that oppose the loving example of Christ. We acknowledge those facts and empathize with those feelings.

But we believe there is a better way than reinterpreting passages against their grain and, once again, recommend the Renew Network's soft complementarian view.

Here are our ten questions in a summary fashion.

1. How did the earliest Christian leaders get it so wrong?
2. Why did God create from scratch—not based on culture—male leadership roles in the Old Testament, in the ministry of Jesus, and in the New Testament church?
3. Why make giftedness, not the created order, the starting point?
4. Why reject the priest/rabbi/synagogue role as a historical background for key texts in 1 Corinthians 11:3–5, 1 Corinthians 14:29–34, and 1 Timothy 2:11–13?
5. How do Jesus and the church mutually submit to each other?
6. Does it bother you that you must redefine the understanding of so many passages and key words?
7. What can you teach from Scripture on what makes a man distinct from a woman?
8. How will you use Scripture as a basis for appointing female elders?
9. Why do churches not grounded in secular Western egalitarianism tend to read these passages so differently?
10. How will you stop the drift to gay, lesbian, and transgender affirmation and other forms of progressivism in your church?

We pray that God will help you to thoughtfully answer each of these questions.

CONCLUSION: A SUMMARY

BOBBY HARRINGTON, RENÉE WEBB SPROLES

This chapter is a summary of what Scripture teaches about gender in leadership roles, specifically within the Christian home and the church. This topic requires careful thought and nuance, so we encourage you to explore these points in more detail as covered in other chapters of this book. What follows is a recap of what has been written by scholars and practitioners at Renew.org, written for those disciples of Jesus who want to read one in-depth distillation:

1. God created males and females to be different.
2. God created male headship (authority) in the beginning.
3. Male headship in the home means that husbands act like Jesus.
4. Wives respond to the headship of their husbands the way the church responds to Jesus.
5. Male headship in the local church is reflected in the teaching-authority and elder roles.
6. Men and women are to submit to and honor the authority of male headship in the church.
7. Honoring Jesus-style male headship will bring blessings on the family and the church.

The male headship viewpoint from Scripture that we will summarize below is broadly in step with the complementarian view of the earliest Christians (who were discipled by the apostles, in the churches of the apostles, with the same language and culture of the apostles) and with the larger, historic Christian consensus:

- For nearly 2,000 years
- For all kinds of cultures
- For all kinds of countries
- For all kinds of Christian traditions

Even now, in most churches around the world, the consensus about male headship prevails. Yes, there are exceptions, but these prove the norm.

Only in the secular, equality-means-interchangeability culture of the West is a different view becoming prevalent.

The alternative view is called egalitarianism, where women can lead in the home and in the church interchangeably with men. While this may be popular and "feel right," egalitarianism typically leads to progressive Christianity, as the scholar Wayne Grudem demonstrated.[157] And progressivism, as many have observed, leads to declines in male participation in churches and declines in convictions on other hard teachings, and it ultimately leads to church decline and spiritual death.[158]

Before we jump into our seven points, we will start with our personal stories regarding gender and the Bible.

OUR PERSONAL STORIES

Our personal stories—and our cultural context—provide a narrative that helps explain to others why we believe what we believe. Recently, thoughtful

157. Wayne Grudem, *Evangelical Feminism: The New Path to Liberalism* (Wheaton: Crossway, 2006). See also the summary of this book in Wayne Grudem, "Is Evangelical Feminism the New Path to Liberalism? Some Disturbing Warning Signs," *Journal for Biblical Manhood and Womanhood*, Spring 2004, www.cbmw.org/wp-content/uploads/2013/05/9-1.pdf (accessed October 17, 2022).

158. See just a sampling of the evidence in the following posts: "Is Progressive Christianity Dangerous," *The Christian Chronicle*, October 1, 2018, www.christianchronicle.org/is-progressive-christianity-dangerous/ (accessed October 17, 2022); R. Albert Mohler, "Why Conservative Churches Are Growing," *The Christian Post*, April 26, 2011, www.christianpost.com/news/why-conservative-churches-are-growing.html (accessed October 17, 2022); and David Millard Haskell, "Why Conservative Churches Grow and Liberal Churches Shrink," *The Dallas Morning News*, December 15, 2016, www.dallasnews.com/opinion/commentary/2016/12/15/why-conservative-churches-grow-and-liberal-churches-shrink/ (accessed October 17, 2022).

books that seek to "explain away" the complementarian view because it allegedly stems from conservative politics/culture have become popular. These books craft a captivating narrative that seeks to undermine the view we advocate. Complementarians have been saying that egalitarians are being led by our culture, and so Beth Allison Bar (*The Making of Biblical Womanhood: How the Subjugation of Women Became Gospel Truth*) and Kristin Kobes Du Mez (*Jesus and John Wayne*) seek to turn the tables by pointing out the ways in which conservative culture influenced complementarians to adopt their views.

The excellent critiques of both Barr and Du Mez by Guy Layfield show the flaws in their narratives.[159] However, we agree that our culture and personal biases can influence us and our interpretations of Scripture—and we must resist. God gave us Scripture to be our reliable and ultimate authority (2 Timothy 3:16–4:5).

BOBBY'S STORY

I (Bobby) grew up as a secular Canadian.

I knew a lot of people in my high school of 2,100 because I was captain of the football team and student council president. But I knew of only three people who actively attended a church—three in the whole school. I graduated high school and went off to the University of Calgary, where I got to know my French professor who was a disciple of Jesus. He showed me why I could trust Scripture as God's Word and what it meant to be a disciple of Jesus. I was baptized on my birthday in March and by August I transferred to Harding University in Searcy, Arkansas, where I started studying Greek as a brand-new Bible major.

159. See Guy Layfield, "Are White Evangelicals Responsible for Corrupting the Faith and Fracturing a Nation? A Review of 'Jesus and John Wayne,'" Renew.org, www.renew.org/are-white-evangelicals-responsible-for-corrupting-the-faith-and-fracturing-a-nation-a-review-of-jesus-and-john-wayne/ (accessed October 17, 2022), and Guy Layfield, "Is Complementarianism Oppressive? A Review of Beth Allison Barr's The Making of Biblical Womanhood," Renew.org, www.renew.org/is-complementarianism-oppressive-a-review-of-beth-allison-barrs-the-making-of-biblical-womanhood/ (accessed October 17, 2022).

Eighteen months after my adult baptism, as my second year of studies as a Bible major began, I signed up for a course to read through and study the Greek text of 1 Timothy. I was still trying to learn about my new faith, and I had only engaged in a cursory reading of the difficulties I might have with certain passages like 1 Corinthians 14 where women are told to be silent, or 1 Timothy 2 where women are forbidden to hold teaching authority over men. In those early months of my faith, I consciously deferred my questions.

But that fall I could no longer ignore a major difficulty with a key text.

As the semester progressed, we came to the Greek text of 1 Timothy 2:11–12a. It says, "A woman should learn in quietness and full submission. I do not permit a woman to teach or to assume authority over a man." I knew that the text was describing what happened in the gathered church, but I didn't know how to handle what it taught. Shortly afterward I took another Greek course on 1 Corinthians. In 1 Corinthians 14, the apostle Paul teaches that during the weighing of prophecy, "women should remain silent" and "they are not allowed to speak" (1 Corinthians 14:34).

I had been discipled by my secular environment to believe that a woman can and should do whatever a man does. Only an unenlightened person would restrict a woman. I did not want to be *that* guy, to be seen as a misogynist.

And yet, I had become a disciple of Jesus.

I was taught to take a posture toward the Word of God similar to Isaiah 66:2b, which says: "These are the ones I look on with favor: those who are humble and contrite in spirit, and who tremble at my word." I wanted to humbly tremble at God's Word—and follow it. But these texts created a big problem for me. And I was convinced it would create *big* barriers as I sought to help my secular family and friends make the decision to trust and follow Jesus with me.

I wrote something like the following in the margin of the Greek text of my Bible at that time: *This is not going to sell well back home.*

Because I had been discipled to obey Scripture in the early days of my journey—no matter what the contrary pressure might be from family, friends, and the world—I resolved to uphold what these texts said (2 Timothy 3:14–4:4). As I had been taught, I decided I would trust God with the problems these texts created for those who do not prioritize the Word of God over human wisdom. I concluded that God must have reasons for this teaching that I did not understand. I concluded that I needed to search for better understanding and/or someone to show the reasons to me.

Since that time, I have become a Bible nerd on this topic (and several others). For several decades, I read almost everything that was published on gender and these passages in the scholarly evangelical literature. *Maybe someone could legitimately explain them in a different, truthful, and yet God-honoring way?* I said to myself.

And I continued to wonder, *Why does God's Word teach these things?*

It has been forty years now, and no one has said or published anything that has led me to believe that I should discard these teachings for the secular worldview I was taught growing up. Instead, as I have studied God's Word and ministered in the local church with godly men and women and their families, I have come to believe that God created an order for the home and church, and that order is in step with how we are wired as men and women. And following God's Word is a better way for people than the way the world teaches. The male-headship view or "soft complementarianism" that I see in these texts, and Scripture as a whole, is more in step with the true nature of men and women and, when followed, it is what works best for families and churches.

RENÉE'S STORY

I (Renée) thought I was an egalitarian.

As I mentioned in Chapter 11, the culture at my church, my Christian school, and even my university was what I would now describe as rigid complementarianism. I grew up hearing things like, "Men are the head of the home" and "Men are supposed to lead women." I never saw a single woman pray, read Scripture, or even speak in gatherings where men were present at church. Only male teachers or boys were allowed to participate in chapel at school, and a female teacher couldn't pray aloud with another male in the room. As a child, and even as a young adult, I lived in this world without question.

However, life inside my family was vastly different. My mom and dad started their own business out of our garage while raising three kids. They relied on each other. They trusted one another. They leveraged each other's strengths. A first-generation Christian, my dad bravely laid down his life for us in Jesus-like ways. He was loyal, reliable, and empowering. My mom responded to this Jesus-like love in submission and respect. She was faithful, diligent, and trustworthy.

My grandparents lived behind us on their farm, and they, too, complemented one another in ways that made them thrive. My mom and my grandmother became my mentors in marriage and in life. Their husbands relied on them and trusted them. They respected and honored their husbands by their constancy and loyalty. Together they both built businesses, families, and homes from the ground up.

At twenty-one years old, I married a man who has loved me with a Christlike, empowering, sacrificial love year after year. (Happy thirtieth, honey!) He chose to know me, understand me, and love me, even when I was hard to love. For years I naïvely assumed most women enjoyed this kind of commitment and self-sacrificing love.

Sadly, they don't.

Submitting to this kind of man, to this kind of love, is a joy. My respect and submission for him and his love and submission toward me have made us a high-functioning team. And we have enjoyed a life of mutual admiration and devotion.

By my late twenties, the dissonance between my church life and my home life began to grow, and my list of questions grew too.

Why does my church believe that women can't read Scripture or pray with men around? Why are men the only ones baptizing people? Why are female teachers relegated to the children's ministry? I fumed. I had been loved out of all sense of proportion at home and quietly excluded at church. Slowly, the resentment began to build. *If that is what complementarianism is,* I thought, *then I'm not that.*

But when I really began to study what God reveals in Scripture about gender, I was surprised. I wasn't egalitarian after all.

I was using that word in response to heavy-handed complementarianism in my school and my church. But because the Bible is the Word of God and has unique and absolute authority in the life of a Christ follower, I had to take what I found and try my best to obey it.

I couldn't conclude that Genesis 1–3 was wrong.
I couldn't conclude that Paul was wrong.
I couldn't conclude that cultural changes superseded Scripture.
I couldn't conclude that my experience (or anyone else's!) was more important than Scripture.

Instead, I concluded that God's complementary design for men and women is good for us. Male and female reflect the image of God in gendered ways in life, marriage, and the Christian community.

WIDER THAN A FEW VERSES

We believe the whole Bible (not just a few sticky passages) upholds a complementarian view of men and women. Egalitarianism is not just an alternative interpretation of a few passages of Scripture. Egalitarianism bends the whole biblical narrative toward the interchangeability of the sexes.

Egalitarianism begins to look a lot like the Western world's predominant views on sex and gender, where:

- Gender itself is no longer tied to biology.
- Nobody can tell their sons what it uniquely means to be a man.
- Nobody can tell their daughters what it uniquely means to be a woman.
- A large number of teens are now confused about whether they should identify as male or female or gender fluid.

- Sexual immorality, bisexuality, and homosexuality are fashionable.
- Marriage itself is in crisis, and many are giving up on it.

Think that's a stretch?

Egalitarians have explained away most of the passages on the uniqueness of gender roles in the Bible that would stop a cultural drift toward progressivism. I (Renée) once sat in a four-hour presentation at a local church where half of the time was devoted to convincing church leadership that passages like 1 Timothy 2 were too hard to understand without a degree in Greek. And even then, they argued, scholars can't be sure that Paul wasn't egalitarian.

So it's no surprise that many churches now say the same things on these topics that the world says.

We encourage you to look at the whole scope of Scripture (Chapter 3 covers this in particular) as well as the difficult biblical texts about men and women in many chapters of this book. We encourage you to try and put aside your cultural biases and upbringings and study the Scriptures to understand God's heart for his people, instead of trying to fit God's Word into our preformed system of beliefs and values.

Instead of following a culture of either rigid traditionalism or progressivism, we want to focus on God's good design for us as men and women. The following points summarize what we've learned in this book.

1. GOD CREATED MALES AND FEMALES TO BE DIFFERENT.

The starting place for a discussion on gender in marriage and the church should be chosen carefully.

How do we decide where to go first?

We start where Jesus and the apostles do: the creation account in Genesis 1–3 (see also Matthew 19:1–9, 1 Corinthians 11:3–16, 14:33–36, and 1 Timothy 2:12–15).

The Genesis 1–3 starting point teaches us to focus on God's created order and the unique descriptions given to Adam and Eve as representatives of humanity.

Egalitarians reject the creation account as a starting place and pick Galatians 3:26–28 instead:

> So in Christ Jesus you are all children of God through faith, for all of you who were baptized into Christ have clothed yourselves with Christ. There is neither Jew nor Gentile, neither slave nor free, nor is there male and female, for you are all one in Christ Jesus.

This is a wonderful section of Scripture that teaches equality in salvation for everyone who has been baptized into Christ. But this passage is *not* about gender roles; it is about our identity and unity in Christ.

We wonder if many egalitarians would continue this train of thought throughout all three comparisons in this passage. Are all the differences between Jews and Gentiles negated? Are slaves and free people interchangeable?

When you take verses like Galatians 3:26–28, which exegetically and contextually are not talking about gender roles, and use them to undermine texts that *are* talking about gender, it is a problem. It's an unsound exegetical and hermeneutical method (see Chapter 9: "Can Women be Elders?").

So we must start in Genesis. Men and women were created to equally reflect the image of God, but in gendered ways, according to Genesis 1:27: "So God created mankind in his own image, in the image of God he created them; male and female he created them."

Sex and gender matter to God.

Some of the first things to notice in Genesis 1:26–28 are the Hebrew words *tselem* and *demuth*, which are translated in most English Bibles as "image" and "likeness." The principle that men and women are made to reflect God is stated *five times* in the opening chapters of Genesis (1:26, 27; 5:1; 9:6).

The second thing to notice is the use of the word "they." Both man *and* woman were made to do the things that reflect God's image.

He could have made one sex to represent himself, but he didn't. He made two. All of us, male and female, are made in his image. Our imaging is like a Venn diagram: male and female reflect God's image in many of the same ways, and yet there are also distinctions between us and how we image God.

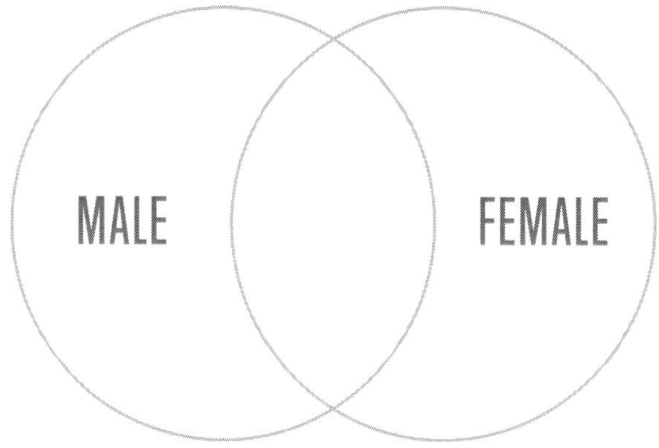

Men and women are similar in that we image God in filling and subduing the earth. We procreate together. We subdue the earth together. We rule every living creature together.

So "image" and "likeness" language are associated with humanity's rule, male and female, over creation on God's behalf. Both men and women are needed to fill the earth. Both men and women are told to *radah* (v. 26), which means to reign or have dominion over all God's creatures.

How do we reign as God's representatives? We tend to God's good creation in every way that builds up, honors, and fulfills his purpose for making it in the first place. We fill the earth through families. We make homes. We create culture. We work. We build just governments and righteous nations.

Every time we do these things, in big ways and small, we reflect the image of our good God.

Jesus reiterated the creation framework when he taught on the foundation of marriage in Matthew 19:4–6 in response to a question:

> "Haven't you read," he replied, "that at the beginning the Creator 'made them male and female,' and said, 'For this reason a man will

> leave his father and mother and be united to his wife, and the two will become one flesh'? So they are no longer two, but one flesh. Therefore what God has joined together, let no one separate."

We were made differently as male and female and we come together in a complementary unity in marriage. Based on these passages, other unions based upon sex changes, adultery, and same sex unions are contrary to God's created order (see Chapters 13 and 14).

Genesis 1–3 is also the text that the New Testament writers return to again and again to note that men and women have unique responsibilities toward one another.

It is an observable, biological truth that men and women are complementary at the deepest levels of their being.

Our brains are different. Our voices are different. Our body shapes, body strengths, and reproductive systems all are different. And even with the skyrocketing number of sex reassignment surgeries, our chromosomes cannot be "reassigned" from one sex to the other. Perhaps the clearest example of complementarity in gender is the fact that each sex has one-half of a reproductive system, requiring the opposite sex to realize its full function. These differences are extensive, and they bear witness to God's creative will for humanity (see more on this in Chapter 1).

Sadly, when sin entered the world, the relationship between the sexes was broken.

While affirming God's created order, we also acknowledge that this order was corrupted in part when our ancestors, Adam and Eve, fell into sin. We image bearers of God have found ourselves in conflict from this point forward, struggling to represent God's nature as we are saddled by evil. Trials and struggles are common as we live in the already-but-not-yet of God's kingdom.

Confusion often exists around God's intended norms regarding identity and sexuality. In the curse of Genesis 3:16, we find that women will have desires for their husbands, which can lead to unrealistic expectations, disappointments, or even manipulation. And men will misuse their authority (headship) to oppress and mistreat women (see more on this in point #2 as well as in Chapter 5).

As with the other consequences of the fall, we must work toward restoration, knowing that full restoration will only come in the new heaven and earth (Revelation 21:1–5).

It should not surprise or scare us, then, when some have attraction for those of their same sex, while others have struggles with gender dysphoria, being born one way biologically but identifying internally with a different sex (see Romans 1:24–27 and Chapters 13–14 of this book).

And then there is the pain. The pain of conflict. The pain of unwanted affections. And the pain of mistreatment at the hands of Christians who wrongly enforce God's norms with judgment and hate, not the love of Jesus—and that description sadly includes many churches.

But God calls us to uphold his created order where we live in step with his teachings on gender, marriage, and LGBTQ+ issues. Each of us has disordered affections and desires, sexual or not, and so each person who chooses Christ must die to their sinful affections rather than give them special status or call them good. God calls us to be faithful to his teachings. And he calls us to love each other and be merciful to each other in our struggles.

God's intentions for the created order are God's best for us. We will point to some of the fruit of God's better way in the following sections.

2. GOD CREATED MALE HEADSHIP (AUTHORITY) IN THE BEGINNING.

Headship is a concept taught in Genesis 1–3. The God-ordained order called "head" has a much richer meaning than frequently used words like *authority, rule,* and *leadership.* These principles are encompassed within the idea of headship, but they are poor synonyms for it. Additionally, leadership and authority are traits that both men and women display in Scripture (for a small sample, see the leadership of women in Romans 16:1–2 and Acts 18:26).

And yet, headship is a unique God-created authority and responsibility to mimic Jesus—to lead and be a head like Jesus—in the home for husbands and in the church for the main preacher/teacher and elders. Headship is how men take responsibility to live out their created fabric in a Jesus-like way that seeks the benefit of families and the local church—and, most of all, seeks to honor God.

Headship is based on the teaching of the creation account in Genesis and the concept of *primogeniture.* God inspired Paul to point to primogeniture when he prescribed gender differences in the church and in marriage (see more in Chapter 4).

What Is Primogeniture?

Primogeniture is the concept that the first created or the firstborn has family leadership responsibility and authority.

God intentionally *created man first,* and he created woman *second,* to complement him. There is a biological poetry that God hard-wired into men and women at creation: we are different and wonderfully complementary (see Chapters 1–2).

As the first created, men were given a set of biological-social strengths that are typically suited to the headship role God created for them in the home and the religious community. Likewise, women were given a set of biological-social strengths that typically suit their complementary role relative to headship. These strengths are not absolute; men and women reveal variations in their biological-social strengths—but they are typical.

In Genesis 2, God created Adam first and gave him the responsibility to tend the garden of Eden and uphold the commandment not to eat from the tree of the knowledge of good and evil (Genesis 2:16–17). God then created the woman to be man's strong help (Genesis 2:18). Their roles are different, but they are equally created in God's image, and they have unity in their relationship as they complement one another. As Genesis 2:24 puts it, "That is why a man leaves his father and mother and is united to his wife, and they become one flesh."

The principle of male headship (primogeniture) is reflected in the following four sections of the New Testament:

First Timothy 2:12–13 describes how headship/primogeniture applies to the main teacher/preacher role in the gathered church: "I do not permit a woman to teach or to assume authority over a man; she must be quiet. For Adam was formed first, then Eve."

First Corinthians 11:3 and 11:8–9 describes how headship/primogeniture applies when women pray and prophesy in the church: "But I want you to realize that the head of every man is Christ, and *the head of the woman is man*, and the head of Christ is God." And, "For man did not come from woman, but woman from man; *neither was man created for woman, but woman for man.*"

First Corinthians 14:34–35 describes how headship/primogeniture applies during the weighing of prophecies in the gathered church. "The law" refers to the creation account that was discussed three chapters earlier in 1 Corinthians 11. "Women should remain silent in the churches. They are not allowed to speak, but must be in submission, as *the law* says."

Ephesians 5:23–24 and 5:31–33 describes how headship/primogeniture applies in marriage: "*The husband is the head of the wife as Christ is the head of the church*. . . . As the church submits to Christ, so also *wives should submit to their husbands in everything*. . . . 'For this reason *a man will leave his father and mother and be united to his wife*, and the two will become one flesh.' This is a profound mystery—but I am talking about Christ and the church. However, each one of you also must *love his wife as he loves himself, and the wife must respect her husband*."

These are the four major sections of the New Testament that discuss the reason for gender distinctions in the gathered church and in the home. These teachings are not based upon changing culture. All four sections uphold the conviction that God's created order is the ground for the biblical doctrine of male headship.

What does this mean?

Men are created by God differently from women, and *consistent with that hardwiring*, they have been given responsibility and authority for Christlike headship in marriage and in certain leadership roles in the local church. It also means women are called to honor and submit to the headship role of their husband and, in the gathered church, to the role of elder and lead teacher/authority, both positions of male leadership (see Chapter 8).

3. MALE HEADSHIP (AUTHORITY) IN THE HOME MEANS HUSBANDS MIMIC JESUS.

The roles of husbands and wives are different. The husband uniquely models himself after Jesus and the wife uniquely models herself after the church. These are not ambiguous or interchangeable roles; as Jesus is the head of the church, the husband is the head of his wife. Jesus' headship is described this way: "God placed all things under his feet and appointed him to be head over everything for the church" (Ephesians 1:22).

A few chapters later, God explicitly teaches husbands to mimic Jesus in his headship role in marriage with his wife in Ephesians 5:25–29:

> Husbands, love your wives, just as Christ loved the church and gave himself up for her to make her holy, cleansing her by the washing with water through the word, and to present her to himself as a radiant church, without stain or wrinkle or any other blemish, but holy and blameless. In this same way, husbands ought to love their wives as their own bodies. He who loves his wife loves himself. After all, no one ever hated their own body, but they feed and care for their body, just as Christ does the church.

Carefully notice the kind of head God teaches a husband to be:

- He gives himself up for his wife.
- He encourages his wife's holiness.
- He encourages his wife's purity and honor.
- He loves his wife like he loves himself.
- He cares and provides for his wife.

Even though Jesus is King of kings and Lord of lords, he is also described as a good shepherd (John 10), a man of sorrows (Isaiah 53), a teacher (Matthew 7), and a lamb (John 1). Jesus reminds his disciples that headship, if it means anything at all, means that they will serve others.

Husbands are called to reject the paths of domineering behavior on the one hand and passive/uncertain behavior on the other (see Chapter 10).

In the last several decades, I (Bobby) have had the opportunity to teach men, and try to live out before them, what it means to be a loving, Christlike, sacrificial head. Here is a summary I used based upon this Ephesians 5 passage (and others related to it), which was slightly modified from the work of Robert Lewis of *BetterMan*.[160] It is called "25 Ways to Be a Jesus-Like Husband in Marriage."

25 WAYS TO BE A JESUS-LIKE HUSBAND IN MARRIAGE

1. He keeps leading and initiating, even when it doesn't go well.
2. He stays alert in seeking to serve and lead, to keep the "blessing-flow" within the family (see 1 Peter 3:7).
3. He accepts spiritual responsibility for his family by personally committing to his own spiritual growth and investing in the growth of his family.
4. He is willing to say "I'm sorry" and "Forgive me" to his family.
5. He lets his wife and children into the interior of his life.
6. He seeks to understand his wife and interacts with her out of that understanding.
7. He seeks his wife's input and counsel, and many times he yields to her view when envisioning the future.
8. He frequently tells his wife what he likes about her and praises her often in public.
9. He prays with and for his wife on a regular basis.
10. He encourages his wife to grow as an individual and ensures time for his wife to pursue her own personal interests.

160. See www.betterman.com/ for more resources from pastor Robert Lewis and his team.

11. He discusses household responsibilities with his wife and makes sure they are reasonably distributed.
12. He provides financially for his family's basic living expenses and consults his wife on all major financial decisions.
13. He keeps his family financially sound and out of harmful debt.
14. He makes sure he and his wife have drawn up a will and arranged a well-conceived plan for their children in case of death.
15. He follows through with commitments he has made to his wife and family.
16. He anticipates the different stages his marriage and his children will pass through.
17. He manages the schedule of the home and anticipates any pressure points.
18. He deals with distractions so he can talk with his wife and family.
19. He initiates meaningful family traditions and regular fun family outings.
20. He takes the lead in establishing with his wife sound, biblically supportable family values.
21. He takes the time to give his children practical instruction about life, which in turn gives them confidence with their peers.
22. He explains sex to each child in a way that gives them a wholesome perspective.
23. He joins a discipling group of men who are dedicated to improving their skills as disciples, husbands, and fathers.
24. He asks for help when he or his family is floundering.
25. He keeps starting over.

The biggest fans of my teaching on male headship in marriage have always been the women. As Jared Ellis points out in Chapter 12, women tend to highly value this kind of discipleship for men. One woman told me in the context of a conversation about biblical submission: "How could I object to submitting to a man who loved me like that?"

4. WIVES RESPOND TO THE HEADSHIP (AUTHORITY) OF THEIR HUSBANDS THE WAY THE CHURCH RESPONDS TO JESUS.

In marriage, a wife submits to her husband the way the church submits to Jesus. Ephesians 5:22–24 makes this clear:

> Wives, submit yourselves to your own husbands as you do to the Lord. For the husband is the head of the wife as Christ is the head of the church, his body, of which he is the Savior. Now as the church submits to Christ, so also wives should submit to their husbands in everything.

In the last decade, I (Renée) have had the opportunity to teach women, and I have tried to live out before them what it means to be a strong, respectful, submissive wife. Here is a summary based upon what we see in Scripture.

25 WAYS A WOMAN IS A STRONG HELPER TO HER HUSBAND

1. She is a capable ally in her husband's headship, using her God-given abilities to help build a high-functioning, complementary team.
2. She guards her husband's reputation by blessing her husband with respect: in her thoughts, in her words, and in her actions, abstaining from complaining about him in casual conversation.
3. She personally commits to her own spiritual growth and cooperates in the spiritual growth of her family.
4. She is ready to say "I'm sorry, please forgive me" to her husband and children.
5. She courageously faces the world shoulder-to-shoulder with her husband, respecting and encouraging his initiating leadership.
6. She intentionally develops her inner beauty by disciplining her reactions and responses to her husband (1 Peter 3:1–6).
7. She gives wise counsel to her husband as they plan for the future.
8. She yields her body to her husband as he also yields his body to her, with neither depriving the other of sexual intimacy except for a time of prayer (1 Corinthians 7:1–5).
9. She prays with and for her husband on a regular basis.
10. She listens attentively to her husband and responds to his concerns.

11. She manages the household with excellence, discussing responsibilities with her husband and ensuring that they are reasonably distributed (1 Timothy 5:14).
12. She faithfully and wisely stewards family time, money, and other resources (1 Timothy 5:14).
13. She sets a positive tone for the home, helping make it a place of peace and joy.
14. She helps her husband stay attuned to the spiritual, physical, and emotional needs of their children.
15. She follows through with commitments she has made to her husband and family.
16. She reacts with calm wisdom toward problems in her husband, trusting in God even when her husband doesn't and resisting the temptation to compare him with other men.
17. She refuses to give way to fear.
18. She cultivates an attitude of contentment for the life she shares with her husband and family.
19. She is interested in her husband's work and is grateful for his contribution to the family's security.
20. She upholds sound, biblically supportable family values.
21. She expresses her ideas and opinions respectfully without belittling or domineering.
22. She is trustworthy; her husband and children know they can depend on her to follow through in word and deed.
23. She joins a discipling group of women who are dedicated to improving their skills as Jesus followers, wives, and mothers.
24. She helps make things right with grace and mercy when family members make mistakes.
25. She keeps starting over.

The submission of wives to the headship of their husbands in marriage is described by Scripture in other unambiguous contexts. Colossians and 1 Peter also make it clear.

> Wives, submit yourselves to your husbands, as is fitting in the Lord. Husbands, love your wives and do not be harsh with them. (Colossians 3:18–19)
>
> Wives, in the same way submit yourselves to your own husbands so that, if any of them do not believe the word, they may be won over without words by the behavior of their wives, when they see the purity and reverence of your lives. (1 Peter 3:1–2)

A Helpful Framework for Submission

The world teaches us that a woman submitting is equal to subservience to her husband.

Submission is seen as wrong, antiquated, unnecessary, and something that may lead to abuse. Genesis 3:16 teaches that women will "desire their husbands." Wives sometimes want more than their husbands can provide. And then men, in their brokenness, will often treat their wives harshly.

"Your desire will be for your husband, and he *will rule over you*," the text teaches us.

It is a function of the curse that many men will misuse their headship. They can either be harsh and domineering with their wives and children (Ephesians 6:4), or indecisive and unsure, like Adam in Eve's temptation, not protecting and watching over their wives (Genesis 3:6).

Because of these extremes, many women flinch at the command to submit to their husbands. And rightly so. In light of this difficulty, 1 Peter 3 provides an important framework. God calls men to a third way: the way of proactive, Jesus-style headship.

First Peter 3:6b teaches women to model themselves after Sarah's example as she submitted to Abraham. It teaches two points of emphasis: "You are her daughters if you do what is right and do not give way to fear."

First, a wife does what is right.

A woman's first loyalty is to Jesus and his teachings. She will not follow her husband in sin. And when she follows her husband in step with Jesus' teachings, she does what is right.

Second, she does not give way to fear.

"Fear not" is the most common command in the Bible. It is difficult for many of us to submit, but a woman often feels particularly vulnerable in submitting to her husband's headship. Young women will need discipleship from older, godly, wise women to learn to do this with grace (Titus 2:4). This passage also assumes a posture of prayer and trust in God. It teaches that submission is often an act of faith in God that renounces fear, especially if a woman struggles to trust her husband's leadership.

Our Problem with These Passages

Scripture is so clear as to be boring when it comes to the principle of submission. God both commands and commends submission. So what's the problem?

We do not like submission. None of us do.

Jesus is commended for his submission to God the Father (Hebrews 5:7) and his parents (Luke 2:51). Through Paul, Jesus teaches all of us to submit to government authorities (Romans 13), for slaves to submit to their masters (Colossians 3:22–25), and for Christians to submit to their church leaders (Hebrews 13:17). All believers are expected to submit to each other out of reverence for Christ (Ephesians 5:21). And submission is for both husbands and wives, even as we express it in distinctly gendered ways (Ephesians 5:21).

As Jim Putman and Chad Harrington show us in their book, *The Revolutionary Disciple*, the revolutionary disciple in North America is the disciple who embraces *humble submission to God-given authorities*.[161] The revolutionary disciple is the disciple who obeys Jesus.

161. Jim Putman and Chad Harrington, *The Revolutionary Disciple: Walking Humbly with Jesus in Every Area of Life* (HIM Publications, 2021).

Rebecca McLaughlin puts the whole teaching about submission in marriage in context:

> Ephesians 5 sticks like a burr in our 21st-century, Western ears. But we must not misread it as justifying "traditional" gender roles. The text doesn't say the husband is the one whose needs come first and whose comfort is paramount. In fact, Ephesians 5 is a withering critique of traditional gender roles, in its original context and today. In the drama of marriage, the wife's needs come first, and the husband's drive to prioritize himself is cut down with the axe of the gospel. . . . And it's a daily challenge to remember what I'm called to in this gospel drama, and to notice opportunities to submit to my husband as to the Lord—not because I'm naturally more or less submissive, or because he is naturally more or less loving, but because Jesus submitted to the cross for me.[162]

So men submit to Jesus in their role as husbands and fathers, loving their wives as Christ loved the church. And women submit to Jesus in their role as wives and mothers, submitting to their husbands and respecting them as they are instructed by God.

Christian egalitarians and our Western culture make a strong case that we must stop the abuse and mistreatment of women.

We agree. Heartily. Strongly. But we differ on the solution. Telling men to be like women and women to be like men does not work. Why? Because it fails to address the core of our problem: the freedom to choose sin.

Jesus explained that misusing our freedom to do what we shouldn't do actually leads to a hidden form of slavery. *True* freedom starts with letting him set us free from our slavery to sin so that we can live how God created us to live.

> To the Jews who had believed him, Jesus said, "If you hold to my teaching, you are really my disciples. Then you will know the

162. Rebecca McLaughlin, *The Secular Creed: Engaging Five Contemporary Claims* (Austin, TX: The Gospel Coalition, 2021). For more on Ephesians 5, see Chapter 10.

> truth, and the truth will set you free." They answered him, "We are Abraham's descendants and have never been slaves of anyone. How can you say that we shall be set free?" Jesus replied, "Very truly I tell you, everyone who sins is a slave to sin. Now a slave has no permanent place in the family, but a son belongs to it forever. So if the Son sets you free, you will be free indeed." (John 8:31–36)

Jesus taught that true freedom means setting aside our natural inclinations and following *God's* will. But he didn't just teach this to us; he modeled it for us.

Jesus, who holds the universe together by the power of his might, can do *anything* that aligns with his holy nature. Yet when it came to following his Father's will, Jesus gave up his freedom, saying, "Not my will but thy will be done." Why? He followed God's will—all the way to the cross—so that *we* could experience true freedom: freedom from sin (Colossians 1:15–17; Matthew 26:39; Luke 22:42; Hebrews 10:10).

No matter our personalities, natural inclinations, or gifts, to be *truly* free, each of us must apply the gospel's guardrails: we say *no* to sin so that we can say *yes* to living life to the full for Jesus (John 10:10; Galatians 2:20). Freedom is not ripping the guardrails off the road, making them up ourselves, or pretending they don't exist. If we do that, we may experience what feels like freedom for a while, but eventually we'll careen off reality's road and into a ditch of one kind or another.

As we hold to the teachings of Jesus, we will enjoy freedom to live our best lives in the areas of marriage, sex, and raising children. In each of these areas, our post-Christian culture will try to persuade us that saying *no* to our desires is slavery. Yet true freedom comes from saying *no* to sin so that we can say *yes* to living the truly good life.

God calls men to reject male domination (we call this "corrupted patriarchy" or "hard complementarianism") on the right as well as the egalitarian impulse (we call this "androgynous confusion") on the left. Scripture points to the third way: the way of proactive, Jesus-style headship.

We have seen the clear fruit of this path in countless situations, and it leads to God's blessings on men, women, and families.

5. MALE HEADSHIP IN THE LOCAL CHURCH IS REFLECTED IN THE TEACHING-AUTHORITY AND ELDER ROLES.

The New Testament repeatedly features males in the teaching-authority structures that are established by God.

While women lead in many ways throughout the Bible, there are notable exceptions to their work (see Chapters 6–9). Women are featured prominently in the ministry of Jesus, but he did not choose them as any of the official twelve disciples/apostles. There are no women in the New Testament who are given the role of evangelist, like Timothy and Titus. The elders of the churches are also male. This is consistent with the teaching of headship/primogeniture as described above.

When the Christians gathered as a church, women did not serve as the authoritative teachers, nor were they to be involved in the evaluation of prophecy (the job of elders), and Paul instructed women in Corinth to wear veils when they prayed and prophesied in the gathering of the church.

Let's look briefly at these three teachings.

1 Timothy 2

In 1 Timothy 2, God speaks through Paul and prohibits women from giving authoritative teaching. These verses in 1 Timothy 2 may be the starkest verses on this subject in Scripture, as they are in direct contrast to contemporary cultural ideals of full female participation in the leadership of any organization—both secular and within the church. Note Paul's words found in 1 Timothy 2:11–14:

> A woman should learn in quietness and full submission. I do not permit a woman to teach or to assume authority over a man; she must be quiet. For Adam was formed first, then Eve. And Adam was not the one deceived; it was the woman who was deceived and became a sinner.

If we read these verses carefully, the key element is the coupling of teaching *and* authority. We believe that the authority role Paul has in mind refers to teaching that represents the authority and guidance of the leadership of the church (Chapters 8 and 9). Stated differently, the teaching restricted to men is the teaching that leads and sets direction for the congregation. In most churches, this is the role of the main preacher/teacher and the elders/pastors. This is also consistent with the Old Testament role of the priests, who were exclusively males and who served as the primary teachers of the law (again, see Chapters 8 and 9).

There are other authoritative roles in the local church that are not found in Scripture. For example, many churches have executive ministers who administer significant delegated authority from the elders, directing the congregation in teaching and practice. While the Bible does not address this particular role, we believe that each position in a church should honor male headship. In fact, everything we do should align—as much as possible—with both the explicit teachings and underlying principles found in the New Testament.

The key question for considering a woman as an executive minister comes down to function: Is she exercising spiritual authority over men? Is she telling men, as the authority, what they should teach or how they should exercise their spiritual leadership? If the answer to these questions is "yes," then it seems to violate the teaching/principle of 1 Timothy 2:11–3:7. If the answer is "no," for example, because it is primarily a business/financial role, then it would not violate those principles (see Romans 16:1–2).

Before we move to 1 Corinthians 11 and 14, here are a few other things to consider:

1. Because the word "pastor" is used in the Bible as a synonym for "elder" (see Acts 20:28; 1 Peter 5:1–2) and the elder/pastor/overseer roles in the New Testament are reserved for qualified men only (see Chapter 9), we recommend using these words as titles for men only. It is clearest and most biblical if we can refer to Bible roles with the words used in the Bible. Those churches who call women "pastors" are using the word in a

way that it is not used in the Bible or the earliest churches, and it creates confusion or the blurring of lines.
2. The word "minister" is equivalent to or fits within the range of meaning for the word "deacon" in Scripture. We recommend that churches use the word "minister" (or the equivalent expressions like "director") for the leadership roles that women (and men who are not elders or the main preacher-teacher) take on as staff positions with a church.
3. In some big churches, some women work on the staff of a church to lead in roles over men and women staff members (and volunteers), but the church has outlined a clear delineation in their roles between spiritual leadership and administrative duties pertaining to their work. This is a good solution.
4. Words have been used in different ways in different church cultures today. Each church is wise to define the words they use in such a way that people understand the complementarian differences between an elder/pastor/overseer and other ministry roles. If the church uses modern terms, not found in the Bible, they still should clarify the differences biblically so that the local church understands clearly distinctions concerning gender and roles.

1 Corinthians 11 and 14

A similar principle is at play in 1 Corinthians. Again, following the principle of headship/primogeniture, God inspires Paul to teach women to show that they are in submission to the male leadership of the church by wearing veils when they pray and prophesy. First Corinthians 11:3–4 sets forth the teaching:

> But I want you to realize that the head of every man is Christ, and the head of the woman is man, and the head of Christ is God. . . . Every woman who prays or prophesies with her head uncovered dishonors her head.

In first-century Corinth, people wore veils in a worship context when they prayed, offered sacrifices, or prophesied *to show that they were in submission to their authority* (see Chapter 6). It is important to note that prophecy is distinguished from teaching in the New Testament.[163]

The act of wearing a veil today does not communicate submission to authority; thus, it does not communicate the same thing it did in first-century Corinth. But the underlying principle of submission to authority does apply today. So in a public gathering of the church, it is important that when women pray, make announcements, read Scripture, or do things that may be comparable to 1 Corinthians 11, they adhere to the principle of honoring the male headship of the church.

This same principle is at work in 1 Corinthians 14 during the weighing and evaluating of prophecy. In Corinth, the practice often created disorder during gatherings. So with reference to these times of weighing and evaluating prophecies, God inspired the apostle Paul to write, "Women should remain silent in the churches. They are not allowed to speak, but must be in submission, as the law says" (1 Corinthians 14:34).

Each of these passages points to a teaching-authority role reserved for qualified males, based upon headship/primogeniture in the creation account.

It should come as no surprise, then, that when the New Testament describes elders (1 Timothy 3:1–6; Titus 1:5–9) and directly addresses people in the elder roles (Acts 20:30; 1 Peter 5:1–2, etc.), it consistently only refers to qualified men. Notice the descriptive words of the qualities that we are instructed to look for when seeking to appoint elders/overseers:

- "Now the overseer is to be. . . faithful to *his* wife, temperate" (1 Timothy 3:2a).
- "He must manage *his* own family well and see that *his* children obey him" (1 Timothy 3:4a).
- "*He* must not be a recent convert" (1 Timothy 3:6a).
- "An elder must be blameless, faithful to *his* wife, a man whose children believe" (Titus 1:6a).
- "*He* must be blameless" (Titus 1:7a).

163. "Prophecy—Yes, But Teaching—No," *CBMW*, July 23, 2007, www.cbmw.org/2007/07/23/prophecy-yes-but-teaching-no/ (accessed October 17, 2022).

- "*He* must be hospitable" (Titus 1:8a).
- "*He* must hold firmly to the trustworthy message as it has been taught" (Titus 1:9a).

Women held many leadership roles in the ancient world (see Chapter 9) and in the early church. They were deacons (Romans 16:1–2), private teachers of doctrine to men (Acts 18:26), and prophets (Acts 21:9) (see Chapter 11). But God inspired Paul, consistent with the principle of primogeniture, to teach that qualified males should be appointed as elders.

6. MEN AND WOMEN ARE TO SUBMIT TO AND HONOR THE AUTHORITY OF MALE HEADSHIP IN THE CHURCH.

When it comes to God-given authority, both men and women are called to submit to and honor that authority (Hebrews 13:17; Romans 13:7).

As we described in the previous section regarding the significance of the veil and submission to authority, God also shows us that the teaching-authority and elder roles in the local church are reserved for qualified men. Women are not to seek these roles, and the women and men who are not performing these roles must submit to and honor the men in those roles.

The three key passages that uphold male teaching-authority explicitly call women to show submission and respect to these men that God has called into this position within the church.

Again, in 1 Timothy 2 the apostle Paul is clear: "A woman should learn in quietness and full submission. I do not permit a woman to teach or to assume authority over a man; she must be quiet" (1 Timothy 2:11–12). In previous chapters we discussed the ways egalitarian scholars seek to explain away this passage to fit contemporary secular ideals and why that is misguided. We also join The Gospel Coalition's Tim Keller in pointing people to the excellent recent commentary on the letters to Timothy and Titus by Robert Yarbrough for his exegetical and historical background work on this passage. He reminds us that Paul's argument is not based on culture, but on the view that "Adam was formed first, then Eve" and it is a declaration "that the creation order is still in effect."[164]

When it says that a woman is to learn in quietness, this "quiet" does not denote silence, but a quiet spirit. Paul is describing a demeanor, admonishing women to respect the male teachers and their authority to teach. And during these public teaching times, they are to learn quietly.

Similarly, 1 Corinthians 11 teaches that when women pray and prophesy, they are to honor headship. Contrary to what some teach, headship in this context does not mean "source," but rather "authority" as we described earlier (see Chapter 6).

- "I want you to realize that the head of every man is Christ, and *the head of the woman is man"* (1 Corinthians 11:3a).
- "Every woman who prays or prophesies with her head uncovered *dishonors her head"* (1 Corinthians 11:5a).
- "A man ought not to cover his head, since he is the image and glory of God; but *woman is the glory of man"* (1 Corinthians 11:7).

The apostle Paul clarifies that the principle of honoring male headship is not just for the Corinthian church; it is to be a universal practice in all the churches: "If anyone wants to be contentious about this, we have no other practice—nor do the churches of God" (1 Corinthians 11:16).

Paul goes on to teach that women must be silent during the weighing of prophecy (1 Corinthians 14:29). He then says, "If they want to inquire about something, they should ask their own husbands at home; for it is disgraceful for a woman to speak in the church" (1 Corinthians 14:35).

Now, let us be clear: women's opinions are valuable for seeing sides of situations that men may be unable to notice. God has placed women in the lives of church leaders to be their strong help. Those women who did not have husbands, it can be assumed, could contact other leaders in the church. Yet most of the women would have had husbands to whom they could ask

164. Robert W. Yarbrough, *The Letters of Timothy and Titus* (Grand Rapids: Wm. B Eerdmans, 2018), 180.

questions about the prophecies. But a woman disrupting this time with questioning would be considered disrespectful of male headship, including the elders of the church (see Chapter 11).

These teachings present all of us with a major stumbling block when it comes to how we think in Western civilization. The world tells us to be noisy and disrespectful when we don't agree with someone. Yet God tells us to be gentle of spirit and to honor the men he has placed in positions of authority.

The Scriptures force us to see that Jesus teaches us to uphold the headship/primogeniture principle and show submission and respect for the male leaders of the local church.

7. HONORING JESUS-STYLE MALE HEADSHIP WILL BRING BLESSINGS ON THE FAMILY AND THE CHURCH.

One natural reaction to these teachings—since they are so different from what we think based on our secular culture—is to question their truthfulness and applicability.

Questioning is an understandable reaction. When I (Bobby) first read these passages, everything within me wanted to reject them. "How can this be?" I once said, and many still say. It is easy to think of them as restrictions instead of an outpouring of God's love for his people, both men and women. Yet, we should seriously consider the following:

- What if the beliefs of our secular culture on these points are wrong?
- What if it is a major mistake to reject male headship/primogeniture?
- What if honoring God's created order leads to blessing?
- What if our rejection of all patriarchy and fear of being misogynists is an overreaction to abuses in the past?
- What if egalitarianism undermines the divine order between men and women?
- What if egalitarianism ultimately overthrows gender and sexual identities that were intended by God?
- What if following these passages of Scripture in faith actually leads to God's best for us?

We believe all seven of these questions point to the wisdom of God's countercultural path—and that our secular culture is wrong in these areas. We are convinced that the cultural acceptance of radical secular egalitarianism is destroying the family, sexuality, and our identity as men and women as God intended.

As John Stonestreet of the Colson Center for Christian Worldview puts it, "Ideas have consequences, and bad ideas have victims."[165]

Our secular culture, and its commitment to complete egalitarianism, is pursuing ideas that ultimately push us to live contrary to God's created order. These ideas are harming countless victims (see Chapters 1, 2, 13, and 14).

But there is hope.

I (Bobby) have been a lead pastor for thirty-four years and the leader of two national disciple making networks for the last several years. I have been given a front-row seat to the results of Jesus-style male headship in the home and in the church.

I (Renée) have experienced Jesus-style male headship in my childhood home and in my marriage. A man who loves like Jesus will listen to me, make space for me to grow and thrive, and sacrifice his comfort for my well-being.

The words in Ephesians 5:33 provide a helpful summary to guide us. As Paul says, "Each one of you also must love his wife as he loves himself, and the wife must respect her husband."

In these words, there is an emphasis on men showing *love* to their wives and women showing *respect* to their husbands. Some wives may feel a need for their spouse to emphasize respect and some husbands may feel a need for their wives to emphasize love, but the exceptions prove the rule. Emmerson Eggerich, PhD, provides more in-depth and practical background on these points.[166] When wives are loved well and husbands are respected well, the results tend to be that:

---

165. John Stonestreet, "When Bad Ideas Get Loose," *Breakpoint*, September 30, 2019, www.breakpoint.org/breakpoint-when-bad-ideas-get-loose/ (accessed October 17, 2022).
166. See more at loveandrespect.com.

- Men rise up and aspire to Jesus-style headship.
- Women provide strong help as they are well-loved and protected by their husbands.
- Men accept a unique responsibility to lead their families, especially as they love and serve their wives.
- Women are inclined to cooperate with their husband's initiating service and love, becoming a powerful ally against the forces of evil that come against their family.
- Men get more involved in church and family life, even as worldly pursuits hold less appeal.
- Women experience less fear, more security, and greater contentment.
- Children are more secure in their family and develop better countercultural attitudes.

Likewise, we see the following in the church when Jesus-style headship is truly honored by men and women:

- Male headship churches challenge men to be worthy of respect in noble headship—and men in turn become more involved. We typically find that in churches that emphasize male headship, the church is composed of 55 percent or more men, and these men are more engaged spiritually than in egalitarian churches. Meanwhile, egalitarian churches do not call men to the challenge of Jesus-style headship—ignoring their hardwiring for respect—and they tend to lose men and become more and more dominated by women.
- Male headship churches hold the line on homosexuality, gender fluidity, and transgenderism. Their culture of upholding Scripture on gender roles is applied consistently so that they uphold what Scripture teaches on these other issues. Meanwhile, egalitarian churches tend to become more and more open to homosexual marriages and transgender activism.
- Children within male headship churches see examples of strong, Christlike men in their lives and in their ministries.

The New Testament describes women prophesying (Acts 21:9), serving as deacons (Romans 16:1–2), mentoring younger women (Titus 2:3–4), making disciples (Matthew 28), and doing other important and visible acts of ministry. Taking the whole of Scripture, women should be empowered for countless vital ministries for their good and God's glory.

By way of summary, the following statement—from the Renew.org faith statement—captures what we believe the Bible teaches regarding gender:

> We believe both men and women were created by God to equally reflect, in gendered ways, the nature and character of God in the world. In marriage, husbands and wives are to submit to one another, yet there are gender specific expressions: husbands model themselves in relationship with their wives after Jesus' sacrificial love for the church and wives model themselves in relationship with their husbands after the church's willingness to follow Jesus. In the church, men and women serve as partners in the use of their gifts in ministry, while seeking to uphold New Testament norms which teach that the lead teacher/preacher role in the gathered church and the elder/overseer role are for qualified men. The vision of the Bible is an equal partnership of men and women in creation, in marriage, in salvation, in the gifts of the Spirit, and in the ministries of the church but exercised in ways that honor gender as described in the Bible.

ABOUT THE CONTRIBUTORS

BOBBY HARRINGTON (DMin, Southern Baptist Theological Seminary) is CEO of Renew.org and Discipleship.org, both national disciple making networks. Bobby is the founding and Lead Pastor of Harpeth Christian Church. He is author or coauthor of more than a dozen books on disciple making.

CHAD RAGSDALE (DMin, Talbot School of Theology) is Academic Dean of Ozark Christian College and has served on its faculty since 2005. He teaches Christian apologetics, philosophy, and biblical interpretation. He has a Bachelor of Arts in Preaching and a Master of Divinity in Contemporary Theology, both from Lincoln Christian University. His Doctor of Ministry is in Engaging Mind and Culture. He is the author of *Christian Convictions: Discerning the Essential, Important, and Personal Elements.*

DANIEL MCCOY (PhD, North-West University) is Editorial Director of Renew.org and part-time professor of philosophy at Ozark Christian College. Among his books are *The Popular Handbook of World Religions* (general editor) and *Real Life Theology* (co-general editor with Bobby Harrington).

DAVID ROADCUP (DMin, Trinity Evangelical Divinity School) is Professor of the Discipleship and Global Outreach Representative with TCM International Institute. He has served the Kingdom in vocational ministry for over fifty years through dozens of ministries in a myriad of roles. His MA is from Cincinnati Bible Seminary, and his DMin is from Trinity Evangelical Divinity School. Dr. Roadcup has authored numerous articles and three books.

ELLEN RADCLIFF has a BA in Interpersonal Communication from East Carolina University and an MA in Counseling from Harding School of

Theology. Ellen has served on the volunteer staff of Strength in Weakness, an organization that strives to bridge the gap between the LGBTQ+ community and God's church through awareness, education, and support. Ellen has helped countless individuals and families navigate the tender topics of sexual identity and gender identity.

EMMA JANE GOODWYN graduated from Homelife Academy in 2016 after being homeschooled for 10 years and graduated with a BA in Graphic Design from Middle Tennessee State University. She is passionate about working with kids and young adults, especially through nannying and tutoring. When not designing, some of her favorite pastimes are picnicking in Centennial Park with her husband Thomas, trying out new recipes, and starting a new sewing project.

GARY L. JOHNSON (DMin, Grace Theological Seminary) is Executive Director of e2: Effective Elders and author of LeaderShift. He has served in pastoral ministry for four decades. In addition to his Doctor of Ministry, he holds a Master of Arts in Church History (Lincoln Christian Seminary) and a Master of Ministry and a Master of Divinity (Cincinnati Bible Seminary).

JARED ELLIS is the preaching minister at Fellowship Regional Church in Iola, KS, with a satellite campus in Caney, KS. He is also the host of a long-form interview podcast show called *The Homilist*, which explores the various aspects of preaching.

JIM ESTEP (PhD, Trinity Evangelical Divinity School) is the Dean of Lincoln Christian Institute. He has been in the ministry since 1985, teaching not only in colleges and seminaries but in churches around the country and internationally. He has two MAs and an MDiv from Cincinnati Christian University, a DMin from Southern Baptist Theological Seminary, and a PhD from Trinity Evangelical Divinity School.

JOHN WHITTAKER (DMin, Gordon-Conwell Theological Seminary) is a disciple of Jesus and a Bible teacher whose goal is to provide what he calls "blue jeans theology"—theology for everyday life. He's been a pastor and Bible college professor and a church planter. He is the creator of the Bible in Life online teaching ministry and of the Listener's Commentary on the New Testament.

MICHELLE EAGLE currently quarterbacks the Discipleship Ministry at Harpeth Christian Church in Franklin, TN. Prior to joining the ministry team at Harpeth, Michelle was a Physician Assistant working with HIV-infected mothers and their children in Jacksonville, FL. After a family move to TN in 2008, Michelle began volunteering in the home groups ministry at Harpeth, which led to a staff administrative position.

PAUL HUYGHEBAERT serves as the Lead Minister for the Grace Chapel Church of Christ in Cumming, GA, just north of Atlanta. Paul holds bachelor's degrees in Bible and Psychology and a master's degree in Professional Counseling. His passion is to see the Church embrace both the message and the mission of Jesus. Paul is a Renew.org Leader and the author of the book *The Way Back: Repentance, the Presence of God, and the Revival the Church So Desperately Needs.*

RENÉE WEBB SPROLES is Director of Cultural Engagement for Renew.org. She is a fifteen-year homeschool veteran, has served as director of The School of Christian Thought at North Boulevard Church, and is a founder and co-director of the Discipleship Tutorial in Murfreesboro, TN. With her husband, David, Renée has co-taught parenting classes for twenty years and currently teaches a marriage and family class of one hundred students each week.

RICHARD OSTER has taught at Harding School of Theology for over forty years. He helps prepare students for work in Christian ministry (and a smaller number for doctoral studies elsewhere) by teaching courses in New Testament Greek and courses in the content of the New Testament. These courses include Acts of Apostles, Pauline letters, book of Revelation, New Testament theology, and historical and cultural backgrounds of the New Testament. He is also an expert on ancient Ephesus.

Made in United States
North Haven, CT
02 May 2023

36138371R00189